The
Eclectic
Gourmet
Guide to
Los Angeles

Also available from Menasha Ridge Press

The Eclectic Gourmet Guide to San Francisco & the Bay Area,
   by Richard Sterling

The Eclectic Gourmet Guide to San Diego,
   by Steve Silverman

The Eclectic Gourmet Guide to New Orleans,
   by Tom Fitzmorris

The Eclectic Gourmet Guide to

Los Angeles

Colleen Dunn Bates

MENASHA
RIDGE
PRESS

Every effort has been made to ensure the accuracy of information throughout this book. Bear in mind, however, that prices, schedules, etc., are constantly changing. Readers should always verify information before making final plans.

Menasha Ridge Press, Inc.
P.O. Box 43059
Birmingham, Alabama 35243

Cover and text design by Suzanne H. Holt

Cover art by Michele Natale

ISBN 0-89732-217-7

Library of Congress Catalog Card Number: 96-16172

Manufactured in the United States of America

10 9 8 7 6 5 4 3 2 1

First Edition

CONTENTS

acknowledgments

My first thanks go to my agent, Betsy Amster, without whom I would never have connected with Menasha Ridge Press. Next, of course, I must thank the good people at Menasha, particularly publisher Bob Sehlinger and associate publisher Molly Burns, two of the most trusting, easygoing people I've ever worked with.

I've worked with more great people in my writing and editing career than I can mention here, so I'll just say thanks to the people who've helped me in my restaurant-reviewing work. Thanks to my editors along the way: Deborah Patton in the early days of the Gault Millau books, when I began my serious eating; Andre Gayot, during the glory days of Gault Millau; my wonderful *L.A. Style* editors, Michael Lassell, Susan LaTempa, and Heidi Dvorak; and my current beloved editor at *Westways,* Susan LaTempa. Thanks also to the California restaurant writers whose writing style, reporting, enthusiasm, and wit have so inspired me: Jonathan Gold, Linda Burum, Anne Lamott, Colman Andrews, Meredith Brody, Ruth Reichl, and, especially, Merrill Shindler and Kitty Morgan, without whose advice and support this book wouldn't have been possible.

Finally, eternal thanks to my family: my mother, Ellie Dunn, for cooking all those wonderful meals I never appreciated and for transferring her love of a good meal out; my father, Joe Dunn, for encouraging me to do whatever I wanted when I grew up; my husband, Darryl, for sharing and inspiring my love for good food; and my little girls, Erin and Emily, for reminding me of the pure joy of a great ice-cream cone.

The
Eclectic
Gourmet
Guide to
Los Angeles

ABOUT THE AUTHOR

Colleen Dunn Bates has been writing about restaurants for nearly 15 years. A coauthor of Gault Millau's first *The Best of Los Angeles,* she went on to become the editor of Gault Millau's entire line of English-language guides for the gourmet. For six years, she was the restaurant critic for *L.A. Style,* visiting all of L.A.'s hottest spots incognito; currently she reviews restaurants for *Westways* magazine. She has written about restaurants, food, and travel for *Travel & Leisure, Cooking Light, Food & Wine, Departures, Shape, Los Angeles, Living Fit,* and *Westworld* magazines, and has contributed to several Gault Millau, Fodor, and Mobil guidebooks.

A sixth-generation Southern Californian, Colleen lives in Pasadena with her husband, Darryl, a film editor and amateur chef, and their two daughters. To balance her love of food, she is an avid walker, surfer, skier, and hiker.

qettiNq it RiqHt

A lot of thought went into this guide. While producing a dining guide may appear to be a straightforward endeavor, I can assure you that it is fraught with peril. I have read dining guides by authors who turn up their noses at anything except four-star French restaurants (of which there are a whole lot fewer than people think). Likewise, I have seen a guide that totally omits Thai and Indian restaurants—among others—because the author did not understand those cuisines. I have read guides absolutely devoid of criticism, written by "experts" unwilling to risk offending the source of their free meals. Finally, I've seen those books that are based on surveys and write-ins from diners whose credentials for evaluating fine dining are mysterious at best and questionable at least.

How, then, do you go about developing a truly excellent dining guide? What is the best way to get it right?

If dining guides are among the most idiosyncratic of reference books, it is primarily because the background, taste, integrity, and personal agenda of each author are problematical. The authors of most dining guides are vocational or avocational restaurant or food critics. Some of these critics are schooled professionals, with palates refined by years of practical experience and culinary study; others are journalists, often with no background in food criticism or cooking, who are arbitrarily assigned the job of reviewing restaurants by their newspaper or magazine publisher. (Although it *is* occasionally possible to find journalists who are also culinary professionals.) The worst cases are the legions of self-proclaimed food critics who mooch their way from restaurant to restaurant, growing fat on free meals in exchange for writing glowing reviews.

1

Ignorance of ethnic cuisine or old assumptions about what makes for haute cuisine particularly plague authors in cities without much ethnic variety in restaurants, or authors who have been writing for years about the same old white-linen, expense-account tourist traps. Many years ago in Lexington, Kentucky, for example, there was only one Chinese restaurant in town and it was wildly successful—in spite of the fact that it was Chinese in name only. Its specialty dishes, which were essentially American vegetable casseroles smothered in corn starch, were happily gobbled up by loyal patrons who had never been exposed to real Chinese cooking. The food was not bad, but it was not Chinese either. Visitors from out of town, inquiring about a good local Chinese restaurant, were invariably directed to this place. As you would expect, they were routinely horrified by the fare.

And, while you might argue that American diners are more sophisticated and knowledgeable nowadays than at the time of the Lexington pavilion, the evidence suggests otherwise. In Las Vegas, for instance, a good restaurant town with a number of excellent Italian eateries, the local Olive Garden (a chain restaurant) is consistently voted the city's best Italian restaurant in a yearly newspaper poll. There is absolutely nothing wrong with the Las Vegas Olive Garden, but to suggest that it is the best Italian restaurant in the city is ludicrous. In point of fact, the annual survey says much more about the relative sophistication of Las Vegas diners than it does about the quality of local Italian restaurants.

But if you pick up a guide that reflects the views of many survey respondents, a *vox populi* or reader's choice compendium, that is exactly the problem. You are dependent upon the average restaurant-goer's capacity to make sound, qualitative judgments—judgments almost always impaired by extraneous variables. How many times have you had a wonderful experience at a restaurant, only to be disappointed on a subsequent visit? Trying to reconcile the inconsistency, you recall that on your previous visit, you were in the company of someone particularly stimulating, and that perhaps you had enjoyed a couple of drinks before eating. What I am getting at is that our reflections on restaurant experiences are often colored by variables having little or nothing to do with the restaurant itself. And while I am given to the democratic process in theory, I have my doubts about depending entirely on survey forms that reflect such experiences.

There are more pragmatic arguments to be made about such eaters' guides as well. If you cannot control or properly qualify your survey respondents, you cannot assure their independence, knowledge, or critical sensitivity. And, since literally anyone can participate in such surveys, the ratings can be easily slanted by those with vested interests. How many bogus responses would it take to dramatically upgrade a restaurant's rating in a survey-based, big city dining guide? Forty or even fewer. Why? Because the publisher receives patron reports (survey responses, readers' calls) covering more restaurants than can be listed in the book. Thus the "voting" is distributed over such a large number of candidate restaurants that the median number of reports for the vast majority of establishments is 120 or fewer. A cunning restaurant proprietor who is willing to stuff the ballot box, therefore, could easily improve his own rating—or lower that of a competitor.

So my mission in the *Eclectic Gourmet Guides* is to provide you with the most meaningful, useful, and accessible restaurant evaluations possible. Weighing the alternatives, I have elected to work with culinary experts, augmenting their opinions with a carefully qualified survey population of totally independent local diners of demonstrated culinary sophistication. The experts I have sought to author the *Eclectic Gourmet Guides* are knowledgeable, seasoned professionals; they have studied around the world, written cookbooks or columns, and closely follow the development of restaurants in their cities. They are well versed in ethnic dining, many having studied cuisines in their native lands. And they have no prejudice about high or low cuisine. They are as at home in a Tupelo, Mississippi catfish shack as in an exclusive French restaurant on New York's Upper East Side. Thus the name *Eclectic Gourmet*.

Equally important, I have sought experts who make every effort to conduct their reviews anonymously, and who always pay full menu prices for their meals. We are credible not only because we are knowledgeable, but also because we are independent.

You, the reader of this *Eclectic Gourmet Guide,* are the inspiration for and, we hope, the beneficiary of our diligence and methodology. Though we cannot evaluate your credentials as a restaurant critic, your opinion as a consumer—of this guide and the restaurants within—is very important to us. A clip-out survey can be found at the back of the book; please tell us about your dining experiences and let us know whether you agree with our reviews.

Eat well. Be happy.

Bob Sehlinger

✠ diniNG iN
✠ los ANGEles

Food lovers in New York and San Francisco will call me a fool for proclaiming Los Angeles as America's current reigning restaurant champ. And it's true that New York has more (and better) temples of fine dining, and San Francisco does the contemporary American restaurant better than any other city. But for sheer culinary joy, for dazzling ethnic diversity, for the pure love of food, L.A. is paradise.

You want seafood dishes from China's northern provinces? We've got 'em. How about Salvadoran pupusas? Or Jamaican conch fritters? Or sashimi from Tokyo's fish markets? Or salsas and ceviches of staggering freshness and variety? Or Irish stew, Korean barbecue, French duck confit, and New Mexican nopales? You name it, we've got it, thanks to L.A.'s extraordinarily diverse population, its access to fresh, affordable produce and food products, and its atmosphere of open-mindedness and creativity.

Aside from the glamorous boîtes of Hollywood fable, Southern California boasts restaurants reflecting dozens of vibrant, food-loving ethnic communities. Along with a respectable Chinatown near downtown, there's a sprawling new Chinese suburban community in the south San Gabriel Valley that hosts dozens of great restaurants. Vietnamese food is plentiful in Santa Ana's Little Saigon, and Korean restaurants abound in central L.A.'s Koreatown. Many restaurants keep kosher in the Fairfax District; farther south on Fairfax is an Ethiopian neighborhood with some good eateries. A West L.A. neighborhood around Sawtelle boasts many great Japanese cafes and noodle houses, while downtown's Little Tokyo offers the full range of Japanese dining experiences. Authentic Indian, Italian, Thai, Middle Eastern, Greek,

French, Hungarian, and Russian restaurants are scattered all over the region. And, of course, there are hundreds upon hundreds of Mexican and Central American restaurants, many tucked into primarily Latino neighborhoods, from East L.A. to Hollywood to Northridge, others found in virtually every community in Southern California.

Los Angeles is also blessed with tremendous economic diversity in its cuisine. If you're game for dropping a couple hundred bucks for a high-style dinner, you'll find a number of restaurants worthy of such an investment. But if you need to stretch a twenty as far as possible, you'll find even more places that will feed you well. You may have to drive a fair piece, and you'll need to bring along a sense of adventure, but the reward can be memorable food—not to mention a richer, fuller understanding of this exciting, polyglot, ever-evolving region.

A NOTE ON WARDROBE

Los Angeles is a famously casual town; you can count on one hand the number of restaurants that would hesitate to seat a man without a tie. You can bet that if Bruce Springsteen shows up at Patina or Eclipse in jeans and a motorcycle jacket, he'll be welcomed with open arms. Conservative suits are common at downtown restaurants, though they're not required; on the flip side, if you wore your solidest Brooks Brothers to such fashion-forward places as Cafe La Boheme, Spago, or The Ivy, you'd be immediately tagged as a tourist or suburban goon. At the vast majority of L.A. restaurants, a woman would feel at home in anything from a little black dress to jeans and a silk shirt. A man will often fit in best with a well-cut sportcoat, but a tie is strictly optional, except at the very few conservatively elegant places (namely, L'Orangerie, the Regent Beverly Wilshire, Rex, Diaghilev, and the Belvedere).

MAKING THE SCENE

If you want to mingle with upper-crust Hollywood and related power people from the worlds of music and fashion, you'll want to frequent a relatively short list of restaurants. Some of the town's major hot spots also happen to have good (if overpriced) food. The most action-packed restaurants that made the grade in this book include **Drai's, The Ivy, Spago, Le Dome, Maple Drive, Matsuhisa, Cicada, Georgia,** and

5

Chinois on Main; you're almost always likely to see at least one famous face at those places. More sedate power restaurants—with less plastic surgery on parade and more serious conversations and meetings—include **Patina, The Grill, Citrus, Pinot, Pinot Hollywood, Gardens,** and **The Belvedere.**

Some of the other heavy-hitter hangouts are not found in the pages that follow, either because they're too new, too volatile (as with some of the nightclub-restaurants), or too prone to serve bad or boring food. After a move across the street and some chef problems, **Morton's** (8764 Melrose Avenue, West Hollywood, (310) 276-5205) has slipped a notch as *the* power-dinner spot in town, eclipsed partly by **Eclipse** (8800 Melrose Avenue, West Hollywood, (310) 724-5959), recently opened by Spago's former maître 'd. Hot newcomers for the young music/club crowd include **Jones** (7205 Santa Monica Boulevard, Hollywood, (213) 850-1727), an ultra-hip retro-Italian; **House of Blues** (8430 Sunset Boulevard, West Hollywood, (213) 650-0247), a terrific music club and a pretty good restaurant; and **Luna Park** (665 N. Robertson Boulevard, West Hollywood, (310) 652-0611), another worthy music club, which at this writing boasted the skilled, architectural cooking of Robert Gadsby. An older showbiz crowd likes **Jimmy's** (201 S. Moreno Drive, Beverly Hills, (310) 879-2394), a fancy but mediocre Continental boîte; others like **The Palm** (9001 Santa Monica Boulevard, West Hollywood, (310) 550-8811) for its big-ticket steaks and lobsters.

Be advised that the trendier the scene, the more likely the restaurant or club will be out of business soon; so call before visiting.

TOURIST pLACES

When visitors arrive in town, they invariably want to rush off to the **Hard Rock Cafe** (Beverly Center, (310) 276-7605). Instead of famous faces, they find other tourists and packs of ten year olds begging their parents for Hard Rock T-shirts. And now L.A. has its own **Planet Hollywood** (9560 Wilshire Boulevard, Beverly Hills, (310) 275-7828), a frenetic tribute to Hollywood celebrities that no real celebrity would ever visit.

Other tourist spots include **Gladstone's 4 Fish** (17300 Pacific Coast Highway, Santa Monica, (310) 454-3474), with a fabulous beachfront location, a party atmosphere, and huge portions of so-so food; **Gladstone's Universal** (CityWalk, (818) 622-3474), which applies the same concept to the depressingly phony CityWalk; **Wolfgang Puck**

6

Cafe, also at CityWalk (818) 985-9653), as well as South Coast Plaza, the USC campus, and Santa Monica; **Geoffrey's** (27400 Pacific Coast Highway, Malibu, (310) 457-1519), a lovely, view-rich California bistro on the coast that has had uneven food; **Thunder Roadhouse** (8371 Sunset Boulevard, West Hollywood, (213) 650-6011), a Hard Rock–on–a–Harley burger joint; and **Dive** (Century City Marketplace, (310) 788-3483), a decent, kid-pleasing submarine-theme restaurant opened by Steven Spielberg and Jeffrey Katzenberg.

NEWCOMERS

A restaurant must have some 18 months' seasoning to warrant inclusion in this book, so a number of interesting newcomers failed to get reviewed. Aside from some mentioned in "Making the Scene" and "Tourist Places" above, the following may well be worth a visit.

The Back Pocket
1651 West Sunflower
Santa Ana   (714) 668-1737
With just nine tables, this new casual offshoot of Gustaf Anders is always booked—and for good reason.

Barney Greengrass
Barney's New York, 9570 Wilshire Boulevard
Beverly Hills   (310) 777-5877
Sleek, chic, and all the rage, this fashionable deli in the heart of the high-fashion world takes classic deli fare to an elegant new level.

Boxer
7615 Beverly Boulevard
Los Angeles   (213) 932-6178
The Asian-influenced California cooking at this new spot has foodies abuzz. Worth a try.

✓ The Buffalo Club
1520 West Olympic Boulevard
Santa Monica   (310) 450-8600

gm courtyard lively/casual

Homey American food created by talented French chef Patrick Healy and served to a show-off crowd of celebs and moguls. The hot spot of the moment.

Cafe Pinot

700 West Fifth Street
Downtown   (213) 239-6500

A new jewel in the Patina crown, this indoor-outdoor beauty serves rustic and modern French fare in the front yard of the splendid Los Angeles Public Library.

Fenix

The Argyle Hotel, 8358 Sunset Boulevard
West Hollywood   (213) 654-7100

Ken Frank of La Toque fame is back, turning out a similarly elegant California-French cuisine.

442

442 North Fairfax Avenue
Los Angeles   (213) 651-4421

Simple, fresh, healthful American cooking, with several good vegetarian choices, is bringing this neighborhood spot a loyal following.

JR Seafood

11901 Santa Monica Boulevard
West Los Angeles   (310) 268-2463

San Gabriel–style Chinese cooking comes to the westside at last.

La Cachette

10506 Little Santa Monica Boulevard
Century City   (310) 470-4992

A very promising French newcomer from a former chef of L'Orangerie and Cicada. Well worth a trip.

Le Colonial

8783 Bonner Drive
West Hollywood   (310) 289-0660

A shabby-swank replica of Jean Denoyer's New York Le Colonial. Modern Vietnamese food for the *Vanity Fair* crowd.

Manhattan Wonton Company

8475 Melrose Place
West Hollywood   (213) 655-6030

Skillfully updated '50s Chinese fare (chow mein, fried rice) and spiffy martinis fuel a high-gloss crowd of young and old Beverly Hills types.

Modada
8115 Melrose Avenue
West Hollywood   (213) 653-4612
Modern-age food for a modern-age crowd, prepared skillfully and with lots of architectural flair by Splichal protégé Sam Marvin.

Nouveau Cafe Blanc
9777 Little Santa Monica Boulevard
Beverly Hills   (310) 888-0108
Fans of the old Cafe Blanc in Silverlake will want to hurry over to its new incarnation, a lovely little cafe serving the same refined French-Japanese food.

Pangeaa
Hotel Nikko, 465 South La Cienega Boulevard
Beverly Hills   (310) 246-2100
An intriguing, out-there international cuisine in the high-tech Hotel Nikko.

Patinette
Museum of Contemporary Art, 250 South Grand Avenue
Downtown   (213) 626-1178
Wonderful lunch fare served on a MOCA patio from the owner/chef of Patina.

Pinot Hollywood
1448 North Gower Street
Hollywood   (213) 461-8800
A handsome canteen for the studio set, with a rambling, comfortable bar and more of Joachim Splichal's winning French fare.

Serenata Gourmet
10924 West Pico Boulevard
West Los Angeles   (310) 441-9667
The superb Mexican cooking of La Serenata di Garibaldi has made it to the westside.

Sylvie
Beverly Prescott Hotel, 1224 South Beverwill Drive
Los Angeles   (310) 772-2999
Sylvie Darr, ex of San Francisco's wonderful Zuni Cafe, is behind this
most promising Provençal/Mediterranean newcomer.

MORE RECOMMENDATIONS

◆ Best Bagels

Goldstein's Bagels
86 W. Colorado Boulevard, Pasadena   (818) 792-2435
I & Joy Bagels
246 N. Beverly Drive, Beverly Hills   (310) 274-5522
Western Bagel
11628 Santa Monica Boulevard, West L.A.   (310) 479-4823

◆ Best Bakeries

Breadworks
7961 W. 3rd Street, L.A.   (213) 930-0047
La Brea Bakery
624 S. La Brea Avenue, L.A.   (213) 939-6813
Pasadena Baking Company
29 E. Colorado Boulevard, Pasadena   (818) 796-9966

◆ Best Barbecue

Dr. Hogly Wogly's Tyler, Texas Barbecue
8136 N. Sepulveda Boulevard, Van Nuys   (818) 780-6701
Phillip's Bar-B-Que
4307 Leimert Boulevard, L.A.   (213) 292-7613
Warren's BBQ
4916 ½ W. Slauson Boulevard, Ladera Heights   (213) 294-2272

◆ Best Breakfasts

Beverly Hills Breakfast Club
9671 Wilshire Boulevard, Beverly Hills   (310) 271-8903

Caffe Latte
see restaurant profile
Du-Par's
12036 Ventura Boulevard, Studio City   (818) 766-4437
Hugo's
see restaurant profile
John O'Groats
10516 W. Pico Boulevard, West L.A.   (310) 204-0692
Old Town Bakery
see restaurant profile
Village Coffee Shop
2695 N. Beachwood Drive, Hollywood   (213) 467-5398

◆ Best Chicken

Koo Koo Roo
8393 Beverly Boulevard, L.A.   (213) 655-9045
255 S. Grand Avenue, Downtown   (213) 620-1800
11066 Santa Monica Boulevard, West L.A.   (310) 473-5858
Zankou Chicken
5065 Sunset Boulevard, Hollywood   (213) 665-7842
1415 E. Colorado Boulevard, Glendale   (818) 244-1937

◆ Best Coffeehouses

Big & Tall Books
7311 Beverly Boulevard, L.A.   (213) 939-5022
Equator
22 Mills Place, Pasadena   (818) 564-8656
Highland Grounds
742 N. Highland Avenue, L.A.   (213) 466-1507
The Novel Cafe
212 Pier Avenue, Santa Monica   (310) 396-8566
Onyx
1804 N. Vermont Avenue, Los Feliz   (213) 660-5820

◆ Best Desserts

L.A. Desserts
113 N. Robertson Boulevard, Beverly Hills   (310) 273-5537

Mani's Bakery
(for low-fat) 519 S. Fairfax Avenue, L.A.   (213) 938-8800
Old Town Bakery
see restaurant profile
Sweet Lady Jane
8360 Melrose Avenue, West Hollywood   (213) 653-7145

◆ Best Gourmet Takeout

Julienne
2649 Mission Street, San Marino   (818) 441-2299
Marmalade
710 Montana Avenue, Santa Monica   (310) 395-9196
Netty's
1700 Silver Lake Boulevard, Silver Lake   (213) 662-8655

◆ Best Hamburgers, Hot Dogs, and Sandwiches

The Apple Pan
10801 W. Pico Boulevard, West L.A.   (310) 475-3585
Falafel King
1059 Broxton Avenue, Westwood   (310) 208-4444
Hampton's
1342 N. Highland Avenue, Hollywood   (213) 469-1090
4301 Riverside Drive, Burbank   (818) 845-3009
Jodi Maroni's Sausage Kingdom
2011 Ocean Front Walk, Venice   (310) 306-1995
1315 Third Street Promenade, Santa Monica   (310) 393-9063
Mo' Better Meaty Meat
5855 W. Pico Boulevard, L.A.   (213) 938-6558
Philippe's
(for French dips) 1001 N. Alameda Street, Downtown   (213) 628-3781
Pink's
711 N. La Brea Avenue, L.A.   (213) 931-4223
Tommy's
2575 W. Beverly Boulevard, L.A.   (213) 389-9060
Wolfe Burgers
46 N. Lake Street, Pasadena   (818) 792-7292

◆ Best Mexican/Central American Fast Food

El Gallo Giro
260 S. Broadway, Downtown   (213) 626-6926
El Tepayac Cafe
812 N. Evergreen Avenue, East L.A.   (213) 268-1960
La Salsa
11075 W. Pico Boulevard, West L.A.   (310) 479-0919,
   and many locations
Pescado Mojado
1701 Sunset Boulevard, L.A.   (213) 413-8712, and many locations
Poquito Mas
3701 Cahuenga Boulevard West, Studio City   (818) 505-0068
Señor Fish
5111 N. Figueroa Street, Highland Park   (213) 257-2498
4803 Eagle Rock Boulevard, Eagle Rock   (213) 257-7167
618 Mission Street, South, Pasadena   (818) 403-0145
Yuca's Hut
2056 N. Hillhurst Avenue, Los Feliz   (213) 662-1214

◆ Best Pizza

Angeli
see restaurant profile
Casa Bianca
1650 Colorado Boulevard, Eagle Rock   (213) 256-9617
Da Pasquale
see restaurant profile
Hard Times Pizza
2664 Griffith Park Boulevard, Silver Lake   (213) 661-5656
Johnnie's NY Pizza
1456 Third Street Promenade, Santa Monica   (310) 395-9062
22333 Pacific Coast Highway, Malibu   (310) 456-1717,
   and many locations

UNDERSTANDING
THE RATINGS

We have developed detailed profiles for the best restaurants (in our opinion) in town. Each profile features an easily scanned heading which allows you, in just a second, to check out the restaurant's name, cuisine, star rating, cost, quality rating, and value rating.

Star Rating. The star rating is an overall rating that encompasses the entire dining experience, including style, service, and ambience in addition to the taste, presentation, and quality of the food. Five stars is the highest rating possible and connotes the best of everything. Four-star restaurants are exceptional and three-star restaurants are well above average. Two-star restaurants are good. One star is used to connote an average restaurant that demonstrates an unusual capability in some area of specialization, for example, an otherwise unmemorable place that has great barbecued chicken.

Cost. Beneath the star rating is an expense description that provides a comparative sense of how much a complete meal will cost. A complete meal for our purposes consists of an entree with vegetable or side dish, and choice of soup or salad. Appetizers, desserts, drinks, and tips are excluded.

Inexpensive	$15 and less per person
Moderate	$16–30 per person
Expensive	$31–40 per person
Very Expensive	Over $40 per person

14

Quality Rating. Below the cost rating appears a number and a letter. The number is a quality rating based on a scale of 0–100, with 100 being the highest (best) rating attainable. The quality rating is based expressly on the taste, freshness of ingredients, preparation, presentation, and creativity of food served. There is no consideration of price. If you are a person who wants the best food available, and cost is not an issue, you need look no further than the quality ratings.

Value Rating. If, on the other hand, you are looking for both quality and value, then you should check the value rating, expressed in letters. The value ratings are defined as follows:

A   Exceptional value, a real bargain
B   Good value
C   Fair value, you get exactly what you pay for
D   Somewhat overpriced
F   Significantly overpriced

lOCATiNq THE RESTAURANT

Just above the restaurant address and phone number is a designation for geographic zone. This zone description will give you a general idea of where the restaurant described is located. For ease of use, we divide Los Angeles into ten geographic zones.

Zone 1.   Westside (West L.A. to the ocean, Marina del Rey
              to Malibu)
Zone 2.   South Bay (Manhattan Beach to Long Beach)
Zone 3.   Golden Triangle (Beverly Hills, Century City, and
              West Hollywood)
Zone 4.   City South (Baldwin Park, Culver City, south L.A.)
Zone 5.   Central City (Hollywood to East L.A.)
Zone 6.   San Gabriel Valley
Zone 7.   San Fernando Valley East (Burbank to Sherman Oaks)
Zone 8.   San Fernando Valley West (Encino to Westlake)
Zone 9.   Orange County North (Anaheim to Corona del Mar)
Zone 10.   Orange County South (Laguna to Dana Point)

The sprawl is vast in L.A., so if you're a visitor, a car is highly recommended. Some of the better hotels in the Beverly Hills area and downtown offer limousine services to shopping and restaurant areas.

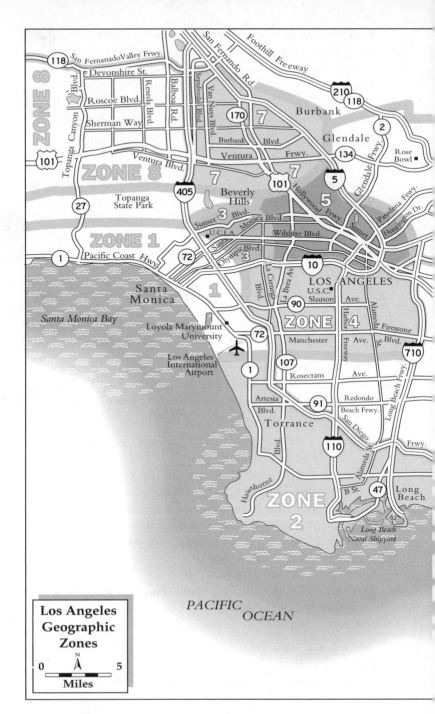

16

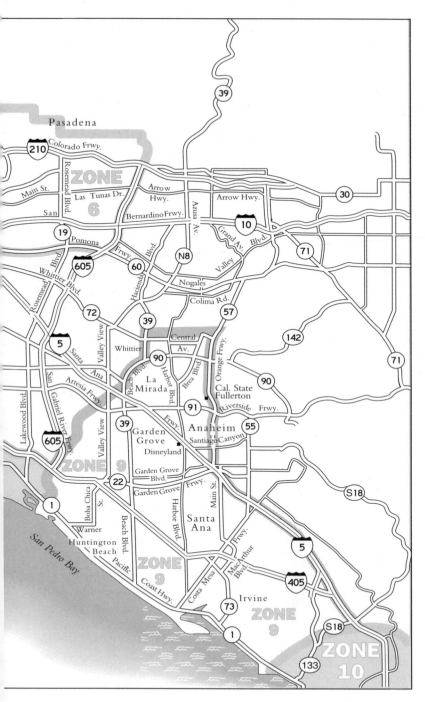

OUR pick of THE bEST los ANGElES RESTAURANTS

Because restaurants are opening and closing all the time in Los Angeles, we have tried to confine our list to establishments—or chefs—with a proven track record over a fairly long period of time. Those newer or changed establishments that demonstrate staying power and consistency will be profiled in subsequent editions.

Also, the list is highly selective. Non-inclusion of a particular place does not necessarily indicate that the restaurant is not good, but only that it was not ranked among the best or most consistent in its genre. Detailed profiles of each restaurant follow in alphabetical order at the end of this chapter.

A NOTE AbOUT SpEllING

Most diners who enjoy ethnic restaurants have noticed subtle variations in the spelling of certain dishes and preparations from one menu to the next. A noodle dish found on almost all Thai menus, for example, appears in one restaurant as *pad thai,* in another as *Phat Thai,* and in a third as *Phad Thai.*

This and similar inconsistencies arise from attempts to derive a phonetic English spelling from the name of a dish as pronounced in its country of origin. While one particular English spelling might be more frequently used than others, there is usually no definitive correct spelling for the names of many dishes. In this guide, we have elected to use the spelling most commonly found in authoritative ethnic cookbooks and other reference works.

We call this to your attention because the spelling we use in this guide could be different than that which you encounter on the menu in a certain restaurant. We might say, for instance, that the *tabbouleh* is good at the Pillars of Lebanon, while at the restaurant itself the dish is listed on the menu as *tabouli*.

Restaurants by Cuisine

Name of Restaurant	Star Rating	Price Rating	Quality Rating	Value Rating	Zone
American (see also New American)					
Saddle Peak Lodge	★★★★	Exp	90	C	8
The Grill on the Alley	★★★½	Exp	87	D	3
Cynthia's	★★★	Mod	81	B	3
Lawry's The Prime Rib	★★★	Mod	81	C	3
17th Street Cafe	★★★	Inexp	80	B	1
Hollywood Canteen	★★★	Mod	80	C	5
Old Town Bakery	★★★	Inexp	80	B	6
Pedals	★★★	Mod	79	C	1
Daily Grill	★★½	Inexp/Mod	79	B	1,3,8
Lincoln Bay Cafe	★★½	Mod	79	B	1
Shenandoah Cafe	★★½	Inexp/Mod	79	B	2
Book Soup Bistro	★★½	Mod	78	C	3
Caffe Latte	★★½	Inexp	78	B	5
The Main Course	★★½	Inexp	78	A	1
Real Food Daily	★★½	Inexp	77	A	1
Roscoe's House of Chicken and Waffles	★★½	Inexp	76	A	4,5,6
Engine Co. No. 28	★★½	Mod	74	C	5
Original Pantry Cafe	★★	Inexp	74	A	5
Musso & Frank	★★	Mod	72	D	5
Argentinian					
Gardel's	★★½	Mod	77	C	5
Asian					
Noodle World	★★	Inexp	78	A	6
Cajun / Creole					
Harold & Belle's	★★★	Mod	80	C	4
Gumbo Pot	★★	Inexp	75	B	5
Caribbean					
Cha Cha Cha	★★½	Mod	77	C	2,5
Cha Cha Cha Encino	★★½	Mod	77	C	8
Chilean					
Rincon Chileno	★★½	Inexp	77	B	5

Restaurants by Cuisine (continued)

Name of Restaurant	Star Rating	Price Rating	Quality Rating	Value Rating	Zone
Chinese					
Yujean Kang's	★★★★	Mod	92	B	6
Ocean Star	★★★★	Mod	91	B	6
Lake Spring Cuisine	★★★½	Inexp	85	B	6
The Mandarin	★★★½	Mod	85	D	3
Ocean Seafood	★★★½	Mod	85	C	5
Wei Fun	★★★	Inexp	85	A	6
Empress Pavilion	★★★	Inexp/Mod	84	B	5
Mon Kee	★★★	Mod	84	B	5
Bamboo	★★★	Inexp	83	B	7
Charming Garden	★★★	Inexp	83	B	6
Dragon Regency	★★★	Inexp	83	B	6
Fu Shing	★★★	Inexp	83	C	6
Yang Chow	★★★	Inexp	83	B	5
Chu's Mandarin Cuisine	★★★	Inexp	82	B	6
Tung Lai Shun	★★★	Inexp/Mod	82	B	6
Seafood Strip	★★★	Inexp/Mod	81	C	6
Plum Tree Inn	★★★	Inexp	79	C	1,5,8
Hu's Szechwan	★★½	Inexp	79	B	4
Jasmine Tree	★★½	Inexp	79	B	1
Mandarin Deli / Mandarin Noodle House	★★½	Inexp	79	A	5,6,8
Fragrant Vegetable	★★½	Inexp	76	B	1
Continental					
Mr. Stox	★★★	Mod	80	C	9
Beaurivage	★★½	Mod/Exp	74	D	1
Cuban					
Versailles	★★	Inexp	75	A	4,5,8
Delicatessen					
Brent's Delicatessen	★★★	Inexp	84	B	8
Art's Delicatessen	★★★	Mod	82	C	7
Langer's	★★½	Inexp	80	B	5
English					
Ye Olde King's Head	★★	Inexp	76	B	1

Name of Restaurant	Star Rating	Price Rating	Quality Rating	Value Rating	Zone
French					
Patina	★★★★★	Exp	98	B	5
L'Orangerie	★★★★★	Very Exp	97	D	3
Citrus	★★★★½	Exp	95	C	5
Pascal	★★★★	Mod/Exp	93	C	9
Pinot	★★★★	Mod	91	C	7
Antoine	★★★★	Exp	90	D	9
Bar Bistro	★★★½	Mod	89	B	5
Lunaria	★★★½	Mod	89	C	3
Xiomara	★★★½	Mod	88	D	6
Cafe Bizou	★★★½	Mod	87	B	7
Le Chardonnay	★★★	Exp	83	C	3
Le Dome	★★★	Mod/Exp	83	D	3
Le Petit Bistro	★★★	Inexp	83	B	3
Barsac Brasserie	★★★	Mod	80	C	7
Drai's	★★★	Exp	80	D	3
Louis XIV	★★½	Mod	79	B	5
French / Japanese					
Carrots	★★★½	Exp	85	D	1
Grill Lyon	★★★	Mod	84	B	5
French / American					
Rockenwagner	★★★★	Exp	94	C	1
Twin Palms	★★★½	Mod	86	B	6
Greek					
Sofi Estiatorian	★★★	Mod	84	B	3
Le Petit Greek	★★★	Mod	80	B	5
Hungarian					
The Players	★★★	Mod	80	C	3
Hungarian Budapest	★★½	Inexp	78	B	5
Indian					
Bombay Cafe	★★★½	Inexp	87	B	1
Bombay Duck	★★★	Mod	82	B	10
Nawab of India	★★★	Inexp	80	A	1

Name of Restaurant	Star Rating	Price Rating	Quality Rating	Value Rating	Zone
Indonesian					
Bali Place	★★	Inexp	75	B	1
International					
Chaya Brasserie	★★★½	Exp	89	C	3
Vida	★★★½	Mod	86	C	5
Gilliland's	★★★	Mod	83	B	1
Nicola	★★★	Mod	83	C	5
Chez Melange	★★★	Mod	82	B	2
Depot	★★★	Mod	82	C	2
Bo kaos	★★	Mod	72	D	3
Italian					
Valentino	★★★★★	Exp/Very Exp	96	C	1
Rex Il Ristorante	★★★★	Exp/Very Exp	93	D	5
Drago	★★★½	Mod	89	C	1
Ca'Brea	★★★½	Mod	87	C	5
Locanda Veneta	★★★½	Mod	87	C	3
Posto	★★★½	Mod/Exp	87	C	7
Remi	★★★½	Mod/Exp	86	D	1
Chianti Cucina	★★★½	Mod	85	B	5
Chianti Ristorante	★★★½	Mod	85	C	5
Primi	★★★½	Mod	85	C	1
Angeli Caffe	★★★	Inexp	86	B	5
Alto Palato	★★★	Mod	85	C	3
Ca'del Sole	★★★	Mod	85	C	7
Il Mito	★★★	Mod	84	C	7
Il Pastaio	★★★	Inexp/Mod	84	A	3,6
Da Pasquale	★★★	Inexp	83	A	3
L'Opera	★★★	Mod	83	C	2
Toscana	★★★	Mod	83	C	1
Trattoria Farfalla	★★★	Inexp/Mod	83	B	5
Hugo's	★★★	Inexp	82	B	3
Il Cielo	★★★	Mod/Exp	82	C	3
Il Ristorante di Giorgio Baldi	★★★	Mod	82	C	1

Name of Restaurant	Star Rating	Price Rating	Quality Rating	Value Rating	Zone
Italian (continued)					
Il Moro	★★★	Inexp	81	A	1
Cicada	★★★	Mod	80	B	3
Il Fornaio	★★★	Inexp/Mod	80	B	3,6,9
Mi Piace	★★★	Inexp	80	B	6
Prego	★★★	Mod	80	B	3
Tutto Mare	★★★	Mod	80	C	9
Farfalla La Brea	★★½	Mod	80	C	5
Caffe Delfini	★★½	Inexp/Mod	79	C	1
La Loggia	★★½	Mod	79	B	7
La Luna	★★½	Mod	79	C	5
Osteria Nonni	★★½	Inexp	79	B	5
Ritrovo	★★½	Mod	79	C	8
Romeo Cucina	★★½	Inexp	79	B	10
Terrazza Toscana	★★½	Mod	79	C	8
Milano's Italian Kitchen	★★½	Inexp	78	A	1,6,8
Toto Caffe Spaghetteria	★★½	Inexp	78	A	1,7
La Pergola	★★½	Mod	77	C	7
Fabiolus	★★½	Inexp	76	A	5
I Cugini	★★½	Mod	76	C	1
Fritto Misto	★★	Inexp	74	A	1
Jamaican					
Coley's Place	★★½	Mod	78	C	4
Japanese					
Matsuhisa	★★★★½	Very Exp	95	C	3
Ginza Sushi-ko	★★★½	Very Exp	90	F	3
Ita-Cho	★★★½	Inexp	88	A	5
Sushi Nozawa	★★★½	Mod	88	C	7
Katsu	★★★½	Mod	86	C	5
Asanebo	★★★	Mod	85	B	7
Katsu 3rd	★★★	Mod	84	C	3
R-23	★★★	Mod	84	B	5
U-Zen	★★★	Mod	84	C	1
Yuu	★★★	Inexp/Mod	83	C	1

Name of Restaurant	Star Rating	Price Rating	Quality Rating	Value Rating	Zone
Teru Sushi	★★★	Mod	80	D	7
Shabu Shabu House	★★½	Inexp	80	B	5
Atch–Kotch	★★½	Inexp	79	A	5
Asahi Ramen	★★½	Inexp	77	A	1
Mishima	★★½	Inexp	77	B	1
Korean					
Nam Kang	★★★	Inexp	83	B	5
Lebanese					
Al Amir	★★★½	Mod	86	B	5
Malaysian					
Kuala Lumpur	★★½	Inexp	79	B	6
Mediterranean					
Splashes	★★★½	Mod	84	C	10
Fino	★★★	Mod	83	B	2
Beaurivage	★★½	Mod/Exp	74	D	1
Mexican					
Border Grill	★★★½	Mod	87	C	1
La Serenata de Garibaldi	★★★½	Mod	87	B	5
El Emperador Maya	★★★	Inexp	85	B	6
La Cabanita	★★★	Inexp	82	A	6
Mexica	★★★	Mod	82	B	5
La Parrilla	★★★	Inexp	81	B	5,8
Lula	★★½	Inexp	79	B	1
Mi Ranchito	★★½	Inexp	78	A	4
Barragan's	★★½	Inexp	77	B	5,6,7
El Cholo	★★½	Inexp	77	B	5
Super Antojitos	★★½	Inexp	74	A	9
Middle Eastern					
Al Amir	★★★½	Mod	86	B	5
Marouch	★★★	Inexp	83	B	5
Shahrezad	★★½	Inexp	79	B	1,8

Name of Restaurant	Star Rating	Price Rating	Quality Rating	Value Rating	Zone
Moroccan					
Koutoubia	★★★	Mod	83	B	1
Marrakesh	★★½	Mod	78	C	7
New American					
Campanile	★★★★½	Exp	95	C	5
Granita	★★★★	Exp	92	C	1
Gardens	★★★★	Very Exp	91	D	3
Hotel Bel-Air	★★★★	Exp	91	C	1
Bistro 45	★★★★	Exp	90	C	6
Parkway Grill	★★★★	Mod	90	C	6
Regent Beverly Wilshire Dining Room	★★★★	Very Exp	90	D	3
The Dining Room	★★★★	Very Exp	89	D	10
The Belvedere	★★★½	Exp	89	C	3
Spago	★★★½	Exp	89	D	3
Michael's	★★★½	Exp	88	C	1
Shiro	★★★½	Mod	88	B	6
Golden Truffle	★★★½	Mod	85	B	9
Woodside	★★★½	Mod	85	B	1
Maple Drive	★★★½	Exp	84	C	3
David Slay's La Veranda	★★★½	Exp	83	D	3
Bistango	★★★	Mod	84	C	9
72 Market Street	★★★	Exp	84	D	1
Hal's Bar & Grill	★★★	Mod	83	B	1
Jackson's	★★★	Exp	83	C	3
Joe's	★★★	Mod	83	B	1
Julienne	★★★	Mod	83	C	6
Muse	★★★	Mod	83	C	5
Reed's	★★★	Mod	83	B	2
Bambu	★★★	Mod/Exp	82	D	1
Diva	★★★	Mod	82	C	9
Crocodile Cafe	★★★	Inexp	80	B	1,6
The Ivy	★★★	Very Exp	80	F	3
The Ivy at the Shore	★★★	Exp	80	D	1
Mr. Stox	★★★	Mod	80	C	9
Flora Kitchen	★★½	Inexp	80	D	5

Restaurants by Cuisine (continued)

Name of Restaurant	Star Rating	Price Rating	Quality Rating	Value Rating	Zone
Out Take Cafe	★★½	Inexp	78	A	7
Atlas Bar & Grill	★★½	Mod	77	C	5
Cafe del Rey	★★½	Mod	75	C	1
California Pizza Kitchen	★★	Inexp	74	B	1,5,6
Nicaraguan					
La Plancha Grill	★★½	Inexp	78	A	5
Pacific Rim					
Chinois on Main	★★★★½	Very Exp	95	C	1
Five Feet	★★★½	Mod	88	C	10
Cinnabar	★★★	Mod	84	C	6
Zenzero	★★★	Mod/Exp	84	D	1
Cafe La Boheme	★★★	Mod	82	C	3
Typhoon	★★½	Inexp/Mod	79	B	1
Peruvian					
Mario's Peruvian	★★★	Inexp	80	B	5
Polish					
Warszawa	★★½	Inexp/Mod	78	B	1
Russian					
Diagilev	★★★½	Very Exp	89	D	3
Uzbekistan	★★	Inexp	75	B	5
Scandinavian					
Gustaf Anders	★★★★	Mod/Exp	94	C	9
Seafood					
Ocean Star	★★★★	Mod	91	B	6
Ocean Seafood	★★★½	Mod	85	C	5
Water Grill	★★★½	Mod/Exp	85	C	5
Ocean Avenue Seafood	★★★	Mod	83	C	1
The Reel Inn	★★	Inexp	77	A	1
Neptune's Net	★★	Inexp	75	A	1
Southern					
Georgia	★★★	Mod	84	C	5
Aunt Kizzy's Back Porch	★★★	Inexp	81	B	1

Name of Restaurant	Star Rating	Price Rating	Quality Rating	Value Rating	Zone
Southwestern					
Abiquiu	★★★★	Mod	92	B	1
Authentic Cafe	★★★	Inexp	85	A	5
Original Sonora Cafe	★★★	Mod	81	D	5
Kachina Grill	★★½	Inexp/Mod	79	C	5
Steakhouse					
Arnie Morton's of Chicago	★★★½	Exp	86	D	3
Ruth's Chris Steak House	★★★	Exp	84	D	3
Thai					
Jitlada	★★★	Inexp	85	B	5
Talesai	★★★	Mod	85	C	3,7
Tommy Tang's	★★★	Mod	82	C	6
Jitlada West	★★★	Inexp	81	B	7
Chan Dara	★★★	Inexp	80	B	1,5
Sanamluang Cafe	★★½	Inexp	80	A	5,7
Thai Ranch	★★½	Inexp	77	B	8
Thai–Chinese					
Vim	★★½	Inexp	80	A	5
Vegetarian					
Real Food Daily	★★½	Inexp	77	A	1
Fragrant Vegetable	★★½	Inexp	76	B	1
Vietnamese					
Dong Kahn	★★★	Inexp	80	A	9
Tay Ho	★★½	Inexp	75	A	9
West African					
Rosalind's	★★½	Inexp	78	B	5

Restaurants by Star Rating

Name of Restaurant	Cuisine	Price Rating	Quality Rating	Value Rating	Zone
Five-Star Restaurants					
Patina	French	Exp	98	B	5
L'Orangerie	French	Very Exp	97	D	3
Valentino	Italian	Exp/Very Exp	96	C	1
Four-and-a-Half Star Restaurants					
Campanile	New American	Exp	95	C	5
Chinois on Main	Pacific Rim	Very Exp	95	C	1
Citrus	French	Exp	95	C	5
Matsuhisa	Japanese	Very Exp	95	C	3
Four-Star Restaurants					
Gustaf Anders	Scandinavian/ New American	Mod/Exp	94	C	9
Rockenwagner	French/ New American	Exp	94	C	1
Pascal	French	Mod/Exp	93	C	9
Rex Il Ristorante	Italian	Exp/Very Exp	93	D	5
Abiquiu	Southwestern	Mod	92	B	1
Granita	New American	Exp	92	C	1
Yujean Kang's	Chinese	Mod	92	B	6
Gardens	New American	Very Exp	91	D	3
Hotel Bel-Air	New American	Exp	91	C	1
Ocean Star	Chinese/Seafood	Mod	91	B	6
Pinot	French	Mod	91	C	7
Antoine	French	Exp	90	D	9
Bistro 45	New American/ French	Exp	90	C	6
Parkway Grill	New American	Mod	90	C	6
Regent Beverly Wilshire Dining Room	New American	Very Exp	90	D	3
Saddle Peak Lodge	American	Exp	90	C	8
The Dining Room	New American/ French	Very Exp	89	D	10
Three-and-a-Half Star Restaurants					
Ginza Sushi-ko	Japanese	Very Exp	90	F	3
Bar Bistro	French	Mod	89	B	5

Name of Restaurant	Cuisine	Price Rating	Quality Rating	Value Rating	Zone
Three-and-a-Half Star Restaurants *(continued)*					
The Belvedere	New American	Exp	89	C	3
Chaya Brasserie	International	Exp	89	C	3
Diagilev	Russian/French	Very Exp	89	D	3
Drago	Italian	Mod	89	C	1
Lunaria	French	Mod	89	C	3
Spago	New American	Exp	89	D	3
Five Feet	Pacific Rim	Mod	88	C	10
Ita-Cho	Japanese	Inexp	88	A	5
Michael's	New American	Exp	88	C	1
Shiro	New American	Mod	88	B	6
Sushi Nozawa	Japanese	Mod	88	C	7
Xiomara	French	Mod	88	D	6
Bombay Cafe	Indian	Inexp	87	B	1
Border Grill	Mexican	Mod	87	C	1
Ca'Brea	Italian	Mod	87	C	5
Cafe Bizou	French	Mod	87	B	7
The Grill on the Alley	American	Exp	87	D	3
La Serenata de Garibaldi	Mexican	Mod	87	B	5
Locanda Veneta	Italian	Mod	87	C	3
Posto	Italian	Mod/Exp	87	C	7
Al Amir	Lebanese	Mod	86	B	5
Arnie Morton's of Chicago	Steakhouse	Exp	86	D	3
Katsu	Japanese	Mod	86	C	5
Remi	Italian	Mod/Exp	86	D	1
Twin Palms	French/American	Mod	86	B	6
Vida	International	Mod	86	C	5
Carrots	French/Japanese	Exp	85	D	1
Chianti Cucina	Italian	Mod	85	B	5
Chianti Ristorante	Italian	Mod	85	C	5
Golden Truffle	New American	Mod	85	B	9
Lake Spring Cuisine	Chinese	Inexp	85	B	6
The Mandarin	Chinese	Mod	85	D	3

Restaurants by Star Rating (continued)

Name of Restaurant	Cuisine	Price Rating	Quality Rating	Value Rating	Zone
Ocean Seafood	Chinese/Seafood	Mod	85	C	5
Primi	Italian	Mod	85	C	1
Water Grill	Seafood/American	Mod/Exp	85	C	5
Woodside	New American	Mod	85	B	1
Maple Drive	New American	Exp	84	C	3
Splashes	Mediterranean	Mod	84	C	10
David Slay's La Veranda	New American/ Italian	Exp	83	D	3

Three-Star Restaurants

Name of Restaurant	Cuisine	Price Rating	Quality Rating	Value Rating	Zone
Angeli Caffe	Italian	Inexp	86	B	5
Alto Palato	Italian	Mod	85	C	3
Asanebo	Japanese	Mod	85	B	7
Authentic Cafe	Southwestern/ New American	Inexp	85	A	5
Ca'del Sole	Italian	Mod	85	C	7
El Emperador Maya	Mexican	Inexp	85	B	6
Jitlada	Thai	Inexp	85	B	5
Talesai	Thai	Mod	85	C	3,7
Wei Fun	Chinese	Inexp	85	A	6
Bistango	New American	Mod	84	C	9
Brent's Delicatessen	Delicatessen	Inexp	84	B	8
Cinnabar	Pacific Rim	Mod	84	C	6
Empress Pavilion	Chinese	Inexp/Mod	84	B	5
Georgia	Southern	Mod	84	C	5
Grill Lyon	French/Japanese	Mod	84	B	5
Il Mito	Italian	Mod	84	C	7
Il Pastaio	Italian	Inexp/Mod	84	A	3,6
Katsu 3rd	Japanese	Mod	84	C	3
Mon Kee	Chinese	Mod	84	B	5
R-23	Japanese	Mod	84	B	5
Ruth's Chris Steak House	Steakhouse	Exp	84	D	3
72 Market Street	New American	Exp	84	D	1
Sofi Estiatorian	Greek	Mod	84	B	3
U-Zen	Japanese	Mod	84	C	1
Zenzero	Pacific Rim	Mod/Exp	84	D	1

Name of Restaurant	Cuisine	Price Rating	Quality Rating	Value Rating	Zone
Three-Star Restaurants *(continued)*					
Bamboo	Chinese	Inexp	83	B	7
Charming Garden	Chinese	Inexp	83	B	6
Da Pasquale	Italian	Inexp	83	A	3
Dragon Regency	Chinese	Inexp	83	B	6
Fino	Mediterranean	Mod	83	B	2
Fu Shing	Chinese	Inexp	83	C	6
Gilliland's	International	Mod	83	B	1
Hal's Bar & Grill	New American	Mod	83	B	1
Jackson's	New American	Exp	83	C	3
Joe's	New American	Mod	83	B	1
Julienne	New American	Mod	83	C	6
Koutoubia	Moroccan	Mod	83	B	1
L'Opera	Italian	Mod	83	C	2
Le Chardonnay	French	Exp	83	C	3
Le Dome	French	Mod/Exp	83	D	3
Le Petit Bistro	French	Inexp	83	B	3
Marouch	Middle Eastern	Inexp	83	B	5
Muse	New American	Mod	83	C	5
Nam Kang	Korean	Inexp	83	B	5
Nicola	International	Mod	83	C	5
Ocean Avenue Seafood	Seafood	Mod	83	C	1
Reed's	New American	Mod	83	B	2
Toscana	Italian	Mod	83	C	1
Trattoria Farfalla	Italian	Inexp/Mod	83	B	5
Yang Chow	Chinese	Inexp	83	B	5
Yuu	Japanese	Inexp/Mod	83	C	1
Art's Delicatessen	Delicatessen	Mod	82	C	7
Bambu	New American	Mod/Exp	82	D	1
Bombay Duck	Indian	Mod	82	B	10
Cafe La Boheme	Pacific Rim	Mod	82	C	3
Chez Melange	International	Mod	82	B	2
Chu's Mandarin Cuisine	Chinese	Inexp	82	B	6
Depot	International	Mod	82	C	2

Name of Restaurant	Cuisine	Price Rating	Quality Rating	Value Rating	Zone
Diva	New American	Mod	82	C	9
Hugo's	Italian	Inexp	82	B	3
Il Cielo	Italian	Mod/Exp	82	C	3
Il Ristorante di Giorgio Baldi	Italian	Mod	82	C	1
La Cabanita	Mexican	Inexp	82	A	6
Mexica	Mexican	Mod	82	B	5
Tommy Tang's	Thai	Mod	82	C	6
Tung Lai Shun	Chinese	Inexp/Mod	82	B	6
Aunt Kizzy's Back Porch	Southern	Inexp	81	B	1
Cynthia's	American	Mod	81	B	3
Il Moro	Italian	Inexp	81	A	1
Jitlada West	Thai	Inexp	81	B	7
La Parrilla	Mexican	Inexp	81	B	5
Lawry's The Prime Rib	American	Mod	81	C	3
Original Sonora Cafe	Southwestern	Mod	81	D	5
Seafood Strip	Chinese	Inexp/Mod	81	C	6
17th Street Cafe	American	Inexp	80	B	1
Barsac Brasserie	French	Mod	80	C	7
Chan Dara	Thai	Inexp	80	B	1,5
Cicada	Italian	Mod	80	B	3
Crocodile Cafe	California	Inexp	80	B	1,6
Dong Kahn	Vietnamese	Inexp	80	A	9
Drai's	French	Exp	80	D	3
Harold & Belle's	Cajun/Creole	Mod	80	C	4
Hollywood Canteen	American	Mod	80	C	5
Il Fornaio	Italian	Inexp/Mod	80	B	3,6,9
The Ivy	New American	Very Exp	80	F	3
The Ivy at the Shore	New American	Exp	80	D	1
Le Petit Greek	Greek	Mod	80	B	5
Mario's Peruvian	Peruvian	Inexp	80	B	5
Mi Piace	Italian	Inexp	80	B	6

Restaurants by Star Rating (continued)

Name of Restaurant	Cuisine	Price Rating	Quality Rating	Value Rating	Zone
Three–Star Restaurants (continued)					
Mr. Stox	New American/ Continental	Mod	80	C	9
Nawab of India	Indian	Inexp	80	A	1
Old Town Bakery	American	Inexp	80	B	6
The Players	Hungarian/ American	Mod	80	C	3
Prego	Italian	Mod	80	B	3
Teru Sushi	Japanese	Mod	80	D	7
Tutto Mare	Italian	Mod	80	C	9
Pedals	American	Mod	79	C	1
Plum Tree Inn	Chinese	Inexp	79	C	1,5,8
Two–and–a–Half Star Restaurants					
Farfalla La Brea	Italian	Mod	80	C	5
Flora Kitchen	New American	Inexp	80	D	5
Langer's	Delicatessen	Inexp	80	B	5
Sanamluang Cafe	Thai	Inexp	80	A	5,7
Shabu Shabu House	Japanese	Inexp	80	B	5
Vim	Thai/Chinese	Inexp	80	A	5
Atch-Kotch	Japanese	Inexp	79	A	5
Caffe Delfini	Italian	Inexp/Mod	79	C	1
Daily Grill	American	Inexp/Mod	79	B	1,3,8
Hu's Szechwan	Chinese	Inexp	79	B	4
Jasmine Tree	Chinese	Inexp	79	B	1
Kachina Grill	Southwestern	Inexp/Mod	79	C	5
Kuala Lumpur	Malaysian	Inexp	79	B	6
La Loggia	Italian	Mod	79	B	7
La Luna	Italian	Mod	79	C	5
Lincoln Bay Cafe	American	Mod	79	B	1
Louis XIV	French	Mod	79	B	5
Lula	Mexican	Inexp	79	B	1
Mandarin Deli/ Mandarin Noodle House	Chinese	Inexp	79	A	5,6,8
Osteria Nonni	Italian	Inexp	79	B	5
Ritrovo	Italian	Mod	79	C	8

Name of Restaurant	Cuisine	Price Rating	Quality Rating	Value Rating	Zone
Romeo Cucina	Italian	Inexp	79	B	10
Shahrezad	Middle Eastern	Inexp	79	B	1,8
Shenandoah Cafe	American	Inexp/Mod	79	B	2
Terrazza Toscana	Italian	Mod	79	C	8
Typhoon	Pacific Rim	Inexp/Mod	79	B	1
Book Soup Bistro	American	Mod	78	C	3
Caffe Latte	American	Inexp	78	B	5
Coley's Place	Jamaican	Mod	78	C	4
Hungarian Budapest	Hungarian	Inexp	78	B	5
La Plancha Grill	Nicaraguan	Inexp	78	A	5
The Main Course	American	Inexp	78	A	1
Marrakesh	Moroccan	Mod	78	C	7
Mi Ranchito	Mexican	Inexp	78	A	4
Milano's Italian Kitchen	Italian	Inexp	78	A	1,6,8
Out Take Cafe	California	Inexp	78	A	7
Rosalind's	West African	Inexp	78	B	5
Toto Caffe Spaghetteria	Italian	Inexp	78	A	1, 7
Warszawa	Polish	Inexp/Mod	78	B	1
Asahi Ramen	Japanese	Inexp	77	A	1
Atlas Bar & Grill	New American/ International	Mod	77	C	5
Barragan's	Mexican	Inexp	77	B	5,6,7
Cha Cha Cha	Caribbean	Mod	77	C	2,5
Cha Cha Cha Encino	Caribbean	Mod	77	C	8
El Cholo	Mexican	Inexp	77	B	5
Gardel's	Argentinian	Mod	77	C	5
La Pergola	Italian	Mod	77	C	7
Mishima	Japanese	Inexp	77	B	1
Real Food Daily	American/ Vegetarian	Inexp	77	A	1
Rincon Chileno	Chilean	Inexp	77	B	5
Thai Ranch	Thai	Inexp	77	B	8
Fabiolus	Italian	Inexp	76	A	5

Name of Restaurant	Cuisine	Price Rating	Quality Rating	Value Rating	Zone
Two-and-a-Half Star Restaurants *(continued)*					
Fragrant Vegetable	Chinese/ Vegetarian	Inexp	76	B	1
I Cugini	Italian	Mod	76	C	1
Roscoe's House of Chicken and Waffles	American	Inexp	76	A	4,5,6
Cafe del Rey	New American	Mod	75	C	1
Tay Ho	Vietnamese	Inexp	75	A	9
Beaurivage	Continental/ Mediterranean	Mod/Exp	74	D	1
Engine Co. No. 28	American	Mod	74	C	5
Super Antojitos	Mexican	Inexp	74	A	9
Two-Star Restaurants					
Noodle World	Asian	Inexp	78	A	6
The Reel Inn	Seafood	Inexp	77	A	1
Ye Olde King's Head	English	Inexp	76	B	1
Bali Place	Indonesian	Inexp	75	B	1
Gumbo Pot	Cajun/Creole	Inexp	75	B	5
Neptune's Net	Seafood	Inexp	75	A	1
Uzbekistan	Russian	Inexp	75	B	5
Versailles	Cuban	Inexp	75	A	4,5,8
California Pizza Kitchen	California	Inexp	74	B	1,5,6
Fritto Misto	Italian	Inexp	74	A	1
Original Pantry Cafe	American	Inexp	74	A	5
Bo kaos	International	Mod	72	D	3
Musso & Frank	American	Mod	72	D	5

Restaurants by Zone

Name of Restaurant	Star Rating	Price Rating	Quality Rating	Value Rating
Zone 1—Westside				
◆ *American*				
17th Street Cafe	★★★	Inexp	80	B
Daily Grill	★★½	Inexp/Mod	79	B
Lincoln Bay Cafe	★★½	Mod	79	B
Pedals	★★★	Mod	79	C
The Main Course	★★½	Inexp	78	A
Real Food Daily	★★½	Inexp	77	A
◆ *Chinese*				
Plum Tree Inn	★★★	Inexp	79	C
Jasmine Tree	★★½	Inexp	79	B
Fragrant Vegetable	★★½	Inexp	76	B
◆ *Continental /Mediterranean*				
Beaurivage	★★½	Mod/Exp	74	D
◆ *English*				
Ye Olde King's Head	★★	Inexp	76	B
◆ *French*				
Rockenwagner	★★★★	Exp	94	C
Carrots	★★★½	Exp	85	D
◆ *Indian*				
Bombay Cafe	★★★½	Inexp	87	B
Nawab of India	★★★	Inexp	80	A
◆ *Indonesian*				
Bali Place	★★	Inexp	75	B
◆ *International*				
Gilliland's	★★★	Mod	83	B
◆ *Italian*				
Valentino	★★★★★	Exp/Very Exp	96	C
Drago	★★★½	Mod	89	C
Remi	★★★½	Mod/Exp	86	D
Primi	★★★½	Mod	85	C
Toscana	★★★	Mod	83	C

Name of Restaurant	Star Rating	Price Rating	Quality Rating	Value Rating
◆ *Italian (continued)*				
Il Ristorante di Giorgio Baldi	★★★	Mod	82	C
Il Moro	★★★	Inexp	81	A
Caffe Delfini	★★½	Inexp/Mod	79	C
Milano's Italian Kitchen	★★½	Inexp	78	A
Toto Caffe Spaghetteria	★★½	Inexp	78	A
I Cugini	★★½	Mod	76	C
Fritto Misto	★★	Inexp	74	A
◆ *Japanese*				
U–Zen	★★★	Mod	84	C
Yuu	★★★	Inexp/Mod	83	C
Asahi Ramen	★★½	Inexp	77	A
Mishima	★★½	Inexp	77	B
◆ *Mexican*				
Border Grill	★★★½	Mod	87	C
Lula	★★½	Inexp	79	B
◆ *Middle Eastern*				
Shahrezad	★★½	Inexp	79	B
◆ *Moroccan*				
Koutoubia	★★★	Mod	83	B
◆ *New American*				
Granita	★★★★	Exp	92	C
Hotel Bel-Air	★★★★	Exp	91	C
Michael's	★★★½	Exp	88	C
Woodside	★★★½	Mod	85	B
72 Market Street	★★★	Exp	84	D
Hal's Bar & Grill	★★★	Mod	83	B
Joe's	★★★	Mod	83	B
Bambu	★★★	Mod/Exp	82	D
Crocodile Cafe	★★★	Inexp	80	B
The Ivy at the Shore	★★★	Exp	80	D
Cafe del Rey	★★½	Mod	75	C
California Pizza Kitchen	★★	Inexp	74	B

Name of Restaurant	Star Rating	Price Rating	Quality Rating	Value Rating
◆ *Pacific Rim*				
Chinois on Main	★★★★½	Very Exp	95	C
Zenzero	★★★	Mod/Exp	84	D
Typhoon	★★½	Inexp/Mod	79	B
◆ *Polish*				
Warszawa	★★½	Inexp/Mod	78	B
◆ *Seafood*				
Ocean Avenue Seafood	★★★	Mod	83	C
The Reel Inn	★★	Inexp	77	A
Neptune's Net	★★	Inexp	75	A
◆ *Southern*				
Aunt Kizzy's Back Porch	★★★	Inexp	81	B
◆ *Southwestern*				
Abiquiu	★★★★	Mod	92	B
◆ *Thai*				
Chan Dara	★★★	Inexp	80	B
Zone 2—South Bay				
◆ *American*				
Shenandoah Cafe	★★½	Inexp/Mod	79	B
◆ *Caribbean*				
Cha Cha Cha	★★½	Mod	77	C
◆ *International*				
Chez Melange	★★★	Mod	82	B
Depot	★★★	Mod	82	C
◆ *Italian*				
L'Opera	★★★	Mod	83	C
◆ *Mediterranean*				
Fino	★★★	Mod	83	B
◆ *New American*				
Reed's	★★★	Mod	83	B

Name of Restaurant	Star Rating	Price Rating	Quality Rating	Value Rating
Zone 3—Golden Triangle				
◆ *American*				
The Grill on the Alley	★★★½	Exp	87	D
Cynthia's	★★★	Mod	81	B
Lawry's The Prime Rib	★★★	Mod	81	C
Daily Grill	★★½	Inexp/Mod	79	B
Book Soup Bistro	★★½	Mod	78	C
◆ *Chinese*				
The Mandarin	★★★½	Mod	85	D
◆ *French*				
L'Orangerie	★★★★★	Very Exp	97	D
Lunaria	★★★½	Mod	89	C
Le Chardonnay	★★★	Exp	83	C
Le Dome	★★★	Mod/Exp	83	D
Le Petit Bistro	★★★	Inexp	83	B
Drai's	★★★	Exp	80	D
◆ *Greek*				
Sofi Estiatorian	★★★	Mod	84	B
◆ *Hungarian*				
The Players	★★★	Mod	80	C
◆ *International*				
Chaya Brasserie	★★★½	Exp	89	C
Bo kaos	★★	Mod	72	D
◆ *Italian*				
Locanda Veneta	★★★½	Mod	87	C
Alto Palato	★★★	Mod	85	C
Il Pastaio	★★★	Inexp/Mod	84	A
Da Pasquale	★★★	Inexp	83	A
Hugo's	★★★	Inexp	82	B
Il Cielo	★★★	Mod/Exp	82	C
Cicada	★★★	Mod	80	B
Il Fornaio	★★★	Inexp/Mod	80	B
Prego	★★★	Mod	80	B

Name of Restaurant	Star Rating	Price Rating	Quality Rating	Value Rating
♦ *Japanese*				
Matsuhisa	★★★★½	Very Exp	95	C
Ginza Sushi-ko	★★★½	Very Exp	90	F
Katsu 3rd	★★★	Mod	84	C
♦ *New American*				
Gardens	★★★★	Very Exp	91	D
Regent Beverly Wilshire Dining Room	★★★★	Very Exp	90	D
The Belvedere	★★★½	Exp	89	C
Spago	★★★½	Exp	89	D
Maple Drive	★★★½	Exp	84	C
David Slay's La Veranda	★★★½	Exp	83	D
Jackson's	★★★	Exp	83	C
The Ivy	★★★	Very Exp	80	F
♦ *Pacific Rim*				
Cafe La Boheme	★★★	Mod	82	C
♦ *Russian / French*				
Diagilev	★★★½	Very Exp	89	D
♦ *Steakhouse*				
Arnie Morton's of Chicago	★★★½	Exp	86	D
Ruth's Chris Steak House	★★★	Exp	84	D
♦ *Thai*				
Talesai	★★★	Mod	85	C
Zone 4—City South				
♦ *American*				
Roscoe's House of Chicken and Waffles	★★½	Inexp	76	A
♦ *Cajun / Creole*				
Harold & Belle's	★★★	Mod	80	C
♦ *Chinese*				
Hu's Szechwan	★★½	Inexp	79	B

Name of Restaurant	Star Rating	Price Rating	Quality Rating	Value Rating
◆ Cuban				
Versailles	★★	Inexp	75	A
◆ Jamaican				
Coley's Place	★★½	Mod	78	C
◆ Mexican				
Mi Ranchito	★★½	Inexp	78	A
Zone 5—Central City				
◆ American				
Hollywood Canteen	★★★	Mod	80	C
Caffe Latte	★★½	Inexp	78	B
Roscoe's House of Chicken and Waffles	★★½	Inexp	76	A
Engine Co. No. 28	★★½	Mod	74	C
Original Pantry Cafe	★★	Inexp	74	A
Musso & Frank	★★	Mod	72	D
◆ Argentinian				
Gardel's	★★½	Mod	77	C
◆ Cajun / Creole				
Gumbo Pot	★★	Inexp	75	B
◆ Caribbean				
Cha Cha Cha	★★½	Mod	77	C
◆ Chilean				
Rincon Chileno	★★½	Inexp	77	B
◆ Chinese				
Ocean Seafood	★★★½	Mod	85	C
Empress Pavilion	★★★	Inexp/Mod	84	B
Mon Kee	★★★	Mod	84	B
Yang Chow	★★★	Inexp	83	B
Mandarin Deli / Mandarin Noodle House	★★½	Inexp	79	A
Plum Tree Inn	★★★	Inexp	79	C

Name of Restaurant	Star Rating	Price Rating	Quality Rating	Value Rating
◆ *Cuban*				
Versailles	★★	Inexp	75	A
◆ *Delicatessen*				
Langer's	★★½	Inexp	80	B
◆ *French*				
Patina	★★★★★	Exp	98	B
Citrus	★★★★½	Exp	95	C
Bar Bistro	★★★½	Mod	89	B
Grill Lyon	★★★	Mod	84	B
Louis XIV	★★½	Mod	79	B
◆ *Greek*				
Le Petit Greek	★★★	Mod	80	B
◆ *Hungarian*				
Hungarian Budapest	★★½	Inexp	78	B
◆ *International*				
Vida	★★★½	Mod	86	C
Nicola	★★★	Mod	83	C
◆ *Italian*				
Rex Il Ristorante	★★★★	Exp/Very Exp	93	D
Ca'Brea	★★★½	Mod	87	C
Angeli Caffe	★★★	Inexp	86	B
Chianti Cucina	★★★½	Mod	85	B
Chianti Ristorante	★★★½	Mod	85	C
Trattoria Farfalla	★★★	Inexp/Mod	83	B
Farfalla La Brea	★★½	Mod	80	C
La Luna	★★½	Mod	79	C
Osteria Nonni	★★½	Inexp	79	B
Fabiolus	★★½	Inexp	76	A
◆ *Japanese*				
Ita-Cho	★★★½	Inexp	88	A
Katsu	★★★½	Mod	86	C
R-23	★★★	Mod	84	B

Name of Restaurant	Star Rating	Price Rating	Quality Rating	Value Rating
◆ Japanese (continued)				
Shabu Shabu House	★★½	Inexp	80	B
Atch-Kotch	★★½	Inexp	79	A
◆ Korean				
Nam Kang	★★★	Inexp	83	B
◆ Mexican				
La Serenata de Garibaldi	★★★½	Mod	87	B
Mexica	★★★	Mod	82	B
La Parrilla	★★★	Inexp	81	B
Barragan's	★★½	Inexp	77	B
El Cholo	★★½	Inexp	77	B
◆ Middle Eastern				
Al Amir	★★★½	Mod	86	B
Marouch	★★★	Inexp	83	B
◆ New American				
Campanile	★★★★½	Exp	95	C
Muse	★★★	Mod	83	C
Flora Kitchen	★★½	Inexp	80	D
Atlas Bar & Grill	★★½	Mod	77	C
California Pizza Kitchen	★★	Inexp	74	B
◆ Nicaraguan				
La Plancha Grill	★★½	Inexp	78	A
◆ Peruvian				
Mario's Peruvian	★★★	Inexp	80	B
◆ Russian				
Uzbekistan	★★	Inexp	75	B
◆ Seafood				
Ocean Seafood	★★★½	Mod	85	C
Water Grill	★★★½	Mod/Exp	85	C

Name of Restaurant	Star Rating	Price Rating	Quality Rating	Value Rating
◆ Southern				
Georgia	★★★	Mod	84	C
◆ Southwestern				
Authentic Cafe	★★★	Inexp	85	A
Original Sonora Cafe	★★★	Mod	81	D
Kachina Grill	★★½	Inexp/Mod	79	C
◆ Thai				
Jitlada	★★★	Inexp	85	B
Chan Dara	★★★	Inexp	80	B
Sanamluang Cafe	★★½	Inexp	80	A
Vim	★★½	Inexp	80	A
◆ West African				
Rosalind's	★★½	Inexp	78	B
Zone 6—San Gabriel Valley				
◆ American				
Old Town Bakery	★★★	Inexp	80	B
Roscoe's House of Chicken and Waffles	★★½	Inexp	76	A
◆ Asian				
Noodle World	★★	Inexp	78	A
◆ Chinese				
Yujean Kang's	★★★★	Mod	92	B
Ocean Star	★★★★	Mod	91	B
Lake Spring Cuisine	★★★½	Inexp	85	B
Wei Fun	★★★	Inexp	85	A
Charming Garden	★★★	Inexp	83	B
Dragon Regency	★★★	Inexp	83	B
Fu Shing	★★★	Inexp	83	C
Chu's Mandarin Cuisine	★★★	Inexp	82	B
Tung Lai Shun	★★★	Inexp/Mod	82	B

Name of Restaurant	Star Rating	Price Rating	Quality Rating	Value Rating
♦ Chinese (continued)				
Seafood Strip	★★★	Inexp/Mod	81	C
Mandarin Deli / Mandarin Noodle House	★★½	Inexp	79	A
♦ French				
Xiomara	★★★½	Mod	88	D
Twin Palms	★★★½	Mod	86	B
♦ Italian				
Il Pastaio	★★★	Inexp/Mod	84	A
Il Fornaio	★★★	Inexp/Mod	80	B
Mi Piace	★★★	Inexp	80	B
Milano's Italian Kitchen	★★½	Inexp	78	A
♦ Malaysian				
Kuala Lumpur	★★½	Inexp	79	B
♦ Mexican				
El Emperador Maya	★★★	Inexp	85	B
La Cabanita	★★★	Inexp	82	A
Barragan's	★★½	Inexp	77	B
♦ New American				
Bistro 45	★★★★	Exp	90	C
Parkway Grill	★★★★	Mod	90	C
Shiro	★★★½	Mod	88	B
Crocodile Cafe	★★★	Inexp	80	B
California Pizza Kitchen	★★	Inexp	74	B
♦ Pacific Rim				
Cinnabar	★★★	Mod	84	C
♦ Thai				
Tommy Tang's	★★★	Mod	82	C
Zone 7—San Fernando Valley East				
♦ Chinese				
Bamboo	★★★	Inexp	83	B

Name of Restaurant	Star Rating	Price Rating	Quality Rating	Value Rating
◆ *Delicatessen*				
Art's Delicatessen	★★★	Mod	82	C
◆ *French*				
Pinot	★★★★	Mod	91	C
Cafe Bizou	★★★½	Mod	87	B
Barsac Brasserie	★★★	Mod	80	C
◆ *Italian*				
Posto	★★★½	Mod/Exp	87	C
Ca'del Sole	★★★	Mod	85	C
Il Mito	★★★	Mod	84	C
La Loggia	★★½	Mod	79	B
Toto Caffe Spaghetteria	★★½	Inexp	78	A
La Pergola	★★½	Mod	77	C
◆ *Japanese*				
Sushi Nozawa	★★★½	Mod	88	C
Asanebo	★★★	Mod	85	B
Teru Sushi	★★★	Mod	80	D
◆ *Mexican*				
Barragan's	★★½	Inexp	77	B
◆ *Moroccan*				
Marrakesh	★★½	Mod	78	C
◆ *New American*				
Out Take Cafe	★★½	Inexp	78	A
◆ *Thai*				
Talesai	★★★	Mod	85	C
Jitlada West	★★★	Inexp	81	B
Sanamluang Cafe	★★½	Inexp	80	A
Zone 8—San Fernando Valley West				
◆ *American*				
Saddle Peak Lodge	★★★★	Exp	90	C
Daily Grill	★★½	Inexp/Mod	79	B

Name of Restaurant	Star Rating	Price Rating	Quality Rating	Value Rating
◆ *Caribbean*				
Cha Cha Cha Encino	★★½	Mod	77	C
◆ *Chinese*				
Plum Tree Inn	★★★	Inexp	79	C
Mandarin Deli/Mandarin Noodle House	★★½	Inexp	79	A
◆ *Cuban*				
Versailles	★★	Inexp	75	A
◆ *Delicatessen*				
Brent's Delicatessen	★★★	Inexp	84	B
◆ *Italian*				
Ritrovo	★★½	Mod	79	C
Terrazza Toscana	★★½	Mod	79	C
Milano's Italian Kitchen	★★½	Inexp	78	A
◆ *Mexican*				
La Parrilla	★★★	Inexp	81	B
◆ *Middle Eastern*				
Shahrezad	★★½	Inexp	79	B
◆ *Thai*				
Thai Ranch	★★½	Inexp	77	B
Zone 9—Orange County North				
◆ *French*				
Pascal	★★★★	Mod/Exp	93	C
Antoine	★★★★	Exp	90	D
◆ *Italian*				
Il Fornaio	★★★	Mod	80	B
Tutto Mare	★★★	Mod	80	C
◆ *Mexican*				
Super Antojitos	★★½	Inexp	74	A

Restaurants by Zone (continued)

Name of Restaurant	Star Rating	Price Rating	Quality Rating	Value Rating
◆ *New American*				
Golden Truffle	★★★½	Mod	85	B
Bistango	★★★	Mod	84	C
Diva	★★★	Mod	82	C
Mr. Stox	★★★	Mod	80	C
◆ *Scandinavian*				
Gustaf Anders	★★★★	Mod/Exp	94	C
◆ *Vietnamese*				
Dong Kahn	★★★	Inexp	80	A
Tay Ho	★★½	Inexp	75	A
Zone 10—Orange County South				
◆ *Indian*				
Bombay Duck	★★★	Mod	82	B
◆ *Italian*				
Romeo Cucina	★★½	Inexp	79	B
◆ *Mediterranean*				
Splashes	★★★½	Mod	84	C
◆ *New American/French*				
The Dining Room	★★★★	Very Exp	89	D
◆ *Pacific Rim*				
Five Feet	★★★½	Mod	88	C

Recommended for Late Night Dining

Restaurant	Cuisine	Star Rating	Price Rating	Quality Rating	Value Rating	Zone
Caffe Luna	Italian	★★½	Inexp	78	B	5
Cha Cha Cha Encino	Caribbean	★★½	Mod	77	C	8
Il Fornaio	Italian	★★★	Inexp/ Mod	80	B	3,6
Kate Mantilini	American	★★½	Inexp	76	B	3
Le Petit Bistro	French	★★★	Inexp	83	B	3
L'Opera	Italian	★★★	Mod	83	C	2
Louis XIV	French	★★½	Mod	79	B	5
Mi Piace	Italian	★★★	Inexp	80	B	6
Noodle World	Asian	★★	Inexp	78	A	6
Original Pantry Cafe	American	★★	Inexp	74	A	5
Prego	Italian	★★★	Mod	80	B	3
Uzbekistan	Russian	★★	Inexp	75	B	5

Recommended for Business Dining

Restaurant	Cuisine	Star Rating	Price Rating	Quality Rating	Value Rating	Zone
Abiquiu	Southwestern	★★★★	Mod	92	B	1
The Belvedere	New American	★★★½	Exp	89	C	3
Ca'del Sole	Italian	★★★	Mod	85	C	7
Campanile	New American	★★★★½	Exp	95	C	5
Chaya Brasserie	International	★★★½	Exp	89	C	3
Citrus	French	★★★★½	Exp	95	C	5
David Slay's La Veranda	New American/ Italian	★★★½	Exp	83	D	3
Engine Co. No. 28	American	★★½	Mod	74	C	5
Gardens	New American	★★★★	Very Exp	91	D	3
The Grill on the Alley	American	★★★½	Exp	87	D	3
Grill Lyon	French/Japanese	★★★	Mod	84	B	5
Jackson's	New American	★★★	Exp	83	C	3
Le Dome	French	★★★	Mod/Exp	83	D	3

Recommended for Business Dining (continued)

Restaurant	Cuisine	Star Rating	Price Rating	Quality Rating	Value Rating	Zone
L'Opera	Italian	★★★	Mod	83	C	2
Lunaria	French	★★★½	Mod	89	C	3
The Mandarin	Chinese	★★★½	Mod	85	D	3
Maple Drive	New American	★★★½	Exp	84	C	3
Muse	New American	★★★	Mod	83	C	5
Nicola	International	★★★	Mod	83	C	5
Ocean Star	Chinese/Seafood	★★★★	Mod	91	B	6
Parkway Grill	New American	★★★★	Mod	90	C	6
Patina	French	★★★★★	Exp	98	B	5
Pinot	French	★★★★	Mod	91	C	7
Terrazza Toscana	Italian	★★½	Mod	79	C	8
Twin Palms	French/American	★★★½	Mod	86	B	6
Valentino	Italian	★★★★★	Exp/ Very Exp	96	C	1
Water Grill	Seafood/ American	★★★½	Mod/Exp	85	C	5
Yujean Kang's	Chinese	★★★★	Mod	92	B	6

Recommended for Dining with a View

Restaurant	Cuisine	Star Rating	Price Rating	Quality Rating	Value Rating	Zone
Cafe del Rey	New American	★★½	Mod	75	C	1
Geoffrey's	New American	★★½	Exp	78	C	1
Gladstone's	American	★★	Mod	72	B	1
I Cugini	Italian	★★½	Mod	76	C	1
Le Dome	French	★★★	Mod/Exp	83	D	3
Ocean Avenue Seafood	Seafood	★★★	Mod	83	C	1
Pedals	American	★★★	Mod	79	C	1
Riva	New American	★★★	Exp	82	C	1
The Tower	French	★★★	Very Exp	80	D	5
Typhoon	Pacific Rim	★★½	Inexp/Mod	79	B	1

Recommended for Quiet and Romantic Dining

Restaurant	Cuisine	Star Rating	Price Rating	Quality Rating	Value Rating	Zone
Beaurivage	Continental/ Mediterranean	★★½	Mod/Exp	74	D	1
The Belvedere	New American	★★★½	Exp	89	C	3
Cafe La Boheme	Pacific Rim	★★★	Mod	82	C	3
Carrots	French-Japanese	★★★½	Exp	85	D	1
Chianti Ristorante	Italian	★★★½	Mod	85	C	5
Diagilev	Russian/French	★★★½	Very Exp	89	D	3
Gardens	New American	★★★★	Very Exp	91	D	3
Hotel Bel-Air	New American	★★★★	Exp	91	C	1
Il Cielo	Italian	★★★	Mod/Exp	82	C	3
Katsu	Japanese	★★★½	Mod	86	C	5
La Pergola	Italian	★★½	Mod	77		7
Le Chardonnay	French	★★★	Exp	83	C	3
L'Orangerie	French	★★★★★	Very Exp	97	D	3
Lunaria	French	★★★½	Mod	89	C	3
Michael's	New American	★★★½	Exp	88	C	1
Patina	French	★★★★★	Exp	98	B	5
Pinot	French	★★★★	Mod	91	C	7
Talesai	Thai	★★★	Mod	85	C	3,7
Valentino	Italian	★★★★★	Exp/ Very Exp	96	C	1
Xiomara	French	★★★½	Mod	88	D	6
Yujean Kang's	Chinese	★★★★	Mod	92	B	6

RESTAURANT
profiles

Abiquiu

Zone 1   Westside
1413 5th Street, Santa Monica
(310) 395-8611

<table>
<tr><td colspan="2">Southwestern</td></tr>
<tr><td colspan="2">★★★★</td></tr>
<tr><td colspan="2">Moderate</td></tr>
<tr><td>Quality 92</td><td>Value B</td></tr>
</table>

Reservations:	Accepted
When to go:	Happy Hour is a relative bargain
Entree range:	$12–18
Payment:	Major credit cards
Service rating:	★★★★
Friendliness rating:	★★★★
Parking:	Valet available
Bar:	Full service
Wine selection:	Very good
Dress:	Gap to Armani
Disabled access:	Yes
Customers:	Architects, designers, foodies
Lunch:	Monday–Friday, 11:30 A.M.–2 P.M.
Dinner:	Every night, 5–10 P.M.

Atmosphere / setting: A dramatic contemporary space defined by a two-story undulating rosewood wall, huge sheets of plate glass to the street, and an open staircase to the wonderful bar and tamale bar in the loft. Warmth is added with white linens and humble New Mexican religious art.

House specialties: Bowl of Red, a dreamy red-corn posole soup; crispy blue-corn tacos stuffed with duck confit, pine nuts, and onions, with a superb green salsa and a rocket salad; Enchiladas Papas Fritas, a free-form "enchilada" that layers crisp, paper-thin sheets of fried potato, buttery mashed sweet potatoes, and incredibly delicious marinated pork loin; buñuelos, a Mexican donutlike dessert with banana.

Other recommendations: Taquitos Godzilla, tiny multicolored taco shells filled with shrimp, Japanese cucumber, pickled ginger, and wasabe; Banzai Tamale, a traditional tamale topped with Asian vegetables and Chinese air-dried duck; homemade sorbets.

Summary & comments: A few good things came out of the big '94 earthquake, like the reworking of John Sedlar's too-precious Bikini (which suffered considerable damage) into the less-expensive, homier Abiquiu. You'll giggle when you're first presented with the Brobdingnagian plates and food-as-art presentations that Sedlar loves, but you'll be knocked out by the skill with which he combines the powerful flavors of the Southwest and Asia. Considered the father of modern Southwestern cooking, Sedlar is still clearly in his prime.

Al Amir

Zone 5   Central City
5750 Wilshire Boulevard, Suite 195
(213) 931-8740

Lebanese	
★★★½	
Moderate	
Quality 86	Value B

Reservations:	Accepted
When to go:	Any time
Entree range:	$10.95–15.95
Payment:	Major credit cards
Service rating:	★★★★
Friendliness rating:	★★★★
Parking:	Valet available at night
Bar:	Full service
Wine selection:	Californian, French, and Lebanese
Dress:	Business
Disabled access:	Yes
Customers:	Lebanese expatriates, businesspeople
Lunch / Dinner:	Monday–Thursday, 11:30 A.M.–10 P.M.; Friday, 11:30 A.M.–11 P.M.
Dinner:	Saturday, 6–11 P.M.

Atmosphere / setting: *Al Amir* means "The Prince," and a prince would indeed feel at home in this elegant office-building restaurant, with its tuxedoed waiters, heavy silver, rich linens, and etched-glass room dividers.

House specialties: Dozens of exceptional mezze, including kabis (Lebanese pickles); kibbeh nayeh (raw lamb mixed with wheat, onions, and spices); kibbeh maqli (lamb meatballs with pine nuts in a wheat shell); and fried lamb brains with lemon and spices.

Other recommendations: Such Middle Eastern standards as hummus, falafel, tabbouleh, and fresh homemade pita; schwarma; Lebanese pastries.

Entertainment & amenities: Live music and belly dancing Friday and Saturday nights at 9:30.

Summary & comments: L.A.'s preeminent Middle Eastern restaurant, Al Amir boasts a fleet of highly skilled chefs and a dazzling roster of mezze, the Lebanese appetizers that most diners combine to make a meal. There's a whole lot of luxury and seductive flavors for the price.

Alto Palato

Zone 3   Golden Triangle
755 North La Cienega Boulevard
West Hollywood
(310) 657-9271

Italian	
★★★	
Moderate	
Quality 85	Value C

Reservations:	Accepted
When to go:	Any time
Entree range:	$9–20
Payment:	Major credit cards
Service rating:	★★★
Friendliness rating:	★★★
Parking:	Valet available
Bar:	Full service
Wine selection:	Good Italians
Dress:	Casual to chic
Disabled access:	Yes
Customers:	Locals
Lunch/Dinner:	Monday–Friday, noon–10:30 P.M.
Dinner:	Sunday, 5–10:30 P.M.

Atmosphere / setting: Through a contemporary courtyard and past a chic little bar is the pretty dining room, with high ceilings, white linens, candlelight, and dramatic modern art.

House specialties: Superb pizzas, like the one made with thin potato slices and sautéed onions, or the prosciutto and greens; calamari fritti; housemade gelato that may be the best in town.

Other recommendations: Fresh, generous green salads; simple, authentically Italian pastas.

Summary & comments: Mauro Vincenti, who also owns downtown's super-luxe Rex, has struggled with this space, which he has changed from Pazzia to Fennel to this latest incarnation. The trendy hordes still aren't beating a path to his door, which is good news for the regulars, who never have to wait for a table. The pizzas, exceptionally thin of crust and sublime of topping, are worth the trip alone, and the gelati is swell, too. Good, simple Italian fare in a stylish but blessedly quiet settting.

Angeli Caffe

Zone 5   Central City
7274 Melrose Avenue
(213) 936-9086

	Italian
	★★★
	Inexpensive
	Quality 86 Value B

Reservations:	Accepted
When to go:	Any time
Entree range:	$7.50–13.50
Payment:	Major credit cards
Service rating:	★★★
Friendliness rating:	★★★
Parking:	Valet
Bar:	Beer and wine only
Wine selection:	Limited—Italian
Dress:	Casual
Disabled access:	Yes
Customers:	Artists, intellectuals
Lunch/Dinner:	Monday–Friday, 11:30 A.M.–10:30 P.M.; Saturday, noon–11 P.M.
Dinner:	Sunday, 5–10:30 P.M.

Atmosphere / setting: One of the early projects of cutting-edge L.A. architects Morphosis, this two-room cafe is notable for its jutting steel beams and simple black tables and chairs. A lively spot for people-watching and talking about your latest finds on the Internet.

House specialties: Steaming pizza bread; deceptively simple pastas and salads; and superb individual pizzas—the pizza ai tre formaggi, spiked with prosciutto, is heavenly.

Other recommendations: Regulars return for the roast chicken or the grilled chicken topped with tomato and arugula; also worthy are the cacciucco livornese, a heady bowl of fish soup, the daily fresh-fish special, and, when offered, the roast pork with fennel.

Summary & comments: One of the pioneers of the authentic Italian movement, Angeli remains home to what may be the best pizza in town. The rest of the food is terrific, too. Angeli vies with Chianti/Chianti Cucina for best Italian on Melrose, and it's a cool hangout for a cafe lunch or a casual dinner.

ANTOINE

Zone 9   Orange County North
Sutton Place Hotel,
    4500 MacArthur Boulevard,
    Newport Beach
(714) 476-2001

French	
★ ★ ★ ★	
Expensive	
Quality 90	Value D

Reservations:	Advised
When to go:	Any time
Entree range:	$24–34
Payment:	Major credit cards
Service rating:	★ ★ ★ ★ ★
Friendliness rating:	★ ★ ★ ★ ★
Parking:	Valet available
Bar:	Full service
Wine selection:	High-end French and Californians
Dress:	Dressed-up
Disabled access:	Yes
Customers:	Businesspeople and special-occasion celebrants
Dinner:	Tuesday–Thursday, 6–10 P.M.;
	Friday and Saturday, 6–10:30 P.M.

Atmosphere / setting: Conservative, muted, and European in style. Archways connect three quiet rooms replete with mirrored walls, soft colors, elegant oil paintings, upholstered furniture, and extravagant flowers.

House specialties: Steamed Maine lobster on linguine with tarragon sauce; tenderloin of beef with purple-mustard crust; Norwegian salmon with polenta and asparagus coulis.

Other recommendations: Crispy sweetbreads with green beans and mango relish; saddle of lamb with eggplant caviar; napoleon crème brûlée; old-fashioned brownie sundae.

Entertainment & amenities: Guitarist on weeknights.

Summary & comments: A great place for impressing clients or wooing would-be loved ones, Antoine has consistently matched its luxe setting and service with cooking that would surely rate a Michelin star if it were served in Paris. A deeply luxurious restaurant serving skillfully prepared modern French standards.

Honors / awards: Best Dining Experience, *Orange Coast* magazine; *Wine Spectator* Award of Excellence.

Arnie Morton's of Chicago

Steakhouse	
★★★½	
Expensive	
Quality 86	Value D

Zone 3   Golden Triangle
435 South La Cienega Boulevard
(310) 246-1501

Reservations:	Recommended
When to go:	Any time
Entree range:	$15.95–28.95
Payment:	Major credit cards
Service rating:	★★★★
Friendliness rating:	★★★★
Parking:	Valet available
Bar:	Full service
Wine selection:	Large and pricey
Dress:	Business or upscale
Disabled access:	Yes
Customers:	Prosperous carnivores
Dinner:	Monday–Saturday, 5:30–11 P.M.;
	Sunday, 5–10 P.M.

Atmosphere / setting: Rather plain, in a comfortable, masculine, American way. The real decor is found on the rolling cart laden with your meal's raw ingredients: hunks of beef and chicken, lobsters, baking potatoes, fat asparagus.

House specialties: Prime rib, several cuts of first-rate steak, veal and lamb chops, and dauntingly large lobsters are the main draw.

Other recommendations: Massive baked potatoes; oysters; fresh berries with sabayon sauce; New York cheesecake.

Summary & comments: Meat lovers can argue for hours about whether the best steak in town is served at this L.A. branch of the Chicago steakhouse or at Ruth's Chris or The Palm. Suffice it to say that the meat here can hold its own with the best, and sometimes is the best, depending on the day.

Art's Delicatessen

Zone 7 San Fernando Valley East	Delicatessen
12224 Ventura Boulevard, Studio City	★★★
(818) 762-1221	Moderate
	Quality 82 Value C

Reservations:	For large parties
When to go:	Any time; lunch and weekend breakfast are crowded
Entree range:	$8–13
Payment:	Major credit cards
Service rating:	★★
Friendliness rating:	★★
Parking:	Hard to find
Bar:	Beer and wine
Wine selection:	Limited
Dress:	Casual
Disabled access:	Yes
Customers:	All types: showbiz, seniors, upscale Valley families
Open:	Sunday–Thursday, 6:30 A.M.–11 P.M.; Friday and Saturday, 6:30 P.M.–midnight

Atmosphere / setting: A sprawling, bustling deli with plenty of booths, all shiny and new since the recent post-earthquake rebuilding.

House specialties: Art's assorted fish plate for two (lox, cod, whitefish, bagels, and all the fixings) is a cherished Southern California institution. Almost as beloved are the corned beef and pastrami sandwiches, triple-decker sandwiches, and chicken soup.

Other recommendations: The earthquake rebuilding inspired Art to add some fancy, nondeli dinner entrees, like seared ahi and steak.

Summary & comments: A couple of newcomers (Jerry's Deli and Barney Greengrass) have stolen a bit of Art's deli thunder, but it remains one of the best places in town for a nosh.

Asahi Ramen

Zone 1   Westside
2027 Sawtelle Boulevard, West L.A.
(310) 479-2231

	Japanese
	★★½
	Inexpensive
	Quality 77 Value A

Reservations:	Not accepted
When to go:	Any time
Entree range:	$4.25–6.50
Payment:	No credit cards
Service rating:	★★
Friendliness rating:	★★
Parking:	Self
Bar:	Bring your own
Wine selection:	None
Dress:	Casual
Disabled access:	Limited
Customers:	Japanese businesspeople, locals
Lunch/Dinner:	Monday–Wednesday and Friday–Sunday,
	11:30 A.M.–8:30 P.M.

Atmosphere / setting: A simple, cheerful Japanese noodle shop that never lacks for business.

House specialties: Delicious pork-filled gyoza (dumplings); fresh udon and soba noodles, both hot and cold, with various broths and toppings.

Other recommendations: Wonton ramen.

Summary & comments: One of several noodle houses in West L.A.'s "Little Tokyo," Asahi will deeply satisfy your *Tampopo* cravings. A good, quick, very cheap meal.

ASANEBO

Zone 7   San Fernando Valley East
11941 Ventura Boulevard, Studio City
(818) 760-3348

Japanese	
★★★	
Moderate	
Quality 85	Value B

Reservations:	Accepted
When to go:	Any time
Entree range:	$5–9 for small dishes
Payment:	VISA, MC
Service rating:	★★★
Friendliness rating:	★★★★
Parking:	In front
Bar:	Beer and saké
Wine selection:	Good hot and cold saké list
Dress:	Casual
Disabled access:	Yes
Customers:	Neighborhood folks, Japanese chefs
Dinner:	Monday–Thursday, 6–10 P.M.;
	Friday and Saturday, 6–11 P.M. Closing times
	may vary.

Atmosphere / setting: It looks like any of a hundred pod-mall sushi joints, complete with counter, but no sushi is served. The small room is clean, comfortable, and modest.

House specialties: Sparkling fresh sashimi; crispy shell-on fried shrimp with rock salt; extraordinarily sweet and juicy grilled black cod with citrus flavor; asparagus-stuffed calamari with ponzu sauce.

Other recommendations: Sweet steamed Dungeness crab sashimi with yuzu (lemon-lime) dipping sauce; agedashi tofu, fried and placed in a soy-ginger broth.

Summary & comments: After a decade of sushi mania, L.A. is ready to embrace a broader definition of Japanese food. Asanebo is one of the new wave of authentic koryori-ya restaurants, specializing in small dishes and saké. Two chefs, both of whom cooked at Matsuhisa and Itacho, turn out first-rate food at modest prices. Let the friendly staff know you're interested, and they'll help you build a memorable meal.

Atch-Kotch

Zone 5   Central City
1253 North Vine Street, Hollywood
(213) 467-5537

	Japanese
	★★½
	Inexpensive
	Quality 79 Value A

Reservations:	Not accepted
When to go:	A good Hollywood lunch spot
Entree range:	$5–12
Payment:	VISA, MC
Service rating:	★★★
Friendliness rating:	★★★
Parking:	Self
Bar:	Beer and saké
Wine selection:	Saké
Dress:	Casual
Disabled access:	Yes
Customers:	Hollywood-area office and studio workers, other locals
Lunch/Dinner:	Monday–Saturday, 11:30 A.M.–10 P.M.

Atmosphere/setting: A minimall cafe with black lacquer tables, black chairs, Japanese art, and a few small counters.

House specialties: California rolls; daily sashimi specials; cold buckwheat-noodle salads; a complex mix-and-match system of ramen noodle dishes, in fine miso, shoyu, or clear broths, with such toppings as grated garlic, sweet corn, or fresh egg.

Other recommendations: Udon, soba, and somen noodles, hot or cold, with such toppings as curry or shiitake mushrooms; shrimp fried rice; gyoza; chef's daily special ozen dinner

Summary & comments: Hungry Hollywood workers, faced with limited restaurant choices, have found this pleasant little Japanese cafe and made it their own. The carefully made noodle dishes—some of which are fairly spicy—are the big draw, but all the food is good.

Atlas Bar & Grill

Zone 5 Central City	New American / International
3760 Wilshire Boulevard	★★½
(213) 380-8400	Moderate
	Quality 77 Value C

Reservations:	Accepted
When to go:	Any time; late is hipper
Entree range:	$8–19
Payment:	VISA, MC, AMEX
Service rating:	★★
Friendliness rating:	★★★
Parking:	Valet available
Bar:	Full service
Wine selection:	Average
Dress:	Stylish
Disabled access:	Yes
Customers:	At lunch, hip businesspeople; at dinner, trendy folks from all walks
Lunch:	Monday–Friday, 11:30 A.M.–3 P.M.
Dinner:	Monday–Thursday, 6–11 P.M.; Friday and Saturday, 6 P.M.–midnight

Atmosphere / setting: Set in the beautifully restored Wiltern, an L.A. art deco landmark, the Atlas boasts a setting as stylish as the clientele. Most notable are the Greek-god sculptures hanging overhead.

House specialties: Chicken and sausage gumbo; seared ahi salad; shrimp pesto pizza; jerk chicken or red snapper.

Other recommendations: Crabcakes; angel hair pomodoro; spicy black-pepper shrimp; chocolate mousse.

Entertainment & amenities: Live jazz nightly.

Summary & comments: The food's as trendy as can be, but much of it actually tastes good. Atlas does a good job of filling the upscale-restaurant void in faded mid-Wilshire.

Aunt Kizzy's Back Porch

	Southern
Zone 1 Westside	★★★
Villa Marina Shopping Center,	Inexpensive
4325 Glencoe Avenue,	
Marina del Rey	Quality 81 Value B
(310) 578-1005	

Reservations:	No
When to go:	Early or late; weekend dinner and Sunday brunch are mobbed
Entree range:	$10.95–12.95
Payment:	AMEX
Service rating:	★★★
Friendliness rating:	★★★★
Parking:	In front
Bar:	None
Wine selection:	None
Dress:	Casual
Disabled access:	Yes
Customers:	Everyone; Sunday brunch brings a well-dressed after-church crowd of African-American families
Brunch:	Sunday, 11 A.M.–3 P.M.
Lunch/Dinner:	Monday–Thursday, 10 A.M.–10 P.M.; Friday, 10 A.M.–11 P.M.
Dinner:	Saturday, 4–11 P.M.; Sunday, 4–10 P.M.

Atmosphere / setting: Tucked in a corner of a sprawling, confusing mall, Aunt Kizzy's is a cluttered, homey place. But rows of celebrity photos acknowledge that we're not in rural Georgia. Judging by the number of times the staff sings along with Stevie Wonder's happy-birthday song blaring on the sound system, this is one of the most popular birthday-party spots in town.

House specialties: The fried chicken and tender smothered pork chops are well worth the damage they'll do to your arteries.

Other recommendations: Fried catfish, meat loaf with Creole red gravy, collard greens, lemonade, peach cobbler, and wonderful bread pudding.

Summary & comments: Arrive hungry and ready for a good time at this lively bastion of Southern comfort food.

AuthentIc CafE

	Southwestern / New American
	★★★
	Inexpensive
	Quality 85 Value A

Zone 5   Central City
7605 Beverly Boulevard
(213) 939-4626

Reservations:	No
When to go:	Always crowded
Entree range:	$7–13
Payment:	VISA, MC
Service rating:	★★★
Friendliness rating:	★★★
Parking:	Street
Bar:	None
Wine selection:	None
Dress:	Casual
Disabled access:	Yes
Customers:	A funky, young mix of foodies
Lunch / Dinner:	Monday–Thursday, 11:30 A.M.–10 P.M.;
	Friday, 11:30 A.M.–11 P.M.;
	Saturday, 10 A.M.–11 P.M.;
	Sunday, 10 A.M.–10 P.M.

Atmosphere / setting: Colorful, noisy, and crowded with artistically dressed young folk at tiny tables. A new addition has made things more comfortable.

House specialties: Santa Fe salad, a sort of Southwestern tostada; chicken casserole with cornbread crust; soft taco platter; wood-grilled chicken with mole sauce.

Other recommendations: Lots of good choices for vegetarians, from vegetable soft tacos to spicy vegetables with kung pao sauce over brown rice.

Summary & comments: The Authentic is an L.A. trendsetter, serving inventive, vividly flavorful Cal-Mex-Asian food at graduate-student prices. An essential L.A. experience.

Bali Place

	Indonesian
	★★
	Inexpensive
	Quality 75 Value B

Zone 1   Westside
2530 Overland Avenue, West L.A.
(310) 204-4341

Reservations: Accepted
When to go: Any time
Entree range: $5–15
Payment: VISA, MC, AMEX
Service rating: ★★
Friendliness rating: ★★★
Parking: Lot
Bar: None; bring your own
Wine selection: None
Dress: Casual
Disabled access: Yes
Customers: Culinary adventurers
Lunch/Dinner: Monday, Tuesday, Thursday, and Friday,
                        11:30 A.M.–10 P.M.; Saturday and Sunday,
                        noon–10 P.M.

Atmosphere/setting: A no-frills minimall cafe.

House specialties: Gado gado, a vegetable-based salad with tofu, egg, and shrimp chips with a peanut dressing; grilled fish cakes wrapped in banana leaves; fish with lemongrass and shrimp paste.

Other recommendations: Squid-fried chicken; beef stew; glass noodles; shaved ice topped with fruit.

Summary & comments: An admirable L.A. emissary for the spicy, complex cooking of Indonesia.

Bamboo

	Chinese
	★★★
	Inexpensive
	Quality 83 Value B

Zone 7   San Fernando Valley East
14010 Ventura Boulevard,
   Sherman Oaks
(818) 788-0202

Reservations:	Accepted
When to go:	Any time
Entree range:	$8.25–13.75
Payment:	Major credit cards
Service rating:	★★★
Friendliness rating:	★★★
Parking:	Valet available
Bar:	Full service
Wine selection:	Limited
Dress:	Casual
Disabled access:	Yes
Customers:	Valley residents
Lunch/Dinner:	Sunday–Thursday, 11:30 A.M.–10:15 P.M.;
	Friday and Saturday, 11:30 A.M.–10:30 P.M.

Atmosphere / setting: Two bright and cheerful dining rooms, with white linens on the tables and fish swimming in tanks.

House specialties: Spiced Chinese cabbage; pan-fried dumplings; kung pao chicken; vivid jade chicken; Hunanese lamb; hot spicy eggplant.

Other recommendations: Pan-fried noodles; dry-fried string beans; hot braised shrimp.

Summary & comments: Valleyites who don't want to schlep to San Gabriel are fortunate to have Bamboo, an inviting neighborhood restaurant that brings authentic Hunanese, Taiwanese, and Szechwan flavors to Sherman Oaks.

BAMBU

		New American
Zone 1 Westside		★★★
Country Mart,		Mod/Exp
3835 Cross Creek Road, Malibu		
(310) 456-5464		Quality 82 Value D

Reservations:	Accepted
When to go:	Any time
Entree range:	$17–28
Payment:	Major credit cards
Service rating:	★★★
Friendliness rating:	★★★
Parking:	Valet available
Bar:	Full service
Wine selection:	Good
Dress:	Malibu chic
Disabled access:	Yes
Customers:	High-energy, high-style Malibu locals
Lunch:	Tuesday–Sunday, 11:30 A.M.–3 P.M.
Dinner:	Tuesday–Thursday and Sunday, 5:30–10 P.M.;
	Friday and Saturday, 5:30–11 P.M.

Atmosphere / setting: A bustling, contemoporary, people-watching paradise, with a sushi bar on one end, a booze bar on the other, and an open kitchen in between.

House specialties: Lobster salad; a full range of sushi and sashimi; sea bass with sesame-seed crust; french fries dusted with chile powder; tiramisu.

Other recommendations: Spicy Thai chicken wontons; Indonesian rack of lamb; flourless chocolate cake.

Summary & comments: The scene, the people-watching, and the sushi bar may presage hopeless trendiness instead of good food, but chef Lisa Stalvey, ex of Spago, knows her way around the Asian-Italian-Latin-American hodgepodge that makes up modern American cooking. A good place to see Malibu in action, and eat good food, too.

70

Bar Bistro

Zone 5   Central City
Citrus Restaurant,
    6703 Melrose Avenue
(213) 857-0034

<table>
<tr><td></td><td>French</td></tr>
<tr><td></td><td>★★★½</td></tr>
<tr><td></td><td>Moderate</td></tr>
<tr><td></td><td>Quality 89   Value B</td></tr>
</table>

Reservations:	Accepted
When to go:	Any time
Entree range:	$9.50–14
Payment:	Major credit cards
Service rating:	★★★★
Friendliness rating:	★★★★
Parking:	Valet
Bar:	Beer and wine
Wine selection:	Quality, affordable French and Californian
Dress:	Casual to elegant
Disabled access:	Yes
Customers:	Upper-echelon Hollywood, assorted beautiful people
Lunch:	Monday–Friday, noon–2:30 P.M.
Dinner:	Monday–Thursday, 6:30–10 P.M.; Friday, 6:30–10:30 P.M.; Saturday, 6–10:30 P.M.

Atmosphere / setting: What used to be Siberia at Citrus—the dreary inside dining room—has been transformed into a welcoming bistro, warmed with such country touches as hanging bunches of dried flowers. In casual bistro style, tables are small and closely packed.

House specialties: Duck salad; famous mashed potatoes; whole roasted chicken, crisp-skinned and aromatic; sautéed salmon with creamy spinach and onions; apple tart.

Other recommendations: Every dish on the short menu is excellent.

Summary & comments: Diners on an expense account head to the left when they enter Citrus; those watching their wallets head to the right, to this outstanding bistro, where they're served unassuming but flawlessly prepared contemporary French bistro standards. Haute L.A. at Van Nuys prices.

BARRAGAN'S

	Mexican
	★★½
	Inexpensive
	Quality 77 Value B

Zone 5   Central City
1538 West Sunset Boulevard, Echo Park
(213) 250-4256

Zone 6   San Gabriel Valley
814 South Central Avenue, Glendale
(818) 243-1103

Zone 7   San Fernando Valley East
730 North Victory Boulevard, Burbank
(818) 848-2325

Reservations:	Accepted
When to go:	Any time
Entree range:	$6.25–10.95 for complete dinner
Payment:	VISA, MC, CB, DC (payment varies by branch)
Service rating:	★★
Friendliness rating:	★★★
Parking:	Self
Bar:	Full service
Wine selection:	Limited
Dress:	Casual
Disabled access:	Yes
Customers:	All sorts
Open:	Monday–Saturday, 7:30 A.M.–10:30 P.M.; Sunday, 7:30 A.M.–10 P.M. (Burbank and Glendale branches open at 8 A.M.

Atmosphere / setting: The Echo Park Barragan's, the best of the bunch, is stereotypically Mexican: a dark, rambling space with big, deep booths.

House specialties: Excellent margaritas; arroz con pollo; tasty carne asada or carnitas plates; saucy chicken enchiladas; crab enchiladas; traditional birria.

Other recommendations: Good breakfasts: menudo; huevos rancheros; chorizo and eggs; even American pancakes.

Summary & comments: This solid, family-run minichain does a great job with the Cal-Mex comfort-food classics, from combination plates to arroz con pollo to frothy margaritas. The Echo Park branch seems the most authentic, but all will happily satisfy a rice-and-beans or huevos rancheros craving.

BARSAC BRASSERIE

Zone 7   San Fernando Valley East
4212 Lankershim Boulevard,
    North Hollywood
(818) 760-7081

French

★★★

Moderate

Quality 80   Value C

Reservations:	Accepted
When to go:	Any time
Entree range:	$9.95–15.25
Payment:	Major credit cards
Service rating:	★★★
Friendliness rating:	★★★
Parking:	Valet available
Bar:	Full service
Wine selection:	Good, affordable French selections
Dress:	Casual
Disabled access:	Yes
Customers:	From nearby studios
Lunch:	Monday–Friday, 11:30 A.M.–2:30 P.M.
Dinner:	Monday–Saturday, 5:30–10 P.M.

Atmosphere / setting: A comfortable, contemporary bistro with white-washed exposed ceilings, black chairs, white linens, and a bar.

House specialties: Smoked salmon plate; white beans and smoked duck salad; penne with tomato, basil, garlic, and Kalamata olives; thick-cut pork chop with mustard–horseradish sauce.

Other recommendations: Daily specials; chopped spinach salad; grilled halibut with red bell pepper sauce.

Summary & comments: The bloom's a little off of the rose at this bistro, whose food has evolved from classic French bistro to commonplace Italian-French-Californian cafe. But it remains a welcome hangout in a restaurant-poor neighborhood near Universal Studios, and the cooking is entirely competent.

BEAURIVAGE

Continental / Mediterranean	
★★½	
Mod / Exp	
Quality 74	Value D

Zone 1   Westside
26025 Pacific Coast Highway, Malibu
(310) 456-5733

Reservations:	Advised
When to go:	Summer evenings
Entree range:	$13–25
Payment:	Major credit cards
Service rating:	★★★
Friendliness rating:	★★★★
Parking:	Street; valet on weekends
Bar:	Full service
Wine selection:	Good
Dress:	Upscale
Disabled access:	Yes
Customers:	Romantics
Brunch:	Sunday, 11 A.M.–3 P.M.
Dinner:	Sunday–Thursday, 5–10 P.M.;
	Friday and Saturday, 5–11 P.M.

Atmosphere / setting: A lovely Mediterranean cottage across Pacific Coast Highway from the coast, with a bougainvillea-draped patio that's a California dream.

House specialties: Gazpacho; steamed mussels with white wine, shallots, and parsley; grilled rack of lamb with Mediterranean herbs; filet mignon with choice of sauces.

Other recommendations: Smoked salmon; daily fish specials; pappardelle with wild-rabbit ragout.

Entertainment & amenities: Pianist or duo weeknights, strolling guitarists weekends.

Summary & comments: Although the Mediterranean / Continental food is just fine, the real draw here is the romance in the setting and service. An ideal spot for an anniversary or a third date.

THE Belvedere

Zone 3 Golden Triangle	New American
Peninsula Hotel,	★★★½
9882 Little Santa Monica Boulevard,	Expensive
Beverly Hills	Quality 89 Value C
(310) 273-4888	

Reservations:	Accepted
When to go:	For breakfast
Entree range:	$18–26
Payment:	Major credit cards
Service rating:	★★★★★
Friendliness rating:	★★★★★
Parking:	Valet available
Bar:	Full service
Wine selection:	Quality and expensive
Dress:	Business to Hollywood rumpled
Disabled access:	Yes
Customers:	Moguls, dowagers, wealthy travelers
Breakfast:	Every day, 6:30–11:30 A.M.
Brunch:	Sunday, 11 A.M.–3 P.M.
Lunch:	Monday–Friday, 11:30 A.M.–3:30 P.M.
Dinner:	Every night, 6:30–10:30 P.M.

Atmosphere / setting: Subdued and ultra-luxe, done in soft greens and peach, with the finest tableware and linens. Large windows overlook a lovely trellised patio.

House specialties: Menu changes seasonally. Lobster consommé with lemongrass; miso-marinated scallops on ginger risotto; roasted farm chicken with garlic jus; couscous pudding with poached figs and maple syrup ice cream.

Other recommendations: The power-breakfasters stick with bagels and fruit, but the orange hotcakes are terrific.

Entertainment & amenities: Harp music at brunch.

Summary & comments: This deeply luxurious hotel dining room languished in relative obscurity until the Creative Artist Agency moved next door, and now it's considered *the* breakfast-meeting spot in town. Lunch and dinner aren't too shabby, either—and prices are reasonable compared to the city's other luxury restaurants.

Bistango

	New American
Zone 9 Orange County North	★★★
The Atrium,	Moderate
19100 Von Karman Avenue, Irvine	
(714) 752-5222	Quality 84 Value C

Reservations:	Advised
When to go:	Any time
Entree range:	$9–20
Payment:	Major credit cards
Service rating:	★★★
Friendliness rating:	★★★
Parking:	Valet available
Bar:	Full service
Wine selection:	Good Californians
Dress:	Business at lunch, high-style at night
Disabled access:	Yes
Customers:	Businesspeople, couples at night
Lunch:	Monday–Friday, 11:30 A.M.–3 P.M.
Dinner:	Monday–Thursday, 5:30–10:30 P.M.;
	Friday and Saturday, 5:30–11 P.M.;
	Sunday, 5:30–10 P.M.

Atmosphere / setting: Sleek and urbane, with a granite bar, a small bandstand and dance floor, and high-caliber art shows that change every three months.

House specialties: Menu changes frequently. Frequent winners include crab cakes with mizuna greens and mango salsa; any seafood pasta, perhaps fusilli with butterfly shrimp, asparagus, lemon zest, and olive oil; lamb T-bone with Pinot Noir sauce and garlic mashed potatoes; vanilla crème brûlée with raspberries and cookies.

Other recommendations: Good pizzas, perhaps with shrimp, pancetta, corn, and tomato; three-tomato salad with milk mozzarella, red onion, and basil; grilled ahi tuna on crisp vegetables with sesame-soy vinaigrette.

Entertainment & amenities: Latin guitarist Monday–Tuesday, good live jazz Wednesday–Sunday.

Summary & comments: This ambitious place tries to be three things at once: jazz club, art gallery, and top-flight contemporary American restaurant. The surprise is how well it succeeds at all three. The art is exciting, the music usually enjoyable and sometimes exceptional, and the food consistently good. Jeremiah Tower (of Stars fame) helped create the kitchen and menu; chef Paul Gstrein does the master proud.

Bistro 45

	New American/French
Zone 6 San Gabriel Valley	★★★★
45 South Mentor Avenue, Pasadena	Expensive
(818) 795-2478	Quality 90 Value C

Reservations:	Accepted
When to go:	Any time
Entree range:	$18–25
Payment:	VISA, MC, AMEX
Service rating:	★★★★
Friendliness rating:	★★★★
Parking:	Valet available
Bar:	Full service
Wine selection:	Extensive international collection
Dress:	Upscale
Disabled access:	Yes
Customers:	Upper-crust Pasadenans
Lunch:	Tuesday–Friday, 11:30 A.M.–2:30 P.M.
Dinner:	Tuesday–Thursday, 6–9:30 P.M.; Friday, 6–11 P.M.; Saturday, 5:30–11 P.M.; Sunday, 5–9 P.M. Winemaker dinner first Monday of the month.

Atmosphere / setting: On a quiet Pasadena side street away from the Old Town hordes, this renovated art deco building is sleek and sophisticated, yet eminently comfortable. The space is broken into several dining areas, and the setting is lively but not too noisy. Pasadena's stodgiest citizens rub elbows with its progressives and prosperous artisans.

House specialties: Menu changes seasonally. Warm goat cheese salad with field greens, caramelized apples, and Niçoise olives; bouillabaisse for two; fish du jour with crispy skin, whole roasted garlic, and balsamic sauce; caramelized apple tart.

Other recommendations: Grilled portobello mushrooms with tiger shrimp, spinach, and cumin sauce; pan-roasted venison chop with goat cheese and roast sage sauce; cassoulet; chocolate soup.

Summary & comments: This smart, snappy California-French restaurant combines the best of the old and new. It's located in a spiffy old art deco building and offers a dreamy collection of robust French classics like cassoulet and onion soup, but some well-prepared contemporary dishes and a sense of style in the decor and staff prevent stodginess.

Honors / awards: Nation's Top 100 Restaurants, *Condé Nast Traveler.*

Bo kAOS

Zone 3 Golden Triangle	International
8689 Wilshire Boulevard, Beverly Hills	★★
(310) 659-1200	Moderate
	Quality 72 Value D

Reservations:	Essential
When to go:	Early if you want to eat quietly, late to make the scene
Entree range:	$11–19
Payment:	Major credit cards
Service rating:	★★★
Friendliness rating:	★★★★
Parking:	Valet available
Bar:	Full service
Wine selection:	Limited but choice
Dress:	Black
Disabled access:	Yes
Customers:	Beverly Hills trust-fund babies
Dinner:	Every night, 7:30 P.M.–2 A.M.

Atmosphere / setting: The dim lighting, subtly painted woodwork, paper lanterns, and Pier One–style Asiana combine with some success to evoke a backwater Singapore speakeasy. Tables are impossibly tiny.

House specialties: Oyster shooters; aromatic coconut Thai soup; Kingston calamari with spicy green salsa; tender filet mignon with crisp fries.

Other recommendations: Eggplant caviar with sour cream and dill; steamed asparagus wrapped in rib eye steak with sweet saké sauce; steamed mussels.

Entertainment & amenities: Live music on weeknights.

Summary & comments: After 9 P.M., Bo kaos (pronounced boo-kayus) is a scene of major proportions, and it's amusing if you've never seen the young and the spoiled in action. If the Menendez brothers weren't in jail, they'd probably hang out here. But the drinks are great, the oyster bar is fun, the staff is attitude-free, and the eclectic food is better than it needs to be.

Bombay Cafe

	Indian
	★★★½
	Inexpensive
Zone 1 Westside	
12113 Santa Monica Boulevard,	Quality 87 Value B
West L.A.	
(310) 820-2070	

Zone 1   Westside
12113 Santa Monica Boulevard,
    West L.A.
(310) 820-2070

Indian
★★★½
Inexpensive

Quality 87   Value B

Reservations:	Accepted for 6 or more
When to go:	Any time
Entree range:	$8.75–15.50
Payment:	VISA, MC
Service rating:	★★★
Friendliness rating:	★★★★
Parking:	Self
Bar:	Beer and wine
Wine selection:	Limited
Dress:	Casual
Disabled access:	Yes
Customers:	Indian-food addicts
Lunch/Dinner:	Tuesday–Thursday, 11:30 A.M.–10 P.M.; Friday, 11:30 A.M.–11 P.M.
Dinner:	Saturday, 4–11 P.M.; Sunday, 4–10 P.M.

Atmosphere/setting: Set on the second floor of a Westside minimall, the Bombay Cafe makes the most of a generic space, with an open kitchen, lots of mirrors, and a lively, devoted clientele.

House specialties: Menu changes daily. Best bets are all the chutneys; wonderful sindhi chicken, first poached with onion, ginger, chiles, and spices, then sautéed with mango powder, coriander, and cayenne; plump frankies stuffed with lamb; mango ice cream.

Other recommendations: Sev puri, little chips topped with onions, potatoes, and chutneys; reshmi kebabs, tandoor-cooked chicken sausages; smoked bhartha, a puree of eggplant and yogurt; rice pudding.

Summary & comments: Although the mini-mall location doesn't foretell greatness, the Bombay Cafe deserves its reputation as L.A.'s best, most creative Indian restaurant. The vivid, daily-changing roster of Indian street food, snacks, and classic dishes is deeply addictive.

Bombay Duck

Zone 10   Orange County South
231 Ocean Avenue, Laguna Beach
(714) 497-7307

Indian	
★★★	
Moderate	
Quality 82	Value B

Reservations:	Accepted
When to go:	Any time
Entree range:	$6.50–14.95
Payment:	VISA, MC, AMEX
Service rating:	★★★
Friendliness rating:	★★★
Parking:	Self
Bar:	Beer and wine
Wine selection:	Pretty good
Dress:	Casual chic
Disabled access:	Yes
Customers:	Laguna locals
Brunch:	Buffet Sunday, 11 A.M.–3 P.M.
Lunch:	Monday–Saturday, 11 A.M.–3 P.M.
Dinner:	Sunday–Thursday, 5–10 P.M.;
	Friday and Saturday, 5–10:30 P.M.

Atmosphere / setting: A minimalist, contemporary Laguna Beach store-front painted in warm colors, with agreeable art-for-sale on the walls.

House specialties: Marvelous mango-corn soup; Geeta's fresh fish, salmon, or sea bass wrapped in spinach, seasoned, and steamed in a banana leaf; swordfish tikka; lamb vindaloo.

Other recommendations: At lunch, the delicious Bombay roll, naan bread wrapped around tandoori lamb, chicken, or eggplant, with lettuce and tomato; classic tandoor-cooked lamb and chicken.

Summary & comments: Intriguing daily specials and a fresh, creative flair in the kitchen are evidence enough of this Indian bistro's culinary ambition. What the Bombay Cafe is to L.A., Bombay Duck is to Orange County. Modern Indian cooking in a simple Laguna setting.

Book Soup Bistro

	American
Zone 3 Golden Triangle	★★½
8800 Sunset Boulevard,	Moderate
West Hollywood	
(310) 657-1072	Quality 78 Value C

Reservations:	Accepted
When to go:	Crowded on weekend nights
Entree range:	$8.50–17.50
Payment:	Major credit cards
Service rating:	★★
Friendliness rating:	★★
Parking:	Under building
Bar:	Full service
Wine selection:	Californian and Italian
Dress:	Casual
Disabled access:	Yes
Customers:	Bookish sorts
Lunch/Dinner:	Monday–Thursday, noon–10 P.M.;
	Friday, noon–11 P.M.;
	Saturday, 11:30 A.M.–11 P.M.;
	Sunday, 11:30 A.M.–10 P.M.

Atmosphere / setting: Adjacent to one of L.A.'s best bookstores, with a real bistro feel: polished wood, library chairs, black-and-white photos of great writers, and old Sinatra music in the background. Inviting bar/counter.

House specialties: Carrot-ginger soup; charcuterie and crudite for two; marinated flank steak sandwich; turkey meat loaf with mashed potatoes and orange-cranberry compote.

Other recommendations: Fresh fish specials are recommended, and the collection of pastas is inviting.

Summary & comments: A great spot to meet old friends, have a relaxed, satisfying bistro meal, drink a glass or two of Chianti, and argue the relative merits of Susan Sontag and Camille Paglia.

Border Grill

Zone 1   Westside
1445 4th Street, Santa Monica
(310) 451-1655

	Mexican
	★★★½
	Moderate
	Quality 87 Value C

Reservations:	Accepted
When to go:	Any time; peak hours are deafening
Entree range:	$12.50–17.50
Payment:	Major credit cards
Service rating:	★★
Friendliness rating:	★★
Parking:	Valet available
Bar:	Full service
Wine selection:	Limited
Dress:	Casual
Disabled access:	Yes
Customers:	Young Westsiders
Dinner:	Sunday–Thursday, 5:30–10 P.M.;
	Friday and Saturday, 5:30–11 P.M.

Atmosphere / setting: Wildly colorful, dizzyingly noisy, and lots of fun. The long communal table is great for singles or friendly folks.

House specialties: Cold shrimp, lobster, or salmon tacos with cucumber, avocado, radish, and citrus juices; panuchos (black-bean-stuffed tortilla topped with chicken, pickled onion, and avocado); spicy baby-back ribs glazed with honey and lime; tangy margaritas on the rocks. Menu changes seasonally.

Other recommendations: Daily ceviche specials; Border vegetarian platter with rice and beans; Mexican chocolate cream pie.

Summary & comments: Susan Feniger and Mary Sue Milliken came to fame as owner-chefs of City; now they're focusing their considerable talents on this raucous and inventive Mexican restaurant. It may seem like just a margarita bar, but authentic, vivid, wonderful Mexican food is in abundance. Many diners skip the entrees and order a few of the terrific appetizers. A real L.A. experience.

BRENT'S DELICATESSEN

Zone 8   San Fernando Valley West
19565 Parthenia Street, Northridge
(818) 886-5679

Delicatessen
★★★
Inexpensive

Quality 84   Value B

Reservations:	Accepted
When to go:	Any time
Entree range:	$6.95–11.95
Payment:	Major credit cards
Service rating:	★★
Friendliness rating:	★★
Parking:	In front
Bar:	None
Wine selection:	None
Dress:	Casual
Disabled access:	Yes
Customers:	Everyone: blue collar to studio exec
Open:	Every day, 6 A.M.–9 P.M.

Atmosphere / setting: An always-bustling minimall restaurant, recently remodeled after the quake, with comfy booths, green plaid carpeting, ceiling fans, and gleaming deli and dessert cases.

House specialties: Fish platters (lox, smoked whitefish, barbecued cod); juicy pastrami Ruebens; fresh roast turkey sandwiches and entrees; hefty burgers; chocolate four-layer cake; peanut butter–chocolate chip cookies.

Other recommendations: Omelettes; cole slaw; cheese blintzes; corned beef; potato pancakes; Brent's special club sandwich; bundt cakes.

Summary & comments: Beloved in the north Valley for its exceptional consistency and quality, Brent's is one of the finest delis in Southern California. It would take a year to eat your way through the massive menu, but you'd have a great time in the process.

CA'BREA

Zone 5   Central City
346 South La Brea Avenue
(213) 938-2863

Italian	
★★★½	
Moderate	
Quality 87	Value C

Reservations:	Advised
When to go:	Any time
Entree range:	$8.25–21.95
Payment:	Major credit cards
Service rating:	★★★
Friendliness rating:	★★★
Parking:	Valet available
Bar:	Full service
Wine selection:	Good
Dress:	Casual to upscale
Disabled access:	Yes
Customers:	Hollywood toilers, designers, local businesspeople
Lunch:	Monday–Friday, 11:30 A.M.–2:30 P.M.
Dinner:	Monday and Tuesday, 5:30–10:30 P.M.;
	Wednesday and Thursday, 5:30–11 P.M.;
	Friday and Saturday, 5:30 P.M.–midnight

Atmosphere / setting: A handsome, vaguely Tuscan setting with a long bar, an always-hectic main dining area, and a quieter upstairs nook. Good lighting and good art.

House specialties: Homemade Venetian spaghetti with seafood, porcini, and a tomato sauce; baby-back ribs on a bed of sage-flecked beans; risotto with porcini; caramel cream with fudge.

Other recommendations: Osso buco with polenta fritters; any dish featuring the small homemade cheeses; gnocchi.

Summary & comments: First came Locanda Veneta, an extraordinary Venetian restaurant that was too small to handle its countless fans. Then came this larger, more chaotic but still wonderful trattoria, home to some of the best, most authentic Italian food in the West. The only concern is that the newest additions to the group—Il Moro and Ca'del Sole—will spread the talents of the owner / chef and his partner / manager too thin. But so far, so good.

84

Ca'del Sole

	Italian
Zone 7 San Fernando Valley East	★★★
4100 Cahuenga Boulevard,	Moderate
North Hollywood	
(818) 985-4669	Quality 85 Value C

Reservations:	Advised
When to go:	Any time
Entree range:	$7.95–16.95
Payment:	VISA, MC, AMEX
Service rating:	★★★
Friendliness rating:	★★★
Parking:	Valet available
Bar:	Full service
Wine selection:	Good Italians
Dress:	Casual to upscale
Disabled access:	Yes
Customers:	Disney/Warner people and Studio City residents
Lunch/Dinner:	Monday–Friday, 11:30 A.M.–11:30 P.M.
Dinner:	Saturday, 5:30–11:30 P.M.

Atmosphere/setting: A warren of rooms: a dark, inviting bar; a couple of handsome, beamed dining rooms with whitewashed brick walls, muted tapestry banquettes, and a fireplace; and a back-room Siberia for unknowns.

House specialties: Bigoli (Venetian spaghetti) with sautéed shellfish, white wine, and tomato sauce; salmon braised with radicchio and prosecco wine; chicken sausage with braised onion confit and polenta.

Other recommendations: Seasonally changing risottos; osso buco with grilled polenta; pear tart with caramel sauce.

Summary & comments: Part of the ever-expanding Italian empire run by Locanda Veneta creators Antonio Tomassi and Jean-Louis DiMori, Ca'del Sole became an unofficial commissary for the Valley's studio set within moments of opening. Yes, it's another chic Italian, but the cooking is skillful, the ingredients good, and the menu irresistible.

CAFÉ BIZOU

Zone 7 San Fernando Valley East	French
14016 Ventura Boulevard, Sherman Oaks	★★★½
(818) 788-3536	Moderate
	Quality 87 Value B

Reservations:	Accepted
When to go:	Peak hours are mobbed
Entree range:	$10.95–14.95
Payment:	Major credit cards
Service rating:	★★★
Friendliness rating:	★★★
Parking:	Valet available
Bar:	Full service
Wine selection:	Decent, but most bring their own
Dress:	Casual chic
Disabled access:	Yes
Customers:	Stylish Valleyites
Lunch:	Monday–Friday, 11:30 A.M.–2:30 P.M.
Dinner:	Monday–Friday, 5:30–11 P.M.;
	Saturday, 5–11:30 P.M.; Sunday, 5–11 P.M.

Atmosphere / setting: Artistically spare, with white walls, black-and-white photographs, small tables, and simple furnishings.

House specialties: Lobster and salmon ravioli in lobster sauce; roasted monkfish on risotto with fried carrots in lobster sauce; steak au poivre with vegetables, mashed potatoes, and a peppered veal sauce.

Other recommendations: The romaine salad with honey-mustard dressing, just $1 if you order an entree; black tagliolini with grilled shrimp, tomatoes, and basil; sautéed sesame-seed-coated salmon on a bed of potato pancakes and mushrooms in red wine sauce.

Summary & comments: Ever since the chef from the late Cafe Katsu opened this minimalist-looking and minimally priced bistro, the crowds have been relentless. This is high-quality but bargain-basement French-California cooking—the sort of thing you'd expect at a Four Seasons hotel dining room at less than half the price. The seafood and pasta dishes are particularly memorable. Wine lovers flock here because of the give-away $2 corkage fee. One of the city's brightest newcomers.

Cafe del Rey

New American	
★★½	
Moderate	
Quality 75	Value C

Zone 1   Westside
4451 Admiralty Way, Marina del Rey
(310) 823-6395

Reservations:	Accepted
When to go:	Any time
Entree range:	$15–28
Payment:	VISA, MC, AMEX
Service rating:	★★★
Friendliness rating:	★★★
Parking:	In front
Bar:	Full service
Wine selection:	Good by-the-glass list
Dress:	Casually upscale
Disabled access:	Yes
Customers:	Marina locals, date-night couples
Brunch:	Sunday, 10:30 A.M.–2:30 P.M.
Lunch:	Monday–Saturday, 11:30 A.M.–2:30 P.M.; light lunch served until 4 P.M.
Dinner:	Monday–Saturday, 5:30–10 P.M.; Sunday, 5–9:30 P.M.

Atmosphere / setting: The main draw here is the enchanting view of the marina, especially at sunset and during the day on weekends. Inside is an airy, open, very California setting.

House specialties: Kung pao Thai shellfish sausage; sashimi salad; black spaghetti with shrimp and scallops; warm chocolate cake.

Other recommendations: Hamburger with Vermont cheddar; pita-bread quesadilla with cheddar, wild mushrooms, and grilled vegetables.

Entertainment & amenities: Pianist.

Summary & comments: The excesses and overcomplications of California cuisine are too much in evidence, but the simpler dishes can be quite good. And there's always that lovely waterfront setting.

Cafe La Boheme

Zone 3   Golden Triangle
8400 Santa Monica Boulevard,
   West Hollywood
(213) 848-2360

Pacific Rim	
★★★	
Moderate	
Quality 82	Value C

Reservations:	Accepted
When to go:	On the later side
Entree range:	$14.50–23
Payment:	Major credit cards
Service rating:	★★★★
Friendliness rating:	★★★★
Parking:	Valet available
Bar:	Full service
Wine selection:	Good sized
Dress:	Theatrically upscale
Disabled access:	Yes
Customers:	Creative free spirits: designers, artists, musicians
Brunch:	Saturday and Sunday, 11 A.M.–2:30 P.M.
Lunch:	Monday–Friday, 11:30 A.M.–2:30 P.M.
Dinner:	Sunday–Thursday, 5:30–10:30 P.M.;
	Friday and Saturday, 5:30–11:30 P.M.

Atmosphere / setting: Theatrically opulent, with massive velvet draperies, romantic Victorian-bordello-style private booths, a large fireplace, beautiful flowers, and a Baron von Frankenstein ambience.

House specialties: Appetizer of seared tuna with soy-wasabe cream; taraco caviar (fish roe) spaghettini; incredibly succulent pork kakuni, braised for eight hours "until all the poisons are removed"; home-style carrot cake.

Other recommendations: Grilled Chilean sea bass in a lobster nantua sauce, with grilled eggplant, tofu, and rock shrimp; three-flavor profiteroles with hot fudge and caramel sauce.

Summary & comments: A strange and wonderful setting, a quirky, dressed-up clientele, and consistently good Pacific new-wave cuisine add up to an offbeat, enjoyable only-in-L.A. restaurant experience.

Caffe Delfini

Zone 1 Westside	Italian
147 West Channel Road, Santa Monica	★★½
(310) 459-8823	Inexp / Mod
	Quality 79 Value C

Reservations: Essential
When to go: Any time
Entree range: $9–20
Payment: VISA, MC
Service rating: ★★★
Friendliness rating: ★★★
Parking: Valet available
Bar: Beer and wine
Wine selection: Many good Italians
Dress: Casual
Disabled access: Yes
Customers: Local
Dinner: Every night, 6–10 P.M.

Atmosphere / setting: Two small, crowded rooms with an infectious Mediterranean feeling and an ever-present crowd.

House specialties: Arugula–radicchio salad; daily fresh fish; vibrant linguine Portofino, with tomato, basil, and shrimp; homemade orange sherbet served in an orange peel.

Other recommendations: Rich pasta e fagioli soup; veal funghi with mushroom sauce; penne arrabbiata with spicy tomato sauce.

Summary & comments: Simple Italian food in a simple beach setting, prepared with considerable skill and served with charm. An inviting, uncomplicated joy.

CAFFE LATTE

Zone 5   Central City
6254 Wilshire Boulevard
(213) 936-5213

American	
★★½	
Inexpensive	
Quality 78	Value B

Reservations:	Not accepted
When to go:	Breakfast, early or late lunch
Entree range:	$7–11
Payment:	VISA, MC
Service rating:	★★
Friendliness rating:	★★
Parking:	Validated lot
Bar:	None
Wine selection:	None
Dress:	Casual
Disabled access:	Yes
Customers:	Office workers and local apartment dwellers
Open:	Monday–Friday, 7 A.M.–9 P.M.
Breakfast/Lunch:	Saturday and Sunday, 8 A.M.–3:30 P.M.

Atmosphere / setting: A rumpled, crowded storefront cafe decorated with bags of coffee beans.

House specialties: Coffee; French toast; pasta Mama, a wonderful breakfast pasta made with eggs; chicken Anaheim sandwich.

Other recommendations: Vegetarian black-bean burger; BLT sandwiches; pancakes; special pastas; Jody Maroni's sausages.

Summary & comments: One of L.A.'s best breakfast spots, Caffe Latte makes a mean cup of coffee, great French toast, and a knockout carbo-loading day starter called pasta Mama. Lunch and dinner are very good, too. Expect a wait at prime lunch hours and at breakfast on weekends.

CAlifoRNiA PizzA KiTcHEN

Zone 1   Westside
11677 San Vicente Boulevard,
   Brentwood
(310) 826-3573

Zone 5   Central City
Wells Fargo Center, 330 South Hope Street, Downtown
(213) 626-2616

Zone 6   San Gabriel Valley
99 North Los Robles Avenue, Pasadena
(818) 585-9020

California	
★★	
Inexpensive	
Quality 74	Value B

Reservations:	Accepted
When to go:	Any time
Entree range:	$5.95–9.50
Payment:	Major credit cards
Service rating:	★★★
Friendliness rating:	★★★
Parking:	Available
Bar:	Beer and wine
Wine selection:	Limited
Dress:	Casual
Disabled access:	Yes
Customers:	Office workers, families
Lunch/Dinner:	Sunday–Thursday, 11:30 A.M.–10 P.M.;
	Friday and Saturday, 11:30 A.M.–11 P.M.

Atmosphere / setting: Branches are usually bright, open, and modern, with tilework and a yellow, black, and white color scheme. There's usually a long counter and plenty of booths.

House specialties: Duck sausage pizza; two-sausage pizza; Peking duck pizza; Thai pizza.

Other recommendations: The least complicated salads and pastas.

Summary & comments: A chain restaurant for those who think they hate chain restaurants, CPK has taken Southern California by storm and is now off to conquer America. The simpler pizzas and salads make a fine meal; avoid the dishes loaded up with too many trendy ingredients.

CAMPANILE

Zone 5   Central City
624 South La Brea Avenue
(213) 938-1447

New American	
★★★★½	
Expensive	
Quality 95	Value C

Reservations:	Accepted
When to go:	Any time
Entree range:	$18–26
Payment:	Major credit cards
Service rating:	★★★★
Friendliness rating:	★★★★
Parking:	Valet available
Bar:	Full service
Wine selection:	Extensive, with many small producers
Dress:	Stylishly casual to upscale
Disabled access:	Yes
Customers:	Showbiz, business, professional
Breakfast:	Monday–Friday, 7:30–11 A.M.;
	Saturday and Sunday, 8 A.M.–1:30 P.M.
Lunch:	Monday–Friday, 11:30 A.M.–2:30 P.M.
Dinner:	Monday–Thursday, 6–10 P.M.;
	Friday and Saturday, 5:30–11 P.M.

Atmosphere / setting: Rather like a comfortable, inviting monastery, this rough-walled Mediterranean building served as Charlie Chaplin's offices in the '20s. There's a courtyard with fountain, a campanile (bell tower), a central dining area, and a couple of quieter mezzanines overlooking the bustle below.

House specialties: Any of the breads; poached mozzarella with pesto and tomato broth; aromatic fish soup; superb grilled prime rib with black olive puree, white beans, and sautéed bitter greens; sourdough chocolate cake with "iced cream."

Other recommendations: White bean soup with roasted tomato; crisp flattened chicken with parsley-garlic salad; ginger shortcakes with huckleberry sauce; ice cream sundaes.

Summary & comments: Contemporary American food doesn't get any better than this. Mark Peel's rustic American-Mediterranean cooking is consistently wonderful, and the desserts and hearty breads created by wife Nancy Silverton are among the country's best. Don't miss breakfast, when light streams through the high windows and diners read their newspapers over extraordinary breakfast pastries. Breads can be purchased to go from the adjacent La Brea Bakery.

CARROTS

Zone 1   Westside
2834 Santa Monica Boulevard,
    Santa Monica
(310) 453-6505

French / Japanese
★★★½
Expensive

Quality 85   Value D

Reservations:	Advised
When to go:	Any time
Entree range:	$17.75–23.75
Payment:	VISA, MC, AMEX
Service rating:	★★★★
Friendliness rating:	★★★
Parking:	In front
Bar:	Beer and wine
Wine selection:	Fair
Dress:	Casually upscale to business
Disabled access:	Yes
Customers:	Spago defectors, prosperous Westsiders
Lunch:	Wednesday–Friday, 11:30 A.M.–3 P.M.
Dinner:	Tuesday–Sunday, 6–10 P.M.

Atmosphere / setting: The facade bears the unpromising stamp of a mini-mall, but inside is a proper dining room—not as elegant as the prices would suggest, but soothing and comfortable nonetheless.

House specialties: Sautéed seafood cake with crab, shrimp, and port wine butter; grilled salmon with red wine and red onion sauce; thinly sliced New York steak with spicy onion sauce. Menu changes seasonally.

Other recommendations: Shrimp wrapped with julienne potato; chicken salad and kaiware with sesame seed vinaigrette; sautéed sea bass with plum wine and tomato sauce.

Summary & comments: When chef Fred Iwasaki left Chinois on Main to open this seemingly modest restaurant, a cadre of loyal (and well-off) regulars followed him. Iwasaki's food is intelligent and always flavorful, a perfect blend of Californian and Japanese sensibilities.

Cha Cha Cha

Zone 2 South Bay	Caribbean
726 Pacific Avenue, Long Beach	★★½
(310) 436-3900	Moderate
Zone 5 Central City	Quality 77 Value C
656 North Virgil Avenue	
(213) 664-7723	

Reservations:	Accepted
When to go:	Any time
Entree range:	$8–14.95
Payment:	Major credit cards
Service rating:	★★
Friendliness rating:	★★★
Parking:	Valet available at night
Bar:	Beer and wine in Los Angeles, full bar in Long Beach
Wine selection:	Fair
Dress:	Casual
Disabled access:	Yes
Customers:	All sorts
Open:	Sunday–Thursday, 8 A.M.–10 P.M.; Friday and Saturday, 8 A.M.–11 P.M.

Atmosphere / setting: A cheerful, color-washed, studiously ramshackle cafe in a battered east Hollywood neighborhood. Infectious Caribbean music plays in the background.

House specialties: Sopes filled with chicken, black beans, vegetables, and Parmesan; empanadas; camarones negros, jumbo shrimp in a dark, fiery pepper sauce; flan. For breakfast, spicy omelets or banana French toast.

Other recommendations: Jerk chicken pizza; ahi Caesar salad; red snapper Vera Cruz.

Summary & comments: Originally a too-cool scene, L.A.'s Cha Cha Cha has settled down to become a comfortable neighborhood hangout serving a spicy, friendly neo-Caribbean cuisine, including a good breakfast. The new Long Beach branch is a bit more upscale.

Cha Cha Cha Encino

Zone 8 San Fernando Valley West	Caribbean
17499 Ventura Boulevard, Encino	★★½
(818) 789-3600	Moderate
	Quality 77 Value C

Reservations:	Accepted
When to go:	Weekend brunch is fun
Entree range:	$7–19
Payment:	Major credit cards
Service rating:	★★
Friendliness rating:	★★★
Parking:	Self
Bar:	Full service
Wine selection:	Fair
Dress:	Casual, colorful
Disabled access:	Yes
Customers:	Valleyites looking for fun
Lunch/Dinner:	Monday–Thursday, 11:30 A.M.–11 P.M.;
	Friday, 11:30–12:30 A.M.;
	Saturday, 10:30–12:30 A.M.;
	Sunday, 10:30 A.M.–11 P.M.

Atmosphere / setting: A Fantasy Island version of a faded Colonial-in-the-tropics canteen, with tropical rhythms, painted concrete floors, and angels everywhere.

House specialties: Good jerk pork; robust mambo gumbo, thick and spicy; very crisp pizza Latina topped with vegetables, salsa, and cheese; camarones negros, sweet prawns in a dark, powerful chile sauce.

Other recommendations: Black-bean tamales with tomatillo sauce; grilled scallop salad with watercress and balsamic.

Entertainment & amenities: Live tropical music Friday and Saturday.

Summary & comments: Although this riotously colorful sugar shack is no longer associated with the original Cha Cha Cha, it's still serving pretty much the same spicy, festive Caribbean food, along with party-time tropical drinks and lots of good cheer.

CHAN DARA

Thai	
★★★	
Inexpensive	
Quality 80	Value B

Zone 1   Westside
11940 West Pico Boulevard, West L.A.
(310) 479-4461

Zone 5   Central City
1511 North Cahuenga Boulevard
(213) 464-8585

Zone 5   Central City
310 North Larchmont Boulevard
(213) 467-1052

Reservations:	Accepted
When to go:	Any time
Entree range:	$5.75–13.95
Payment:	Major credit cards
Service rating:	★★★
Friendliness rating:	★★★
Parking:	Varies
Bar:	Beer and wine
Wine selection:	Fair
Dress:	Casual
Disabled access:	Yes
Customers:	Everyone; the music industry likes the Hollywood branch
Lunch/Dinner:	Monday–Friday, 11 A.M.–11 P.M.
Dinner:	Saturday and Sunday, 5–11 P.M.

Atmosphere/setting: The original Hollywood restaurant is just a couple of plain, simple, rather dated rooms; the other two are more modern and chic, but less homey.

House specialties: All the Thai classics, notably mee krob; satays; beef panang curry; barbecued chicken; and the house salad with chicken, egg, cucumber, and a curry-peanut sauce.

Other recommendations: Crab and shrimp with silver noodles; chicken-coconut soup; lady shrimp; Thai iced tea.

Summary & comments: Thai restaurants come and go, but Chan Dara endures. All three branches serve consistently tasty Thai standards to a stylish crowd; the original location is still the coolest.

Charming Garden

	Chinese
	★★★
	Inexpensive
	Quality 83 Value B

Zone 6   San Gabriel Valley
111 North Atlantic Boulevard,
    Monterey Park
(818) 458-4508

Reservations:	Accepted
When to go:	Any time
Entree range:	$7.90–13
Payment:	VISA, MC
Service rating:	★★★
Friendliness rating:	★★★
Parking:	Self
Bar:	Beer and wine
Wine selection:	Limited
Dress:	Casual
Disabled access:	Yes
Customers:	Chinese and Chinese-Americans
Lunch:	Every day, 11:30 A.M.–2:30 P.M.
Dinner:	Every night, 5:30–10 P.M.

Atmosphere / setting: An upscale mall restaurant with serious, black-suited service, good table linens and carpeting, and a few banquet rooms.

House specialties: Steamed stuff chicken, an incredibly savory whole red-cooked bird; hot-smoked pomfret; delicate minced shrimp in lettuce cup.

Other recommendations: Stir-fried pork with chilies; richly flavorful house special bean curd; any of the spicy chicken dishes.

Summary & comments: This deservedly respected Hunanese takes its food seriously. The setting is subdued and pleasant, the staff intelligent and unusually solicitous, and the cooking—punched up with spices and rich with complex flavors, but not always hot—is first-rate.

Chaya Brasserie

Zone 3	Golden Triangle
8741 Alden Drive, West Hollywood	
(310) 859-8833	

International
★★★½
Expensive

Quality 89   Value C

Reservations:	Advised
When to go:	Any time
Entree range:	$13–25
Payment:	Major credit cards
Service rating:	★★★★
Friendliness rating:	★★★★
Parking:	Valet available
Bar:	Full service
Wine selection:	Good
Dress:	Stylishly casual to upscale
Disabled access:	Yes
Customers:	Music and design industries, Cedars-Sinai doctors
Lunch:	Monday–Friday, 11:30 A.M.–2:30 P.M.
Dinner:	Monday–Thursday, 6–10:30 P.M.;
	Friday and Saturday, 6–11 P.M.;
	Sunday, 6–10 P.M.; late supper
	Tuesday–Saturday to midnight.

Atmosphere / setting: Airy and modern, yet hardly stark. Huge pine-framed mirrors tilt downward to reflect the handsome diners, while bushy bamboo trees climb to the high ceiling. The long bar is a comfortable place to hang.

House specialties: Menu changes seasonally. Seaweed salad; savory pan-fried oysters over rosti potatoes; pan-fried lobster with brown-rice pilaf; grilled chicken Dijon with outstanding french fries; suave ginger crème brûlée.

Other recommendations: Spaghetti with Japanese eggplant; grilled ahi with jalapeño or anchovy butter; roasted lamb chops with mustard coating; flourless chocolate brownie sundae.

Summary & comments: Hard to classify but easy to enjoy, Chaya Brasserie is a French-style brasserie with a Japanese sensibility and a lot of Italian on the menu. In short, it's the quintessential L.A. restaurant. After a decade or so, it remains hip but hardly trendy—the sort of place David Byrne goes to—and the food is as irresistible as ever.

Chez Melange

Zone 2   South Bay
Palos Verdes Inn,
  1716 Pacific Coast Highway,
  Redondo Beach
(310) 540-1222

International	
★ ★ ★	
Moderate	
Quality 82	Value B

Reservations:	Advised
When to go:	Any time
Entree range:	$10–17
Payment:	VISA, MC, AMEX
Service rating:	★ ★ ★
Friendliness rating:	★ ★ ★ ★
Parking:	Self
Bar:	Full service
Wine selection:	Excellent
Dress:	Stylishly casual to upscale
Disabled access:	Yes
Customers:	South Bay folks
Breakfast:	Monday–Friday, 7–11 A.M.
Brunch:	Sunday, 8 A.M.–2:30 P.M.
Breakfast / Lunch:	Saturday, 7:30 A.M.–2:30 P.M.
Lunch:	Monday–Friday, 11:30 A.M.–2:30 P.M.
Dinner:	Sunday–Thursday, 5–10 P.M.;
	Friday and Saturday, 5–11 P.M.

Atmosphere / setting: A comfortable but rather stodgy dining room attached to an upscale motel in the South Bay. There's a caviar-vodka bar and an oyster-Champagne bar.

House specialties: The menu changes daily, but the famed Cajun meat loaf with mashed potatoes is usually on hand, as is the black-bean soup with chorizo and feta cheese, and the Southern fried chicken salad.

Other recommendations: Examples from one menu include moo shu pork with mango wonton crisp; Tuscany chicken breast stuffed with prosciutto, sun-dried tomatoes, and feta; and Hawaiian wahoo marinated in saké, soy, and mirin and served over an Oriental rainbow salad.

Summary & comments: This pioneer brought the South Bay out of surf 'n' turf land and into the Spago '80s, and it's still doing an admirable job of bringing together some of the world's best tastes in a happy culinary jumble. You'll get a lot of California-cuisine bang for your buck here.

Chianti Cucina

Zone 5   Central City
7383 Melrose Avenue
(213) 653-8333

Italian	
★★★½	
Moderate	
Quality 85	Value B

Reservations:	Advised
When to go:	Any time
Entree range:	$8.75–18.95
Payment:	VISA, MC, AMEX
Service rating:	★★★
Friendliness rating:	★★★
Parking:	Valet available
Bar:	Full service
Wine selection:	Good Italians
Dress:	Casual
Disabled access:	Yes
Customers:	Casually stylish professionals, designers, and Hollywood people
Lunch/Dinner:	Monday–Thursday, 11:30 A.M.–11:30 P.M.; Friday and Saturday, 11:30 A.M.–midnight
Dinner:	Sunday, 4–11 P.M.

Atmosphere/setting: A narrow, bright, tile-lined, noisy trattoria with a handful of small tables. It's no place for a large party.

House specialties: Bruschetta with tomatoes, fresh mozzarella, and prosciutto; beef carpaccio; capellini alla checca; vegetable platter with grilled polenta and potato; gnocchi with braised beef and vegetables.

Other recommendations: Linguine with seafood; roasted branzino (sea bass) with potatoes, rosemary, and olive oil; gelato.

Summary & comments: Melrose's popularity (and cachet) may be fading, but the cooking's still going strong at this wonderful trattoria abutting Chianti Ristorante, one of L.A.'s most venerable Italian restaurants. A great spot for a pasta meal and a glass of Barbera.

Chianti Ristorante

Zone 5 Central City	Italian
7383 Melrose Avenue	★★★½
(213) 653-8333	Moderate
	Quality 85 Value C

Reservations:	Accepted
When to go:	Any time
Entree range:	$11–20
Payment:	VISA, MC, AMEX
Service rating:	★★★★
Friendliness rating:	★★★★
Parking:	Valet available
Bar:	Full service
Wine selection:	Good Italian collection
Dress:	Casual to business
Disabled access:	Yes
Customers:	Longtime loyals, romantics, businesspeople
Dinner:	Every night, 5:30–10:30 P.M.

Atmosphere / setting: A reassuringly discreet and old-fashioned room, with welcoming booths, dark (some say gloomy) lighting, and snap-to service.

House specialties: Carpaccio with celery, truffles, and grana; Caesar salad; angel hair with fresh tomato, basil, and garlic; an impressive grilled veal chop.

Other recommendations: Salmon-spinach lasagne; veal cutlet milanese; braised partridge with pancetta and onions.

Summary & comments: Long before the ascent (and now decline) of trendy Melrose, Chianti did an admirable job of feeding and comforting Angelenos. It's still doing a great job making homemade pasta, grilling veal and game, and pouring good Italian wines.

Chinois on Main

<table>
<tr><td>Zone 1   Westside
2709 Main Street, Santa Monica
(310) 392-9025</td><td>Pacific Rim
★★★★½
Very Expensive

Quality 95   Value C</td></tr>
</table>

Reservations:	Strongly advised
When to go:	Any time
Entree range:	$21.50–28
Payment:	Major credit cards
Service rating:	★★★★
Friendliness rating:	★★★
Parking:	Valet available
Bar:	Full service
Wine selection:	Good Californians
Dress:	Stylish
Disabled access:	Yes
Customers:	Chic Westsiders, showbiz, Puck groupies
Lunch:	Wednesday–Friday, 11:30 A.M.–2 P.M.
Dinner:	Monday–Saturday, 6–10:30 P.M.; Sunday, 5:30–10 P.M.

Atmosphere / setting: Wildly colorful, impossibly noisy, and uncomfortably crowded, but indisputedly great fun. The diners can be as amusing and colorful as Barbara Lazaroff's wacky decor.

House specialties: From the "Chinois Classics" side of the menu: fresh goose liver with marinated grilled pineapples; sizzling sea scallops with potato strings, mixed greens, and vinaigrette; whole sizzling catfish with ginger and ponzu sauce; Shanghai lobster with spicy ginger, julienne of green onions, and curry sauce.

Other recommendations: The newer part of the menu changes regularly. Excellent possibilities include stir-fried lamb with wok-fried Maui onion rings in radicchio leaves; smoked duck sausage with black vinegar dressing; crisp Mandarin quail with a tangerine and ginger glaze and a citrus salad; and passion fruit cheesecake.

Summary & comments: Pacific Rim cooking is all the rage now in California, and Wolfgang Puck's Chinois remains the foremost practitioner of the art. And it is, indeed, an art. If you've never experienced this exciting, inventive blend of Chinese, Japanese, and French cooking, a visit to Chinois is a must—even if it means taking out a second mortgage to pay for it.

Chu's Mandarin Cuisine

Zone 6 San Gabriel Valley	Chinese
140 West Valley Boulevard, San Gabriel	★★★
(818) 572-6574	Inexpensive
	Quality 82 Value B

Reservations:	No
When to go:	Any time
Entree range:	$4.50–12
Payment:	VISA, MC
Service rating:	★★
Friendliness rating:	★★
Parking:	Self
Bar:	Beer and wine
Wine selection:	Limited
Dress:	Casual
Disabled access:	Yes
Customers:	Local Chinese, Chinese-Americans
Lunch/Dinner:	Every day, 11:30 A.M.–10 P.M.

Atmosphere / setting: A plain-Jane room in the Great Mall of China in San Gabriel, whose most notable decorative touches are the curious photos of Mr. Chu with Arnold Schwarzenegger.

House specialties: Any of the dishes made with the rarely seen hand-pulled noodles: noodles in black-bean sauce; chicken or seafood noodle soups; chow meins.

Other recommendations: Intensely flavorful shredded pork with garlic; lamb hot pot; savory steamed dumplings; crispy shrimp in spicy salt.

Summary & comments: All the cooking is good at Mr. Chu's, but the real draw are the fresh, slippery, chewy hand-pulled noodles that make the many noodle dishes so wonderful.

Cicada

	Italian
	★★★
	Moderate
	Quality 80 Value B

Zone 3   Golden Triangle
8478 Melrose Avenue, West Hollywood
(213) 655-5559

Reservations:	Advised
When to go:	Any time
Entree range:	$8–17
Payment:	Major credit cards
Service rating:	★★★★
Friendliness rating:	★★★
Parking:	Valet available
Bar:	Full service
Wine selection:	Good
Dress:	Rock 'n' roll grubbies to agent Armani
Disabled access:	Yes
Customers:	Music and movie crowd
Lunch:	Monday–Friday, noon–2:30 P.M.
Dinner:	Monday–Saturday, 6–10:30 P.M.

Atmosphere / setting: An atmospheric faux Tuscan with tile floors, pale walls with hand-painted scenes, loads of French windows, long banquettes, and a large separate bar.

House specialties: A beautiful help-yourself antipasto buffet, available as both an appetizer and main course; crab cakes with fresh corn and a light lemon-caper sauce; spaghetti with fresh tomato sauce and basil; fettuccine with red basil and sun-dried tomato pesto; homemade tiramisu.

Other recommendations: Arugula salad with grilled prawns; spit-roasted chicken with herbs; fettuccine with prosciutto and sweet peas; cappuccino served with cookies.

Entertainment & amenities: Live jazz on Thursday nights.

Summary & comments: With glamorous Stephanie Haymes (formerly of Le Dome and daughter of Dick Haymes) and Bernie Taupin as owners, it's no surprise that Cicada is such a hot spot with music and showbiz people. After a failed attempt to serve rustic French bistro fare, a chef from the departed Il Giardino took over and created an appealing Italian menu based on antipasto and pastas.

104

Cinnabar

Zone 6   San Gabriel Valley
933 South Brand Avenue, Glendale
(818) 551-1155

Pacific Rim
★★★
Moderate

Quality 84   Value C

Reservations:	Accepted
When to go:	Any time
Entree range:	$11.50–18.50
Payment:	VISA, MC, D
Service rating:	★★★★
Friendliness rating:	★★★★
Parking:	Self
Bar:	Full service
Wine selection:	Good
Dress:	Stylishly casual
Disabled access:	Yes
Customers:	Glendale's hippest
Lunch:	Tuesday–Friday, 11:30 A.M.–2:30 P.M.
Dinner:	Tuesday–Thursday, 6–9:30 P.M.;
	Friday and Saturday, 6–10:30 P.M.;
	Sunday, 5:30–9:30 P.M.

Atmosphere / setting: Located in a former warehouse, Cinnabar is a great blend of old and new, combining a spare, modern design with the richly scarred historic bar from downtown's lamented Yee Mee Loo and the upside-down parasols from Pasadena's lamented Cafe Jacoulet.

House specialties: Lemongrass bouillabaisse with a kaffir lime broth and loads of seafood; air-dried duck with rich tamarind beans and mint sauce; tuna and salmon rolled in finely shredded potatoes and roasted.

Other recommendations: Dim sum tasting, with snow crab sui mai, shiitake mushroom eggroll, and more; yellowtail sashimi mille feuille with wasabe-soy vinaigrette.

Summary & comments: For proof that Glendale is more than a Sizzler suburb, come to this oh-so-cool pan-Asian restaurant on Brand's auto row. The staff is solicitous, the bar is wonderful, and the food displays an admirable blend of inventiveness and restraint. Most dishes are offered in half sizes to please grazers.

CITRUS

	French
Zone 5 Central City	★★★★½
6703 Melrose Avenue	Expensive
(213) 857-0034	
	Quality 95 Value C

Reservations:	Essential
When to go:	Any time
Entree range:	$22–28
Payment:	Major credit cards
Service rating:	★★★★
Friendliness rating:	★★★★★
Parking:	Valet available
Bar:	Full service
Wine selection:	Good Californians, some French
Dress:	Upscale
Disabled access:	Yes
Customers:	An L.A. elite, from rock stars to conservative bankers
Lunch:	Monday–Friday, noon–2:30 P.M.
Dinner:	Monday–Thursday, 6:30–10 P.M.; Friday and Saturday, 6:30–10:30 P.M.

Atmosphere / setting: Pure California—an informal, greenery-rimmed covered patio with huge off-white umbrellas; large, flower-dressed tables; a sparkling kitchen on view behind a wall of glass; and always-amusing people-watching. On the other side of the small bar is Bar Bistro, the indoor bistro offshoot.

House specialties: Shiitake mushroom and garlic napoleon; sautéed scallops with Maui onion rings; grilled swordfish with chili quinoa; chicken with a mushroom crust and mushroom sauce; roasted veal with mashed potatoes and horseradish sauce; crunchy napoleon with butterscotch sauce; chocolate-hazelnut bars with vanilla sauce.

Other recommendations: The menu changes frequently. To do it right, ask Michel Richard or chef de cuisine Alain Giraud to prepare a tasting menu; they'll dazzle you.

Summary & comments: Michel Richard probably has more joie de vivre than any other chef in town, and that warm-hearted enthusiasm comes through loud and clear in Citrus's extraordinary contemporary French-American cuisine. Sophisticated and voluptuous, but never pretentious or stodgy, the cooking of Richard and chef Alain Giraud is among the country's finest—and the desserts, created by pastry whiz Richard, may well be the country's finest.

Coley's Place

Zone 4 City South	Jamaican
5035 West Slauson Avenue,	★★½
Ladera Heights	Moderate
(213) 291-7474	Quality 78 Value C

Reservations:	Accepted
When to go:	Before Laker games
Entree range:	$9.25–21
Payment:	VISA, MC, AMEX
Service rating:	★★★
Friendliness rating:	★★★★
Parking:	In front
Bar:	Beer and wine
Wine selection:	Limited
Dress:	Casual to upscale
Disabled access:	Yes
Customers:	Local residents, Westsiders
Lunch/Dinner:	Monday–Saturday, 11 A.M.–10 P.M.;
	Sunday, 11 A.M.–8 P.M.

Atmosphere / setting: The minimall building is bland; the inside is a gracious dining room with greenery and soft lighting.

House specialties: Conch fritters; chicken Lockerton (banana stuffed with chicken and deep-fried); shrimp St. James, with okra and a coconut-cream sauce; peach cobbler.

Other recommendations: Jamaican patties; grilled lobster.

Summary & comments: Hidden in a restaurant-poor but otherwise upscale neighborhood near LAX, Coley's brings Caribbean warmth and good tastes to an appreciative crowd. Not for cholesterol fanatics.

Crocodile Cafe

<table>
<tr><td>Zone 1</td><td>Westside</td></tr>
</table>

101 Santa Monica Boulevard,
  Santa Monica
(310) 394-4783

Zone 6   San Gabriel Valley
140 South Lake Avenue, Pasadena
(818) 449-9900

Zone 6   San Gabriel Valley
626 North Central Avenue, Glendale
(818) 241-1114

<table>
<tr><td></td><td>California</td></tr>
<tr><td></td><td>★★★</td></tr>
<tr><td></td><td>Inexpensive</td></tr>
<tr><td>Quality 80</td><td>Value B</td></tr>
</table>

Reservations:	Not accepted
When to go:	Any time
Entree range:	$7.25–9.45
Payment:	Major credit cards
Service rating:	★★
Friendliness rating:	★★★
Parking:	Varies
Bar:	Beer and wine
Wine selection:	Good by-the-glass choices
Dress:	Casual
Disabled access:	Yes
Customers:	Everybody
Lunch/Dinner:	Sunday–Thursday, 11 A.M.–10 P.M.;
	Friday and Saturday, 11 A.M.–11 P.M.

Atmosphere / setting: All the modern cafe touches: open kitchens with wood-burning pizza ovens, khaki-clad waiters, and noise-reflecting surfaces, including black laminate tables and tile floors.

House specialties: Black bean and sirloin chili; juicy hamburgers; blue corn tostada salad with fresh corn, black beans, and chicken; four-cheese pizza; fettuccine with grilled chicken, roasted pasilla chile, corn, cilantro, and ancho chili cream.

Other recommendations: All the salads; moo shu chicken calzone; marinated flank steak with salsa, black beans, guacamole, and flour tortillas; chocolate brownie pie.

Summary & comments: Based on the tremendous (and deserved) success of first-born Crocodile Cafe in Pasadena, the Crocodile is setting out to conquer Southern California, and perhaps the entire country. The newest branch boasts a great Santa Monica location near the ocean. The Cal-Southwestern-Asian cuisine is fresh, lively, and affordable, the staff is cheery, and the settings are fun.

Cynthia's

Zone 3 Golden Triangle	American
8370 West 3rd Street, West Hollywood	★★★
(213) 658-7851	Moderate
	Quality 81 Value B

Reservations:	Accepted
When to go:	Any time
Entree range:	$9–17
Payment:	VISA, MC, AMEX
Service rating:	★★★
Friendliness rating:	★★★★
Parking:	Valet available at lunch and weekend nights
Bar:	Beer and wine
Wine selection:	Decent
Dress:	Casual
Disabled access:	Yes
Customers:	Third Street locals, low-key showbiz
Lunch:	Monday–Friday, 11 A.M.–3 P.M.
Dinner:	Every night, 5:30–11 P.M.

Atmosphere / setting: A tiny storefront next to the affiliated catering company, warmed with candlelight, interesting art-for-sale, and the owner's effusive charm.

House specialties: Peppery corn chowder; succulent fried chicken with dumplings; roast pork with potato pancakes and fabulous applesauce; fruit cobblers.

Other recommendations: Niçoise salad with seared ahi; meat loaf.

Summary & comments: After Cynthia Hirsch met with considerable success catering for TV and film crews, she opened this cozy storefront and quickly attracted a loyal following for her hearty, tasty neo-American classics. If your mom cooked this well, you'd probably never have moved out.

Daily Grill

Zone 1   Westside
11677 San Vicente Boulevard,
   Brentwood
(310) 442-0044

Zone 3   Golden Triangle
Beverly Connection, 100 North La Cienega Boulevard, West Hollywood
(310) 659-3100

Zone 8   San Fernando Valley West
16101 Ventura Boulevard, Encino
(818) 986-4111

Reservations:	Accepted for 6 or more
When to go:	Any time
Entree range:	$7.95–16.95
Payment:	VISA, MC, AMEX
Service rating:	★★
Friendliness rating:	★★
Parking:	Validated
Bar:	Full service; beer and wine only in Brentwood
Wine selection:	Fair
Dress:	Casual
Disabled access:	Yes
Customers:	Gap-clad baby boomers
Lunch/Dinner:	Monday–Thursday, 11:30 A.M.–11 P.M.; Friday and Saturday, 11:30 A.M.–midnight; Sunday, 11 A.M.–10 P.M.

Atmosphere/setting: This growing chain mimics a romanticized '40s restaurant, with wood booths, white tile, and counter service. They're always crowded, noisy, and lively.

House specialties: Caesar salad; peppery chicken hash; steak tartare; Joe's special with mushrooms; turkey steak with mashed potatoes; rice pudding.

Other recommendations: Calves' liver with bacon and onions; steamed spinach; french fries; fried onions; burgers; double-layer chocolate cake.

Summary & comments: This chain offshoot of Beverly Hills's posh The Grill has met with booming success, thanks to its comforting retro atmosphere and its even more comforting retro American food, heavy on the meat and potatoes and relatively light on the wallet.

545 Richard

Da Pasquale

	Italian
	★★★
Zone 3　　Golden Triangle	Inexpensive
9749 Little Santa Monica Boulevard, Beverly Hills	
(310) 859-3884	Quality 83　　Value A

5 miles)
east of
Wilshire West
avenue Roxbury
(R) 1 block before
to Santa Monica
block west

Reservations:	Advised
When to go:	Any time
Entree range:	$7.50–16
Payment:	VISA, MC, AMEX
Service rating:	★★★
Friendliness rating:	★★★
Parking:	In lot
Bar:	Beer and wine
Wine selection:	Good Italians
Dress:	Casual
Disabled access:	Yes
Customers:	Beverly Hills locals
Lunch:	Monday–Friday, 11:30 A.M.–3 P.M.
Dinner:	Monday–Saturday, 5–10:30 P.M.; Sunday, 5–10 P.M.

parking lot
on Roxbury to left

Atmosphere / setting:　A casual, bright, contemporary storefront in Beverly Hills's shopping district, with light woodwork, windows to the street, and Italian voices in the background.

House specialties:　Antipasto misto, a generous, colorful collection of marinated vegetables; irresistible pizza bread; forthright bucatini all'amatriciana with pancetta and hot pepper; perfect thin-crust pizzas, especially the alla checca, with fresh tomato, and the tre formaggi, with three cheeses and prosciutto.

Other recommendations:　Spaghetti al fruitti di mare; baked chicken with tomato, potato, and onion; homemade tagliolini with pesto; homemade sorbets.

Summary & comments:　Would that every neighborhood Italian cafe have such fresh, uncomplicated, wonderful food. The pizzas vie with Angeli's for best in town (they're virtually identical), and almost every dish is excellent. A real find in overpriced Beverly Hills.

David Slay's La Veranda

New American/Italian
★★★½
Expensive

Quality 83   Value D

Zone 3   Golden Triangle
225 South Beverly Drive, Beverly Hills
(310) 274-7246

Reservations:	Advised
When to go:	Any time
Entree range:	$17–26
Payment:	Major credit cards
Service rating:	★★★★
Friendliness rating:	★★★★
Parking:	Valet available
Bar:	Full service
Wine selection:	Good
Dress:	Upscale
Disabled access:	Yes
Customers:	Prosperous Beverly Hills people, many over 50
Lunch:	Monday–Friday, 11:30 A.M.–2:30 P.M.
Dinner:	Monday–Saturday, 5:30–10:30 P.M.;
	Sunday, 5–9:30 P.M.

Atmosphere / setting: Contemporary, but not cold: cream-colored walls, simple black chairs, good modern art, and skillful lighting. You can hear yourself think and talk.

House specialties: Salmon tartare with sweet onion, capers, and potato pancake; fried spinach tossed with lemon and Parmesan; juicy baked chicken with whole garlic, oregano vinaigrette, and cannellini beans; sautéed calves' liver with caramelized onions.

Other recommendations: Wild rice blini with duck and braised endive; Chilean sea bass with Parmesan crust; chocolate-walnut tart with caramel sauce.

Entertainment & amenities: Occasionally live piano music is offered.

Summary & comments: Despite a recent trashing in the *Los Angeles Times,* David Slay's remains beloved for its clean, mostly unfussy blend of Italian and contemporary American cooking styles. Slay's food is accomplished, and the setting and service make everyone feel good.

DEPOT

Zone 2   South Bay
1250 Cabrillo Avenue, Torrance
(310) 787-7501

International
★★★
Moderate

Quality 82   Value C

Reservations:	Accepted
When to go:	Any time
Entree range:	$9–23
Payment:	Major credit cards
Service rating:	★★★
Friendliness rating:	★★★★
Parking:	Valet available
Bar:	Full service
Wine selection:	Good; also microbrewery beers
Dress:	Casually upscale
Disabled access:	Yes
Customers:	South Bay and Palos Verdes locals
Lunch:	Monday–Friday, 11 A.M.–2:30 P.M.
Dinner:	Tuesday–Thursday, 5:30–10 P.M.;
	Friday, 5:30–10:30 P.M.;
	Saturday, 5–10:30 P.M.; Sunday, 5–9 P.M.

Atmosphere / setting: A once-dilapidated Red Car depot, skillfully transformed into a very handsome restaurant, with whitewashed beams, private booths, and neoclassical wooden pillars.

House specialties: Pinky's BBQ, with "Thai-dyed" chicken, garlic shrimp, Canton pork ribs, and fried rice; lamb trilogy, with a portobello mushroom–red wine sauce and garlic mashed potatoes; triple chocolate cake with espresso sauce.

Other recommendations: Daily-changing seafood specials, especially ahi and salmon; bowtie pasta with smoked chicken, fresh corn, and chili cream; grilled lamb loin and spinach salad; Depot bar, a chocolate fondant.

Summary & comments: A cheerful, inventive Cal-international cuisine is paired to great advantage with a wonderful setting in a restored trolley station. The food is trendy, to be sure, but it works.

Diagilev

Zone 3   Golden Triangle
Bel Age Hotel,
  1020 North San Vicente Boulevard,
  West Hollywood
(310) 854-1111

Russian/French
★★★½
Very Expensive

Quality 89   Value D

Reservations:	Accepted
When to go:	Special occasions
Entree range:	$21–34
Payment:	Major credit cards
Service rating:	★★★★★
Friendliness rating:	★★★★★
Parking:	Valet available
Bar:	Full service
Wine selection:	Good but expensive
Dress:	Upscale (tie)
Disabled access:	Yes
Customers:	Anniversary celebrants, big spenders
Dinner:	Tuesday–Saturday, 6:30–10:30 P.M.

Atmosphere / setting: All the opulence befitting a caviar-and-Champagne hotel restaurant: lush floral displays, abundant mirrors, serious art, thick linens, capacious banquettes.

House specialties: The finest Russian caviars; flavored frozen vodkas, served from a rolling cart; traditional borscht; shashlik caucasien, made with venison instead of lamb.

Other recommendations: Homemade smoked Norwegian salmon; crab bisque; chicken kiev, stuffed with morels and black truffles; luxurious pastries.

Entertainment & amenities: Performances by a pianist and a renowned balalaika player.

Summary & comments: A wonderful place to propose or celebrate that two-picture deal, Diagilev celebrates Russia's good ol' days in grand style. The setting, service, and flavored vodkas are enough to make a person profoundly happy; fortunately, the food doesn't break the mood.

THE DINING ROOM

New American/French

★★★★

Very Expensive

Quality 89   Value D

Zone 10   Orange County South
Ritz-Carlton Hotel,
    33533 Ritz-Carlton Drive,
    Dana Point
(714) 240-5008

Reservations: Accepted
When to go: To celebrate or luxuriate
Entree range: $29–38
Payment: Major credit cards
Service rating: ★★★★★
Friendliness rating: ★★★★★
Parking: Valet available
Bar: Full service
Wine selection: A blue-blood list
Dress: Dressed-up
Disabled access: Yes
Customers: Well-heeled tourists, special-occasion locals
Dinner: Tuesday–Saturday, 6:30–10 P.M.

Atmosphere / setting: Although the hotel has a spectacular site on the Pacific, the Dining Room is bereft of an ocean view. Anything but beachy, the formal, very handsome restaurant reeks with Continental elegance, with large, properly set tables and muted luxury-hotel colors.

House specialties: At press time, the chef was touring southern France to create an entirely new menu, which will follow in the French-Mediterranean footsteps of its predecessor. Past winners included lobster cannelloni with spinach and black truffles; saddle of venison with roasted fruits and natural jus; and leg of lamb with herbs de Provence, white beans, and Madeira curry.

Other recommendations: Memorable desserts have included warm chocolate fritters with vanilla-saffron sauce; and fresh fruit "pearls" marinated in muscat wine and spiced basil.

Summary & comments: The Ritz-Carlton and its main dining room have been criticized for being too stuffy and formal for kicked-back south Orange County, and the critics have a point. But there's no denying the luxuriousness of the setting, the suaveness of the service, and the rich, brilliant flavors of the modern French-Mediterranean cooking. Worth a splurge if you're in the mood for formality.

Diva

New American	
★★★	
Moderate	
Quality 82	Value C

Zone 9   Orange County North
600 Anton Boulevard, Costa Mesa
(714) 754-0600

Reservations:	Advised
When to go:	Great before visiting the Performing Arts Center
Entree range:	$10–19
Payment:	Major credit cards
Service rating:	★★★
Friendliness rating:	★★★★
Parking:	Valet available
Bar:	Full service
Wine selection:	Good
Dress:	Stylish
Disabled access:	Yes
Customers:	Dressed-up theater-goers, people-watchers, and scene-makers
Lunch:	Monday–Friday, 11:30 A.M.–3 P.M.
Dinner:	Monday, 5–9 P.M.; Tuesday–Thursday, 5–10 P.M.; Friday and Saturday, 5–11:30 P.M.; Sunday, 4:30–9 P.M.

Atmosphere / setting: Clean lines meet with rococo colors in this hip hangout, where a huge gilt-framed mirror tilts down to reflect the considerable scene. Lots of hard surfaces, lots of noise.

House specialties: Ahi "towers"—strips of charred ahi built into a pyramid, a trendy but tasty bit of food architecture; roast chicken with mashed potatoes and sweet garlic sauce; white chocolate soufflé with raspberry sauce.

Other recommendations: An excellent vegetarian platter, meat-free but hardly fat-free, including garlic mashed potatoes, grilled eggplant, steamed asparagus, and more.

Summary & comments: Diva ranks as *the* pre-theater spot in Orange County, thanks to its location near the Performing Arts Center, its dynamic design, and its high-concept contemporary food, which mostly avoids being precious or precocious. A happening spot.

Dong Kahn

Zone 9   Orange County North
10451 Bolsa Avenue, Westminster
(714) 839-1014

	Vietnamese
	★★★
	Inexpensive
	Quality 80 Value A

Reservations:	Not accepted
When to go:	Any time; open late
Entree range:	$5–7.50
Payment:	No credit cards
Service rating:	★★
Friendliness rating:	★★
Parking:	Self
Bar:	Beer
Wine selection:	None
Dress:	Casual
Disabled access:	Yes, but it's crowded
Customers:	Primarily Vietnamese
Open:	Every day, 9:30 A.M.–3 A.M.

Atmosphere / setting: A couple of warm, cluttered, almost tacky rooms filled with large round tables and large family groups.

House specialties: Wonderful fried calamari, much like the Italian version; tangy-sweet fish soup with pineapple; all the other rice-noodle soups at lunchtime.

Other recommendations: Best bet is the fixed-price family dinner, where you can try such good tastes as chopped shrimp on sugarcane or chicken with lemongrass.

Summary & comments: This friendly, family-style cafe in Little Saigon offers food that's fresher and tastier than most, with worthy combination dinners that serve as a good introduction to Vietnamese cooking.

DRAGO

	Italian
	★★★½
Zone 1 Westside	Moderate
2628 Wilshire Boulevard, Santa Monica	
(310) 828-1585	Quality 89 Value C

Reservations:	Advised
When to go:	Any time
Entree range:	$9.50–23
Payment:	Major credit cards
Service rating:	★★★★
Friendliness rating:	★★★
Parking:	Valet available
Bar:	Full service
Wine selection:	Very good
Dress:	Casual chic to upscale
Disabled access:	Yes
Customers:	Handsome Westsiders
Lunch:	Monday–Friday, 11:30 A.M.–3 P.M.
Dinner:	Monday–Saturday, 5:30–11 P.M.;
	Sunday, 5:30–10 P.M.

Atmosphere / setting: Santa Monica is reflected in the design much more than Drago's native Sicily. The style is contemporary, the palette pale, the aura elegant; a well-stocked wine cellar is on view behind glass.

House specialties: Rarely seen Sicilian dishes like spaghetti alla bottarga (dried tuna roe); roasted rabbit with black olives and bell peppers; eggplant soufflé; passion fruit crème brûlée.

Other recommendations: Any of the pastas: seafood risotto with black squid ink; orechiette with wild broccoli; pappardelle with lobster and bell pepper sauce.

Summary & comments: Celestino Drago has won a fiercely loyal following, thanks to his consistent, intelligent Italian food, featuring unusual dishes from his birthplace, Sicily. When you've had enough of angel hair with tomato and basil, come here to fall in love with Italian cooking again.

Dragon Regency

Zone 6   San Gabriel Valley
120 South Atlantic Boulevard,
    Monterey Park
(818) 282-1089

Chinese	
★★★	
Inexpensive	
Quality 83	Value B

Reservations:	Accepted for large groups
When to go:	Any time
Entree range:	$5.95–12.95
Payment:	VISA, MC
Service rating:	★★★
Friendliness rating:	★★
Parking:	Self
Bar:	Beer and wine
Wine selection:	Limited
Dress:	Casual
Disabled access:	Yes
Customers:	Mostly Chinese and Chinese-Americans
Lunch/Dinner:	Every day, 11 A.M.–10 P.M.

Atmosphere / setting: A large, pleasant dining room filled with lots of large parties.

House specialties: Crispy double-pleasure (twice-cooked) sole; snake soup; deep-fried oysters; pan-fried crab with garlic and black bean sauce; frog in garlic sauce.

Other recommendations: Steamed chicken with Chinese broccoli; braised whole abalone with oyster sauce; whole fish in various sauces.

Summary & comments: One of the first Cantonese seafood emporiums in L.A.'s new suburban Chinatown, Dragon Regency has been eclipsed in fame by Ocean Star, Seafood City, and others. But its fish are still fresh and its cooks are still very skilled. The banquet menus are a particularly good value.

Drai's

<table>
<tr><td></td><td>French</td></tr>
<tr><td>Zone 3   Golden Triangle</td><td>★★★</td></tr>
<tr><td>730 North La Cienega Boulevard,</td><td>Expensive</td></tr>
<tr><td>West Hollywood</td><td></td></tr>
<tr><td>(310) 358-8585</td><td>Quality 80   Value D</td></tr>
</table>

Reservations:	Advised
When to go:	Weeknights bring more Hollywood hotshots
Entree range:	$13–28
Payment:	Major credit cards
Service rating:	★★★
Friendliness rating:	★★★
Parking:	Valet available
Bar:	Full service
Wine selection:	Interesting but pricey
Dress:	Hollywood chic—from Armani suits to vinyl leggings
Disabled access:	Yes
Customers:	A dazzling parade of face lifts, breast enhancements, name actors, stubble-faced screenwriters, and aging movie moguls
Lunch:	Friday, noon–2:30 P.M.
Dinner:	Every night, 6:30–10:30 P.M.

Atmosphere / setting: Quite lovely—a cozy, parlorlike bar and three connecting dining rooms, all with sepia-colored walls, dark wood trim, impressive oil portraits, and abundant candlelight. The middle dining room and the adjacent rainforest-painted enclosed patio seem to be the coolest places to sit. Request a free-standing table for privacy; banquette seating is uncomfortably close.

House specialties: Flaky tarts, notably one filled with goat cheese and topped with fresh tomato slices and basil; fresh marinated salmon with fennel salad; baked salmon and lobster wrapped in puff pastry; garlicky spinach.

Other recommendations: Baked potato filled with smoked salmon; wonton ravioli with shiitake and chanterelle mushrooms in mushroom sauce; classic mashed potatoes; raspberry gratin.

Summary & comments: At this writing, Drai's is the hottest restaurant in town, at least in the showier showbiz circles. They love the strikingly handsome, soothing bistro setting, the people-watching, and the rich, amply portioned bistro food, and they don't seem to mind the efficient but brusque service. There's no telling how long chef Claude Segal will last here—he moves around a lot—but his style is perfectly suited to this crowd. There's better food to be had in town, but no better scene.

El Cholo

Zone 5   Central City
1121 South Western Avenue
(213) 734-2773

	Mexican
	★★½
	Inexpensive
	Quality 77 Value B

Reservations:	Advised
When to go:	Peak hours get crowded
Entree range:	$7.50–11
Payment:	Major credit cards
Service rating:	★★
Friendliness rating:	★★
Parking:	Valet available
Bar:	Full service
Wine selection:	Limited
Dress:	Casual
Disabled access:	Yes
Customers:	L.A. cross-section
Lunch/Dinner:	Monday–Thursday, 11 A.M.–10 P.M.;
	Friday and Saturday, 11 A.M.–11 P.M.;
	Sunday, 11 A.M.–9 P.M.

Atmosphere / setting: A warren of festive rooms with rough wooden beams, booths, painted stucco walls, and waitresses in traditional (if hokey) Mexican garb.

House specialties: Sweet green-corn tamales, in summer only; classic chicken enchiladas, butted up against lakes of rice and cheesy refried beans; shrimp fajitas; Cuervo Gold margaritas.

Other recommendations: The combination plate—enchilada and taco, tamale or chili relleno—which was invented here; soft tacos with sautéed fresh fish or savory carnitas; salsa verde crab enchiladas.

Summary & comments: Every true Angeleno has a soft spot in his or her heart for this venerable Cal-Mex restaurant, which has been hopping since 1927. The neighborhood may have declined, but El Cholo continues to thrive, thanks to its first-rate margaritas, Mexican-American comfort food, and party atmosphere.

El Emperador Maya

	Mexican
Zone 6 San Gabriel Valley	★★★
1823 South San Gabriel Boulevard,	Inexpensive
San Gabriel	
(818) 288-7265	Quality 85 Value B

Reservations:	Accepted
When to go:	Any time
Entree range:	$7.95–12.95
Payment:	Major credit cards
Service rating:	★★
Friendliness rating:	★★★★
Parking:	On street
Bar:	Beer and wine
Wine selection:	Small but good
Dress:	Casual
Disabled access:	Yes
Customers:	Local, and cochinita pibil junkies
Lunch:	Tuesday–Friday, 11 A.M.–2:30 P.M.
Dinner:	Tuesday–Thursday, 5–9 P.M.;
	Friday and Saturday, 5–10 P.M.;
	Sunday, 4–9 P.M.

Atmosphere / setting: A plain, almost dreary corner storefront with a few tables, a painting of the chef, and framed reviews that extol the food's many virtues.

House specialties: Extraordinary panuchos (small black-bean-stuffed fried tortillas) topped with marinated turkey and pickled cabbage and red onion; cochinita pibil (achiote-rubbed pork wrapped in a banana leaf); calamari steak with garlic-butter-cilantro sauce; caballero pobre, a bread pudding with fresh fruit and apricot sauce.

Other recommendations: Fried bananas; enchiladas with mole; Yucatan combo for three or more; banana flan.

Summary & comments: What looks like just another working-class Mexican joint is home to some of the best Yucatecan cooking in Southern California. From the panuchos to the cochinita to the flan, the flavors are earthy and robust, yet balanced and finessed.

Empress Pavilion

Zone 5 Central City	Chinese
988 North Hill Street,	★★★
Chinatown	Inexp/Mod
(213) 617-9898	Quality 84 Value B

Reservations:	Accepted for dinner
When to go:	Any time
Entree range:	$7.50–17
Payment:	VISA, MC, DC
Service rating:	★★★
Friendliness rating:	★★★
Parking:	In building
Bar:	Full service
Wine selection:	Limited
Dress:	Casual to business
Disabled access:	Yes
Customers:	Downtown workers, Chinese
Open:	Monday–Friday, 9 A.M.–10 P.M.
Breakfast/Lunch:	Saturday and Sunday, 8 A.M.–3 P.M.
Dinner:	Saturday and Sunday, 5:30–10 P.M.

Atmosphere/setting: An ornate Hong Kong–style restaurant with a complex system of sliding decorated dividers that can break the endless 600-seat space into various configurations.

House specialties: An extensive and first-rate dim sum, from sui mai and bao buns to shrimp rice noodle and steamed lotus-seed buns; sautéed prawns with honey-glazed walnuts; Dungeness crab with ginger and green onion; mango pudding.

Other recommendations: Fried prawns in lemon sauce; oysters on the half shell; one of the live fish, perhaps with a black-bean sauce.

Summary & comments: Just when Angelenos were beginning to despair about decaying Chinatown, along came this glorious Hong Kong–style palace. The dim sum is one of the best in town, the seafood is impeccable, and the service is better than the Chinese norm.

ENGINE CO. NO. 28

Zone 5   Central City
644 South Figueroa Street, Downtown
(213) 624-6996

American	
★★½	
Moderate	
Quality 74	Value C

Reservations:	Advised at lunch
When to go:	Dinner is quieter
Entree range:	$10–20
Payment:	Major credit cards
Service rating:	★★★
Friendliness rating:	★★★
Parking:	Validated at lunch, valet at night
Bar:	Full service
Wine selection:	Excellent
Dress:	Business
Disabled access:	Yes
Customers:	Lawyers, bankers, accountants
Lunch/Dinner:	Monday–Friday, 11:15 A.M.–9 P.M.
Dinner:	Saturday and Sunday, 5–9 P.M.

Atmosphere / setting: A carefully restored 1912 firehouse with lots of masculine charm: cozy wood booths with muted tapestry upholstery, scrolled tin ceilings, old black-and-white photos, a striking bar, and Billie Holliday on the stereo.

House specialties: Pan-fried crab cakes; perfect french fries, spiked with chili powder for the adventurous; fat cheeseburgers on sourdough; double-layer chocolate cake.

Other recommendations: Meat loaf with mashed potatoes and greens; whiskey-fennel sausages with wonderful red cabbage.

Summary & comments: A romanticized re-creation of an American chophouse from the turn of the century, the Engine Company is a great spot for burgers, fries, homey American standards, and great American wines. The more complicated dishes and the gimmicky firehouse specials often disappoint.

Fabiolus

Zone 5   Central City
5255 Melrose Avenue
(213) 464-5857

Zone 5   Central City
5750 Melrose Avenue
(213) 461-1549

Zone 5   Central City
6270 Sunset Boulevard, Hollywood
(213) 467-2882

Italian	
★★½	
Inexpensive	
Quality 76	Value A

Reservations:	Accepted
When to go:	Any time
Entree range:	$6.50–16
Payment:	Major credit cards
Service rating:	★★
Friendliness rating:	★★
Parking:	Self
Bar:	Bring your own at first Melrose cafe; beer and wine elsewhere
Wine selection:	Decent
Dress:	Casual
Disabled access:	Yes
Customers:	Local studio employees
Lunch:	Monday–Friday, 11:30 A.M.–3:30 P.M.
Dinner:	Monday–Saturday, 6–10 P.M.

Atmosphere / setting: Three no-frills trattorias devoted to serving good pastas at good prices. Decor is an afterthought.

House specialties: Antipasto plate with marinated cooked vegetables (asparagus, carrots, beets, etc.); penne with eggplant, tomato sauce, and smoked mozzarella; spaghetti with seafood.

Other recommendations: Penne alla vodka; fusilli with peas, mushrooms, ham, and cream; daily special grilled fish with a side of pasta.

Summary & comments: For some mysterious reason, the neighborhoods near Paramount and Gower Gulch—which are full of hungry, highly paid studio employees—have been bereft of good restaurants. Along came the first Fabiolus, which quickly expanded to a minichain of three, all serving very good, very inexpensive pasta to grateful music and showbiz workers.

Farfalla La Brea

Zone 5   Central City
143 North La Brea Avenue
(213) 938-2504

	Italian
	★★½
	Moderate
	Quality 80 Value C

Reservations:	Accepted
When to go:	Any time
Entree range:	$10–16
Payment:	Major credit cards
Service rating:	★
Friendliness rating:	★★
Parking:	Valet available
Bar:	Full service
Wine selection:	Good Italians
Dress:	Casual
Disabled access:	Yes
Customers:	The young, the black-clad, the self-important
Lunch:	Monday–Friday, 11:30 A.M.–2:30 P.M.
Dinner:	Every night, 6–11 P.M.

Atmosphere / setting: A cool, handsome Mediterranean setting with a worn brick wall, fireplace, wood-burning beehive pizza oven, and hard, noise-bouncing surfaces. The upstairs dining room and bar are quieter.

House specialties: Bruschetta; penne alla Norma, with eggplant; tagliolini with sweet shrimp and a very light sauce of garlic and olive oil; rich gnocchi with smoked chicken and sun-dried tomatoes.

Other recommendations: Roast chicken; large thin-crust pizzas; osso buco.

Summary & comments: This busy, trendy trattoria doesn't work as well as its smaller first-born sibling, the original Trattoria Farfalla in Los Feliz—it's too confused, too big, too inconsistent in the kitchen. But most of the time the pastas, roast chicken, and pizza are pretty terrific.

FINO

Zone 2 South Bay	Mediterranean
Hillside Village,	★★★
24530 Hawthorne Boulevard,	Moderate
Torrance	Quality 83 Value B
(310) 373-1952	

Reservations:	Partial; some tables reserved for walk-ins
When to go:	Any time; peak hours are crowded
Entree range:	$10.50–18.50
Payment:	VISA, MC, AMEX
Service rating:	★★★
Friendliness rating:	★★★
Parking:	Self
Bar:	Beer and wine
Wine selection:	Good rustic choices
Dress:	Casual
Disabled access:	Yes
Customers:	South Bay residents
Dinner:	Monday–Thursday, 5–9:30 P.M.;
	Friday and Saturday, 5–10 P.M.;
	Sunday, 4–9 P.M.

Atmosphere / setting: Cozy and convivial, with a real feeling of Greece or southern Italy that will make you forget you're in a minimall.

House specialties: Menu changes frequently. There are many good tapas, including steamed mussels, grilled portobello mushroom, bruschettas with various toppings, and spinach salad; orecchiette with sautéed spinach; brick-flattened chicken with lemon, garlic, and herbs.

Other recommendations: Farfalle with chicken sausage; baked salmon; Fino cioppino, a farfalle pasta with seafood.

Summary & comments: The men behind Chez Melange and Depot have brought the sunny South Bay a welcome taste of the sunny Mediterranean. The joie de vivre here is as seductive as the cuisine, redolent of garlic, herbs, and olive oil.

FIVE FEET

Zone 10   Orange County South
328 Glenneyre Street, Laguna Beach
(714) 497-4955

Pacific Rim
★★★½
Moderate

Quality 88   Value C

Reservations:	Advised
When to go:	Any time
Entree range:	$17.50–22.50
Payment:	Major credit cards
Service rating:	★★★★
Friendliness rating:	★★★
Parking:	Self
Bar:	Beer and wine
Wine selection:	Good
Dress:	Casual chic
Disabled access:	Yes
Customers:	Lively locals, savvy tourists
Lunch:	Friday, 11:30 A.M.–2:30 P.M.
Dinner:	Sunday–Thursday, 5–10 P.M.;
	Friday and Saturday, 5–11 P.M.

Atmosphere / setting: A lively, funky setting for serious food: exposed brick walls, exposed ceiling rafters, open kitchen, and modern art.

House specialties: Menu changes frequently. Dim sum are always worthy—perhaps potstickers with soy-ginger sauce or sui mai filled with shrimp, black mushrooms, and cabbage; coconut prawns with exotic greens and Thai lime dressing; the famed whole catfish, with hot braised sauce or garlic sauce.

Other recommendations: Excellent entrees have included the duet of duck, roasted duck breast, and savory Chinese-style crispy duck with Elysium-raspberry sauce and braised Chinese eggplant; and Cantonese seafood, a beautiful assortment of shellfish and fresh fish stir-fried with sweet peppers and a black-bean sauce.

Summary & comments: Still as exciting as the day it opened, Five Feet is one of California's pioneers of Pacific Rim cooking. As at Chinois, Chinese techniques and flavors provide the culinary foundation, to which owner / chef Michael Kang adds French, Italian, Thai, and American ornaments. The results are almost always profoundly delicious. Worth a trip.

Flora Kitchen

		New American
Zone 5 Central City		★★½
460 South La Brea Avenue		Inexpensive
(213) 931-9900		
		Quality 80 Value D

Reservations:	No
When to go:	Late mornings or afternoons are quiet
Entree range:	$7–15
Payment:	VISA, MC
Service rating:	★
Friendliness rating:	★
Parking:	Self
Bar:	None
Wine selection:	None
Dress:	Hip
Disabled access:	Yes
Customers:	Workers in the local shops and design studios
Open:	Sunday–Thursday, 8 A.M.–11 P.M.;
	Friday and Saturday, 8 A.M.–midnight

Atmosphere / setting: A simple contemporary storefront adjacent to a high-end florist, with high bar-type tables and a lot of takeout business.

House specialties: Daily-changing salads, like roasted peppers with goat cheese or grilled chicken with baby artichokes; seared ahi sandwich with arugula and yellow tomato salsa on La Brea Bakery bread; blueberry cheesecake; marvelous cookies.

Other recommendations: Vegetarian sandwich of mozzarella, tomato, and basil; pear tarte tatin; ginger scones.

Summary & comments: A lunch counter for the Range Rover set, Flora Kitchen makes some of the best sandwiches, cold salads, and desserts in town. They don't come cheap, however, and the service can be lousy. Great takeout and picnic baskets.

FRAGRANT VEGETABLE

Zone 1   Westside
11859 Wilshire Boulevard, West L.A.
(310) 312-1442

Chinese / Vegetarian
★★½
Inexpensive

Quality 76   Value B

Reservations:	Accepted
When to go:	Any time
Entree range:	$7–10
Payment:	VISA, MC, AMEX
Service rating:	★★
Friendliness rating:	★★★
Parking:	Self
Bar:	Beer and wine
Wine selection:	Limited
Dress:	Casual
Disabled access:	Yes
Customers:	Westsiders
Lunch / Dinner:	Sunday–Thursday, 11:30 A.M.–9 P.M.;
	Friday and Saturday, 11:30 A.M.–10 P.M.

Atmosphere / setting: More attractive than the Chinese norm, with Taoist paintings and comfortable seating.

House specialties: Buddha's Cushions, stewed mushrooms with black moss and tofu roll; Vegetable Treasure, a curry casserole with coconut milk; stewed bean curd with chili and black-bean sauce.

Other recommendations: The various faux meat dishes, made with tofu or gluten, such as lemon "duck" and pepper "steak"; Yin Yang soup, with spinach and corn; string beans with hot bean sauce.

Summary & comments: This Buddhist vegetarian cuisine is far more appealing than the brown-rice-with-veggies American vegetarian stuff. Sauces are robust, with ample use of chilis and spices, and the faux meat, poultry, and seafood dishes are better than you'd think.

Fritto Misto

Zone 1 Westside	Italian
601 Colorado Avenue, Santa Monica	★★
(310) 458-2829	Inexpensive
	Quality 74 Value A

Reservations: For 8 or more
When to go: Crowded at peak hours
Entree range: $7–14
Payment: VISA, MC, D
Service rating: ★★
Friendliness rating: ★★★
Parking: Self
Bar: Beer and wine
Wine selection: A few bargain choices, and an amazing
                            $1 corkage fee
Dress: Casual
Disabled access: Yes
Customers: Locals
Lunch/Dinner: Monday–Thursday, 11:30 A.M.–10 P.M.;
                            Friday and Saturday, 11:30 A.M.–10:30 P.M.;
                            Sunday, 5–9:30 P.M.

Atmosphere/setting: A basic storefront cafe crammed with simple tables and lots of happy people.

House specialties: Italian empanadas, stuffed with shrimp and pancetta or chicken and creamed spinach; fritto misto, a mixed fry of shrimp, calamari, and fresh vegetables; garlic shrimp with black and white pasta.

Other recommendations: Design your own mix-and-match pasta, choosing from all sorts of sauces and ingredients; crème brûlée.

Summary & comments: Every neighborhood should have such a friendly, lively, cheap trattoria. The generously served food is homey and tasty, just the thing when you don't feel like cooking.

Fu Shing

Zone 6   San Gabriel Valley
3500 East Colorado Boulevard,
  2nd Floor, Pasadena
(818) 792-8898

> Chinese
> ★★★
> Inexpensive
>
> Quality 83   Value C

Reservations:	Accepted
When to go:	Any time
Entree range:	$7.50–13.95
Payment:	Major credit cards
Service rating:	★★★
Friendliness rating:	★★★
Parking:	Self
Bar:	Full service
Wine selection:	Limited
Dress:	Casual
Disabled access:	Yes
Customers:	Asian and Occidental Pasadenans
Lunch/Dinner:	Every day, 11:30 A.M.–10:30 P.M.

Atmosphere / setting: A pleasant, soothing space, with large tables, plants, and a teal color scheme. In warm weather tables are set on the outdoor terrace.

House specialties: Spicy Szechwan won tons in a chili broth; sweet and pungent shrimp; diced chicken in tangerine sauce; sautéed spinach.

Other recommendations: Shredded pork with preserved cabbage; braised beef stew; kung pao scallops.

Summary & comments: North San Gabriel Valley residents don't have to drive south for great Chinese food now that Fu Shing has arrived in this Pasadena motel / minimall. Well-balanced, powerfully flavorful dishes from many regions, including Szechwan, are served with kindness and finesse in an upscale setting.

Gardel's

	Argentinian
Zone 5 Central City	★★½
7963 Melrose Avenue	Moderate
(213) 655-0891	
	Quality 77 Value C

Reservations:	Accepted
When to go:	Any time
Entree range:	$10.50–16.50
Payment:	VISA, MC, AMEX
Service rating:	★★★
Friendliness rating:	★★★
Parking:	Valet available at night
Bar:	Beer and wine
Wine selection:	Decent
Dress:	Casual
Disabled access:	Yes
Customers:	Hearty eaters, homesick Argentinians
Lunch:	Wednesday–Friday, 11:30 A.M.–2:30 P.M.
Dinner:	Monday–Saturday, 6–11 P.M.

Atmosphere / setting: An upscale but still homey setting with quality table linens, a handsome bar, and, in the background, the seductive tango music of '30s legend Carlos Gardel.

House specialties: Whole roasted heads of sweet garlic, to squeeze onto thick bread; matambre ("hunger killer"), a starter of flank steak rolled around hard-boiled egg, Spanish pimientos, and pickles; parrillada, a daunting mixed grill including Italian and blood sausages, sweetbreads, skirt steak, and short ribs.

Other recommendations: Argentinian empanadas filled with spinach, chicken, or beef; Argentine-style breaded beef; crêpes filled with caramel sauce.

Summary & comments: Cholesterol counters may flourish in L.A., but this meat-eater's paradise continues to flourish as well. Gardel's is L.A.'s only upscale restaurant devoted to the garlicky, tasty, seriously meaty cuisine of Argentina.

Gardens

	New American
	★★★★
Zone 3 Golden Triangle	Very Expensive
Four Seasons Hotel,	
300 South Doheny Drive	Quality 91 Value D
(310) 273-2222	

Reservations:	Accepted
When to go:	Sunday brunch is superb, lunch is a low-key Hollywood spot
Entree range:	$21–32
Payment:	Major credit cards
Service rating:	★★★★★
Friendliness rating:	★★★★★
Parking:	Valet available
Bar:	Full service
Wine selection:	Top names, top prices
Dress:	Hollywood chic to business
Disabled access:	Yes
Customers:	Top-flight businesspeople, movie stars, showbiz
Brunch:	Sunday, 10 A.M.–2:30 P.M.
Breakfast/Lunch:	Tuesday–Saturday, 6 A.M.–2:30 P.M.
Dinner:	Tuesday–Sunday, 5:30–11:30 P.M.

Atmosphere / setting: Luxurious and conservative, with a subtle gray-and-yellow color scheme, silk and velvet fabrics, Limoges china, huge flower displays, eighteenth-century Italian oil paintings, and a greenery-filled terrace.

House specialties: The buffet Sunday brunch ($39), perhaps the best in town; vegetarian dim sum; risotto of grilled vegetables with lemon oil; roast rack of lamb with creamy polenta, grilled fresh green beans, and rosemary jus.

Other recommendations: Wok-charred swordfish with a ragout of vegetables and basil emulsion; daily fresh fish, like Pacific halibut with orzo pasta and sun-dried tomatoes; chicken pot pie with butter crust; deep-dish apple pie.

Entertainment & amenities: Jazz ensemble during Sunday brunch; piano in adjacent lounge nightly.

Summary & comments: Deeply luxurious but free of Hollywood flash, Gardens is the sort of place Michelle Pfeiffer would meet an interviewer for lunch, away from the industry hordes at the Ivy and Le Dome. The quality of the ingredients and service are top-drawer, and the blend of contemporary American, Asian, and Mediterranean dishes works beautifully. The lighter, healthier "alternative cuisine" dishes taste like anything but diet food.

Honors / awards: The hotel is a Mobil 5-star and AAA 5-diamond award-winner.

GEORGIA

Zone 5   Central City
7250 Melrose Avenue
(213) 933-8420

Southern	
★★★	
Moderate	
Quality 84	Value C

Reservations:	Accepted
When to go:	Any time
Entree range:	$11–19.50
Payment:	VISA, MC, AMEX
Service rating:	★★★
Friendliness rating:	★★★
Parking:	Valet available
Bar:	Full service
Wine selection:	Varied and good
Dress:	Stylish
Disabled access:	Yes
Customers:	A wonderful multiethnic mix
Lunch:	Monday–Friday, noon–3 P.M.
Dinner:	Monday–Saturday, 6:30–11 P.M.;
	Sunday, 5:30–10 P.M.

Atmosphere / setting: It feels like a particularly elegant jazz club, dimly lit
and enveloping, with dark velvet banquettes, wood wainscoting, ceiling fans, rich
fabric wallpaper, and muted wall sconces.

House specialties: Georgia roll, grits rolled with aged cheddar, wild mushrooms and herbs over a bed of sautéed spinach; partially deboned Southern fried
chicken with collard greens and macaroni and cheese; fried green tomatoes;
Georgia peach cobbler.

Other recommendations: House smoked catfish on spicy wild rice corn
cakes; house smoked barbecued ribs; spicy peppered broiled shrimp with a hard
crab bourbon sauce.

Entertainment & amenities: Weekend jazz and blues in the cafe.

Summary & comments: Yet another celebrity restaurant, but in this case
one of the best. Owned by an odd assortment including Denzel Washington,
Connie Stevens, Lou Adler, and Eddie Murphy, Georgia has a terrific atmosphere,
appealing house drinks (Georgia peach daiquiri), and deeply satisfying Southern
American food. True, prices are steep for such down-home cooking, and the
service is erratic, but the experience delivers.

Gilliland's

International
★★★
Moderate

Quality 83   Value B

Zone I   Westside
2424 Main Street, Santa Monica
(310) 392-3901

Reservations:	Accepted
When to go:	Any time; Sunday brunch is lovely
Entree range:	$11–17
Payment:	Major credit cards
Service rating:	★★★
Friendliness rating:	★★★★
Parking:	Self
Bar:	Full service
Wine selection:	Good
Dress:	Casual
Disabled access:	Yes
Customers:	Locals
Brunch:	Sunday, 10 A.M.–2:30 P.M.
Lunch:	Monday–Saturday, 11:30 A.M.–2:30 P.M.
Dinner:	Monday–Saturday, 5:30–10:30 P.M.;
	Sunday, 5–10 P.M.

Atmosphere / setting: A welcoming neighborhood cafe, with a cool patio in back.

House specialties: Blarney cheese-and-onion tart; Mexican corn tamale; Irish beef stew braised in Guinness stout; fruit cobblers.

Other recommendations: Watercress and arugula salad; rack of lamb with daily-changing sauce; chocolate ganache cake.

Summary & comments: An enduring pioneer, Belfast-born Gerri Gilliland was one of the first in town to bring together extremely diverse cuisines—in this case, from Ireland, Mexico, Asia, and the Mediterranean—with great success. Inventive yet homey, Gilliland's is the kind of place you can return to regularly.

Ginza Sushi-ko

Zone 3 Golden Triangle	Japanese
Two Rodeo, 218 Via Rodeo,	★★★½
Beverly Hills	Very Expensive
(310) 247-8939	Quality 90 Value F

Reservations:	Mandatory
When to go:	Any time
Entree range:	No entrees; dinner runs $150 or more per person
Payment:	VISA, MC, AMEX
Service rating:	★★★★
Friendliness rating:	★★★
Parking:	Valet available
Bar:	Beer and saké
Wine selection:	Good sakés
Dress:	Casual to business
Disabled access:	Yes
Customers:	Japanese businessmen, wealthy sushi junkies
Lunch:	Monday–Friday, 11:30 A.M.–2 P.M.
Dinner:	Monday–Saturday, 5–10 P.M.

Atmosphere / setting: A small, excessively spare restaurant above McCormick and Schmick's, comprising only a small counter and one tatami room.

House specialties: There's no menu; diners are served whatever sushi the chef is making that day, based on his supply of rare and exotic seafood and his creative fancy. He presents you with dishes until you've had enough—then he presents you with the bill.

Summary & comments: Owner/chef Masa Takayama has no peer in the West when it comes to procuring the rarest, most prized fresh fish and working them into extraordinary sushi creations. But are these delicacies really worth $200 apiece for dinner? For heavily padded expense accounts or the very wealthy only.

Golden Truffle

New American

★★★½

Moderate

Zone 9	Orange County North
1767 Newport Boulevard, Costa Mesa	
(714) 645-9858	

Quality 85   Value B

Reservations:	Advised
When to go:	When you're feeling creative
Entree range:	$11–18
Payment:	Major credit cards
Service rating:	★★★★
Friendliness rating:	★★★★
Parking:	Self
Bar:	Beer and wine
Wine selection:	Very good
Dress:	Casual-chic to stylish
Disabled access:	Yes
Customers:	Lots of foodie regulars
Lunch:	Tuesday–Saturday, 11:30 A.M.–2:30 P.M.
Dinner:	Tuesday–Saturday, 5:30–10 P.M.

Atmosphere / setting: A couple of storefront rooms with an inviting bistro feel: covered tables, bistro chairs, an open kitchen, and large windows that keep the room bright by day. At night the candlelit rooms are more intimate.

House specialties: Menu changes monthly. Popular recurring dishes include Jamaican jerk chicken salad; prime Angus fillet "Senna style" (in honor of the deceased race-car driver) with a spicy Brazilian sauce; roast gypsy chicken with fresh herbs and natural juices.

Other recommendations: The best way to eat here is to ask chef Greeley to surprise you. He'll do just that, creating dishes using a happy cacophony of flavors and ingredients, from curries to truffles, lobster to Caribbean pickles, ginger-wasabe sauce to prosciutto Alfredo sauce.

Summary & comments: Chef Alan Greeley burns with joie de vivre and culinary passion, and he loves nothing more than to be given free reign by a food-loving customer. If you place yourself in his hands, you'll have an American / Caribbean / Italian / Asian mishmash dinner that will be memorable, if sometimes uneven. If you order off the menu or from the huge list of daily specials, you'll have a similar, if slightly less intense, experience. The menu is very reasonably priced.

GRANITA

Zone 1 Westside	New American
23725 West Malibu Road, Malibu	★★★★
(310) 456-0488	Expensive
	Quality 92 Value C

Reservations:	Advised
When to go:	Any time
Entree range:	$18–26
Payment:	VISA, MC, D, CB
Service rating:	★★★★
Friendliness rating:	★★★★
Parking:	Valet available
Bar:	Full service
Wine selection:	Fine Californians
Dress:	Casual chic
Disabled access:	Yes
Customers:	Malibu locals, Johnny Carson in jeans
Lunch:	Wednesday–Friday, 11:30 A.M.–2 P.M.; Saturday and Sunday, 11 A.M.–2 P.M.
Dinner:	Monday–Thursday, 6–10 P.M.; Friday, 6–11 P.M.; Saturday, 5:30–11 P.M.; Sunday, 5:30–10 P.M.

Atmosphere / setting: *The Little Mermaid* on acid—a submarine riot of colorful, wavelike tile work, fish tanks, and wacky ocean-related artworks. Every detail is extraordinary (don't miss the bathrooms). The crowd is almost as amusing— a tanned, lively bunch in $200 jeans and designer baseball caps.

House specialties: Potato Galette with salmon, dill crème fraiche, and caviar; Wolfgang Puck's famed California pizzas, which remain wonderful; pots de creme.

Other recommendations: Chinese duck with peach chutney; daily fish specials, like sizzling scorpion fish with soy-ginger glaze; clams with Chinese black-bean sauce; daily changing granitas (fruit ices).

Summary & comments: Spago has more of a name, and Chinois more of a high-falutin' culinary reputation, but Granita is the most relaxed and enjoyable restaurant in Wolfgang Puck's fast-growing culinary kingdom. It's easier to get a table than at Spago (though plenty of stars drop by), the staff is friendlier, the setting is pure California fantasy, and the food is consistently delicious. Well worth a drive up the coast on a sun-splashed summer day.

The Grill on the Alley

	American
	★★★½
	Expensive
	Quality 87 Value D

Zone 3   Golden Triangle
9560 Dayton Way, Beverly Hills
(310) 276-0615

Reservations:	Advised
When to go:	Any time
Entree range:	$18.50–32.50
Payment:	Major credit cards
Service rating:	★★★★
Friendliness rating:	★★★★
Parking:	Valet available
Bar:	Full service
Wine selection:	Limited and pricey
Dress:	Upscale
Disabled access:	Yes
Customers:	Beverly Hills stockbrokers, middle-age showbiz
Lunch / Dinner:	Monday–Thursday, 11:30 A.M.–11 P.M.;
	Friday and Saturday, 11:30 A.M.–midnight

Atmosphere / setting: A replica of an upscale, manly chophouse from many decades ago, à la Tadich's in San Francisco, with large, high wooden booths, brass details, an open-counter kitchen, and white-aproned waiters.

House specialties: Oysters on the half shell; Caesar salad; a perfect hamburger; T-bone steak; broiled Chilean sea bass; lyonnaise potatoes; pecan pie.

Other recommendations: Cobb salad; meat loaf; broiled chicken with garlic; crab cakes; cheesecake.

Summary & comments: If you love traditional American food and don't get hives at the thought of paying $4.75 for a baked potato, hurry on over to this wonderful bastion of Yankee comfort food. Everyone feels good in the cozy wooden booths, and the food is reliably tasty.

Grill Lyon

Zone 5   Central City
Honda Plaza, 424 East 2nd Street,
    Little Tokyo
(213) 620-1223

French/Japanese
★★★
Moderate

Quality 84   Value B

Reservations:	Advised
When to go:	Lunch is a good deal
Entree range:	$20 for prix-fixe dinner
Payment:	VISA, MC
Service rating:	★★★
Friendliness rating:	★★★★
Parking:	Self
Bar:	Beer and wine
Wine selection:	Small but choice
Dress:	Casual to business
Disabled access:	Limited
Customers:	Japanese businesspeople, downtown executives
Lunch:	Monday–Friday, noon–2:30 P.M.
Dinner:	Monday–Saturday, 5:30–8:45 P.M.

Atmosphere / setting: A tiny minimall storefront with a counter, a couple of tables, an open kitchen, and a spare Japanese aesthetic.

House specialties: Carefully composed green salads; mussel soup; lamb chops with port wine sauce; braised beef oxtail; homemade soufflé cheesecake.

Other recommendations: Vegetable cream soups; duck a l'orange; papaya cake; pear in red wine.

Summary & comments: In this personal, intimate restaurant, you get a floor show—watching the owner / chef cook your meal with deft precision. His French food is filtered through a Japanese sensibility, and the result is light, carefully considered, and extremely flavorful. A special little hideaway.

Gumbo Pot

Zone 5   Central City
Farmer's Market,
    6333 West 3rd Street
(213) 933-0358

Cajun/Creole
★★
Inexpensive

Quality 75   Value B

Reservations:	Not accepted
When to go:	Lunch or late–afternoon snack
Entree range:	$5.50–7.50
Payment:	No credit cards
Service rating:	★★
Friendliness rating:	★★
Parking:	Self
Bar:	None
Wine selection:	None
Dress:	Casual
Disabled access:	Yes
Customers:	A wonderful L.A. cross-section
Open:	Monday–Saturday, 8:30 A.M.–6:30 P.M.; Sunday, 9 A.M.–5 P.M.

Atmosphere / setting: A typical Farmer's Market self-service counter, with a bustling sea of humanity all around.

House specialties: Sugary beignets; hefty muffuletta sandwiches; robust gumbo yaya with andouille sausage, chicken, and shrimp; jambalaya.

Other recommendations: Sweet potato salad with apples, pecans, and raisins; po' boys; cornbread flecked with corn kernels, cheese, and chilis.

Summary & comments: Forget the greasy pizza and gooey spaghetti at some of Farmer's Market's other lunch counters—come here for first-rate, bargain-basement Cajun and Creole favorites. The gumbo is particularly good.

GUSTAF ANDERS

	Scandinavian / New American
Zone 9 Orange County North	★★★★
South Coast Plaza Village,	Mod / Exp
1651 Sunflower Avenue, B-21,	
Santa Ana	Quality 94 Value C
(714) 668-1737	

Reservations:	Advised
When to go:	Any time
Entree range:	$16–26
Payment:	Major credit cards
Service rating:	★★★★★
Friendliness rating:	★★★★★
Parking:	Self
Bar:	Full service
Wine selection:	Good but peculiar and pricey
Dress:	Dressed-up
Disabled access:	Yes
Customers:	Orange County elite, foodies from L.A.
Lunch:	Monday–Saturday, 11:30 A.M.–2 P.M.
Dinner:	Monday–Saturday, 5:30–10 P.M.

Atmosphere / setting: Part of the endless South Coast Plaza, Gustaf Anders is cool and Scandinavian, with comfortable leather chairs, good art on the walls, and good jazz on the stereo.

House specialties: The justly famed gravad lax, either the traditional version with dill-mustard sauce or the amazing grilled version with a morel sauce; superb parsley salad with sun-dried tomatoes, garlic, and Parmesan; extraordinary calves' liver, an almost Southwestern sauté with garlic, onions, mushrooms, and mild chilis; saffron-raisin ice cream.

Other recommendations: Don't miss the exceptional homemade breads and crackers; wonderful sugar- and salt-cured salmon with creamed dill potatoes; herb-sautéed sturgeon on a bed of steamed vegetables with a caper, tomato, and shallot sauce; lemon tart.

Summary & comments: "Great Scandinavian cooking" doesn't exactly leap to mind when considering California's food highlights, but Gustaf Anders is both a great Scandinavian restaurant and a great California restaurant. Inventive yet meticulous, intellectual yet satisfying, this is a wonderful, consistent cuisine. Worth a considerable detour.

Hal's Bar & Grill

Zone 1   Westside
1349 Abbot Kinney Boulevard, Venice
(310) 396-3105

New American
★★★
Moderate

Quality 83   Value B

Reservations:	Accepted
When to go:	Weekend brunch is particularly nice
Entree range:	$15–22
Payment:	VISA, MC, AMEX
Service rating:	★★★
Friendliness rating:	★★★
Parking:	Valet available for dinner
Bar:	Full service
Wine selection:	Good and affordable
Dress:	Casual hip
Disabled access:	Yes
Customers:	Upscale boho Venice: architects, artists, musicians
Brunch:	Saturday and Sunday, 10 A.M.–3 P.M.
Lunch:	Monday–Friday, 11:30 A.M.–3 P.M.
Dinner:	Every night, 6–10:30 P.M.

Atmosphere / setting: A particularly inviting warehouse space, with exposed rafters, a long bar counter, jazz on the stereo, and often-impressive local art on the walls.

House specialties: Menu changes weekly. Good choices might include the house Cobb salad for lunch; Caesar salad for dinner; simple grilled venison; grilled half chicken with garlic and rosemary oil and crisp french fries; grilled tuna on a bed of basmati rice with corn, zucchini, and thyme.

Other recommendations: All the homemade desserts are wonderful, especially the ice cream sundaes, peanut butter–chocolate cake, and vanilla cream tart with fresh berries.

Summary & comments: The West Beach Cafe and 72 Market Street may have bigger reputations, but Hal's beats them at their own game. The setting is artsy, friendly, and relaxed; the prices are reasonable; the bar is a place for a drink and a conversation, not an obnoxious scene; and the friendly updated American food is quite fine.

Harold & Belle's

Zone 4   City South
2920 West Jefferson Boulevard,
    South-Central L.A.
(213) 735-9023

Cajun/Creole	
★★★	
Moderate	
Quality 80	Value C

Reservations:	Advised
When to go:	When you're really hungry
Entree range:	$14.95–28.95
Payment:	Major credit cards
Service rating:	★★★
Friendliness rating:	★★★★
Parking:	Self
Bar:	Full service
Wine selection:	Limited
Dress:	Upscale
Disabled access:	Yes
Customers:	African-Americans, homesick Southerners
Lunch/Dinner:	Monday–Thursday, noon–10 P.M.;
	Friday, noon–11 P.M.; Saturday, 1–11 P.M.;
	Sunday, 1–10 P.M.

Atmosphere / setting: Crowded and high-spirited, with a dressed-up, date-night clientele.

House specialties: Louisiana hot links; powerful file gumbo with shrimp, crab, sausage, and ham; fried catfish; shrimp Creole in a rich red sauce; peach cobbler; bread pudding with rum sauce.

Other recommendations: Dinners come with heaps of starters and sides: choose the thick clam chowder to start; best accompaniments are corn on the cob and the tasty potato salad.

Entertainment & amenities: Good live jazz on Friday and Saturday nights.

Summary & comments: When your heart's in New Orleans but your body's stuck in L.A., reserve a table at this very fine Creole restaurant. Just don't eat for a day or two before, for you'll be buried in a mountain of rich, deeply satisfying food.

Hollywood Canteen

American	
★★★	
Moderate	
Quality 80	Value C

Zone 5   Central City
1006 Seward Street, Hollywood
(213) 465-0961

Reservations:	Accepted
When to go:	Lunch is busy, dinner quiet
Entree range:	$8.25–19
Payment:	VISA, MC, AMEX
Service rating:	★★★
Friendliness rating:	★★
Parking:	Valet available
Bar:	Full service
Wine selection:	Pretty good
Dress:	Casual
Disabled access:	Yes
Customers:	Studio and post-production workers, music biz
Lunch:	Monday–Friday, 11:30 A.M.–3 P.M.
Dinner:	Monday–Thursday, 5:30–10 P.M.; Friday and Saturday, 6–11 P.M.

Atmosphere / setting: A good-looking neo-'40s diner with a horseshoe counter, dark wood, a skillful use of mirrors and lighting, and a very pleasant walled patio in back.

House specialties: Tasty hamburgers; risotto with wild mushrooms; grilled swordfish Mediterranean style; tiramisu.

Other recommendations: Good salads with organic field greens; pasta with fresh tomato and basil; grilled salmon; crème brûlée.

Summary & comments: This clubby, cozy bar and grill on a grungy side street has become a sort of off-site commissary for many film, TV, and music workers. At night, it's the sort of place that Bruce Springsteen and Patti Scialfa would sneak into for a quiet dinner. The American-Italian fare is as comfortable as the setting.

Hotel Bel-Air

Zone 1   Westside
Bel-Air Hotel,
    701 Stone Canyon Road, Bel Air
(310) 472-1211

New American
★ ★ ★ ★
Expensive

Quality 91   Value C

Reservations:	Accepted
When to go:	Any time
Entree range:	$16–24
Payment:	Major credit cards
Service rating:	★ ★ ★ ★ ★
Friendliness rating:	★ ★ ★ ★ ★
Parking:	Valet available
Bar:	Full service
Wine selection:	Extensive and expensive
Dress:	Upscale (tie)
Disabled access:	Yes
Customers:	Well-heeled Westside matrons by day, wealthy couples and anniversary celebrants by night
Breakfast:	Monday–Saturday, 7 A.M.–11:30 P.M.
Brunch:	Sunday, 11 A.M.–2 P.M.
Lunch:	Monday–Saturday, noon–3:30 P.M.
Dinner:	Every night, 6:30–11 P.M.

Atmosphere / setting: Nestled in the sylvan Santa Monica Mountain foothills in a neighborhood rife with mansions and Bentleys, the Hotel Bel-Air is a truly enchanting fantasy. Outside are ponds, swans, and opulent landscaping; inside are richly upholstered chairs, warm colors, and eminently tasteful art.

House specialties: At breakfast or the famed brunch, huevos rancheros or lemon pancakes with raspberry syrup and fresh raspberries; at lunch, roast salmon salad with fresh shaved fennel, artichokes, pine nuts, and an herb vinaigrette; at dinner, sea bass with herb-potato crust and basil sauce. The formal afternoon tea is the finest in town.

Other recommendations: Any of the luxurious sandwiches; apple-cranberry cobbler.

Entertainment & amenities: Piano music at dinner.

Summary & comments: Everything—storybook setting, intelligent California cuisine, dedicated service—comes together at this opulent hotel restaurant. Whether you're on the patio on a sunny day or by the fireplace on a chilly evening, there's no better—or pricier—spot in town for romance.

Hugo's

Zone 3 Golden Triangle	Italian
8401 Santa Monica Boulevard,	★★★
West Hollywood	Inexpensive
(213) 654-4088	Quality 82 Value B

Reservations:	Accepted
When to go:	Breakfast is the best
Entree range:	$6.50–13
Payment:	VISA, MC, AMEX
Service rating:	★★★
Friendliness rating:	★★★
Parking:	Self
Bar:	Beer and wine
Wine selection:	Decent
Dress:	Casual
Disabled access:	Yes
Customers:	Showbiz, rock 'n' rollers, assorted cool people
Open:	Sunday–Thursday, 7:30 A.M.–10 P.M.;
	Friday and Saturday, 7:30 A.M.–10:30 P.M.

Atmosphere / setting: A bright, open, rather plain cafe, with long glass deli cases and plateglass windows to the street.

House specialties: Pasta Mama, a fabulous, cholesterol-laden dish of fresh pasta, scrambled eggs, Parmesan, and parsley; pumpkin pancakes; pasta pomodoro, with fresh tomatoes; chicken piccata; low-fat lentil stew; low-fat vegetarian Tantric burger.

Other recommendations: Chicken and eggplant sandwich; eggs carbonara, with prosciutto and green onions; several pretty good fat-free desserts.

Summary & comments: Although this very hip pasta cafe is still famed for its fat-supercharged pasta Mama and eggs carbonara, Hugo's has gone healthy, to considerable success. Some ancient Indian vegetarian recipes have been updated and adapted, and several low-fat pasta and other dishes are quite satisfying.

Hungarian Budapest

Zone 5   Central City
7986 Sunset Boulevard, Hollywood
(213) 654-3744

	Hungarian
	★★½
	Inexpensive
	Quality 78 Value B

Reservations:	Accepted
When to go:	Any time
Entree range:	$10–15
Payment:	AMEX, DC
Service rating:	★★★
Friendliness rating:	★★★
Parking:	Self
Bar:	Beer and wine
Wine selection:	Limited
Dress:	Casual
Disabled access:	Yes
Customers:	Hungarians, working-class showbiz and music industry
Dinner:	Tuesday–Sunday, 4–11 P.M.

Atmosphere / setting: Next to the ever-popular Gaucho Grill in a Hollywood pod mall, this is a basic modern storefront restaurant, gussied up with flowers and white linens.

House specialties: Pungent, smoky goulash; stuffed cabbage; veal paprikash with dumplings; palacsinta torte, a delicious walnut-chocolate pastry.

Other recommendations: Hungarian salami sandwiches; consommé with liver dumplings.

Summary & comments: All the rich, gut-sticking classics from Hungary are here, lightened up a little (but not too much) for American sensibilities. The flavors, and sometimes the accents of neighboring diners, are wonderfully authentic.

Hu's Szechwan

	Chinese
	★★½
	Inexpensive
	Quality 79 Value B

Zone 4   City South
10450 National Boulevard, Palms
(310) 837-0252

Reservations:	Not accepted
When to go:	Early or late to avoid crowds
Entree range:	$6–9
Payment:	VISA, MC, DC
Service rating:	★★
Friendliness rating:	★★
Parking:	Self
Bar:	None
Wine selection:	Bring your own
Dress:	Casual
Disabled access:	Limited
Customers:	Locals
Lunch:	Monday–Saturday, 11:30 A.M.–2:30 P.M.
Dinner:	Every night, 5–10:30 P.M.

Atmosphere / setting: A nondescript dining room in a nondescript residential neighborhood.

House specialties: Sweat-inducing Szechwan dumplings; curried chicken; dried-fried string beans with ground pork; kung pao chicken.

Other recommendations: Mandarin chicken salad; tangy-sweet-hot shrimp with a Szechwan tomato sauce.

Summary & comments: Many Angelenos got their first taste of fiery Szechwan cooking at this Palms hole-in-the-wall, which is still turning out fine kung pao and other spicy standards.

I CUGINI

	Italian
	★★½
	Moderate
	Quality 76 Value C

Zone 1   Westside
1501 Ocean Avenue, Santa Monica
(310) 451-4595

Reservations:	Accepted
When to go:	Before sunset to enjoy the view
Entree range:	$9.75–19.95
Payment:	Major credit cards
Service rating:	★★
Friendliness rating:	★★★
Parking:	Valet available
Bar:	Full service
Wine selection:	Very good
Dress:	Casual chic
Disabled access:	Yes
Customers:	Westsiders, some beach-going tourists
Lunch/Dinner:	Sunday–Thursday, 11:30 A.M.–10:30 P.M.; Friday and Saturday, 11:30 A.M.–11:30 P.M.

Atmosphere/setting: Rather like a professionally decorated seventeenth-century Tuscan wine cellar: arches, artfully aged walls painted with Italian city scenes, a huge open kitchen, a busy bar, and a lovely patio offering glimpses of the Pacific.

House specialties: Menu changes regularly. Possiblities include calamari fritti with spicy red sauce; seafood pizza; and pizza with spicy chicken, white cheese, and spinach.

Other recommendations: Littleneck clams baked in the wood oven with pancetta, bell pepper, and garlic; spaghettini alla Genovese, with pesto, potatoes, green beans, and pecorino-romano cheese.

Summary & comments: Great looks, a great location, and a happening bar make I Cugini a Santa Monica hot spot. The cooking ranges from the earthy and delicious to the inconsistent and bland; pizzas are reliably wonderful.

Il Cielo

	Italian
	★★★
	Mod/Exp
	Quality 82 Value C

Zone 3   Golden Triangle
9018 Burton Way, Beverly Hills
(310) 276-9990

Reservations:	Accepted
When to go:	Warm evenings
Entree range:	$15–30
Payment:	Major credit cards
Service rating:	★★★
Friendliness rating:	★★★★
Parking:	Valet available
Bar:	Full service
Wine selection:	Varied
Dress:	Casual chic to upscale
Disabled access:	Yes
Customers:	Starry-eyed lovers
Lunch:	Monday–Saturday, 11:30 A.M.–3 P.M.
Dinner:	Monday–Thursday, 6–10 P.M.;
	Friday and Saturday, 6–11 P.M.

Atmosphere / setting: All the charm of a little Tuscan inn, tucked away on Burton Way's opulent condo row. Inside, rooms are cozy and romantic, with fresco-like painted walls, beams, flowers, and flickering candles; even more romantic is the stone patio, complete with trickling fountain, lush gardens, and a view to the heavens.

House specialties: Capellini with Maine lobster and white wine; fettuccine with porcini mushrooms; grilled branzino (Italian sea bass) with fresh herbs; tiramisu.

Other recommendations: Tagliolini with soft-shell crab and Madeira wine; grilled baby rack of lamb; semifreddo.

Summary & comments: It's no wonder Il Cielo ("the sky") is busy most Sundays with weddings—it's a seriously romantic restaurant, one of the best in town for initiating or rekindling an affair. The elegant Italian food, especially the seafood, is just as romantic as the setting.

Il Fornaio

	Italian
	★★★
	Inexp / Mod
	Quality 80 Value B

Zone 3   Golden Triangle
301 North Beverly Drive, Beverly Hills
(310) 550-2030

Zone 6   San Gabriel Valley
24 West Union Street, Pasadena
(818) 683-9797

Zone 9   Orange County North
18051 Von Karman Avenue, Irvine
(714) 261-1444

Reservations:	Advised
When to go:	Any time
Entree range:	$7.75–17.95
Payment:	Major credit cards
Service rating:	★★★
Friendliness rating:	★★★★
Parking:	Valet available; validated in Irvine
Bar:	Full service
Wine selection:	Good Californians and Italians
Dress:	Casual chic
Disabled access:	Yes
Customers:	Attractive, smartly dressed locals, businesspeople
Open:	*Beverly Hills and Pasadena:* Monday–Thursday, 7 A.M.–11 P.M.; Friday, 7 A.M.–midnight; Saturday, 8 A.M.–midnight; Sunday, 9 A.M.–11 P.M. *Irvine:* Monday–Thursday, 11:30 A.M.–11 P.M.; Friday and Saturday, 11:30 A.M.–midnight; Sunday, 11:30 A.M.–10 P.M.

Atmosphere / setting: The restaurants are striking, with contemporary lighting, pale woods, and lots of white.

House specialties: Melanzane (grilled eggplant with goat cheese, sun-dried tomatoes, and sweet onions); lasagne d'anatra; rotisserie chicken.

Other recommendations: Simple, thin-crust pizzas; fresh mozzarella rolled with speck, ricotta, arugula, and toasted pine nuts; focaccia with Gorgonzola, pine nuts, basil, and onions; terrine of three chocolates.

Summary & comments: This savvy restaurant group grew out of a chain of popular bread bakeries in Italy. The settings are always a knockout, the service snappy, and the wines-by-the-glass tasty. Most important, the food is light, flavorful, and very appealing. What McDonald's is to the 5-year-olds, Il Fornaio is to baby boomers—a fun, consistent, affordable chain that always makes you happy.

Il Mito

<table>
<tr><td>Zone 7   San Fernando Valley East
11801 Ventura Boulevard, Studio City
(818) 762-1818</td><td>Italian
★★★
Moderate

Quality 84   Value C</td></tr>
</table>

Reservations:	Advised
When to go:	Any time
Entree range:	$8–19
Payment:	VISA, MC, AMEX
Service rating:	★★★
Friendliness rating:	★★★
Parking:	Valet available
Bar:	Full service
Wine selection:	Good Italians
Dress:	Casual chic
Disabled access:	Yes
Customers:	Black-clad hipsters from the Valley studios
Lunch:	Monday–Friday, 11:30 A.M.–2:30 P.M.
Dinner:	Monday–Friday, 6–10 P.M.; Saturday, 6–10:30 P.M.

Atmosphere / setting: Two chic, architecturally compelling, but uncomfortably crowded rooms, with a congested bar.

House specialties: Parma-style onion soup with toasted croutons and Parmesan; risotto with fresh river shrimp, saffron, and turmeric; grilled veal T-bone with fresh herbs.

Other recommendations: Insalata della casa, a Caesar variation; ravioli stuffed with lobster in a lemon-cream sauce; boneless free-range chicken with Malaysian mustard sauce.

Summary & comments: Michael Fekr gained a following when he cooked at Locanda Veneta, and he's even more popular now as proprietor of this very fine (if cramped) trattoria. His dishes are creative but uncluttered, and flavors are right on the mark.

Il Moro

Zone 1   Westside
11400 West Olympic Boulevard,
   West L.A.
(310) 575-3530

Italian	
★★★	
Inexpensive	
Quality 81	Value A

Reservations:	Yes
When to go:	Any time
Entree range:	$6.95–12.95
Payment:	Major credit cards
Service rating:	★★★
Friendliness rating:	★★★
Parking:	Valet available
Bar:	Beer and wine
Wine selection:	Good by-the-glass selection
Dress:	Casual
Disabled access:	Yes
Customers:	Young, stylish office workers and locals
Lunch:	Monday–Friday, 11:30 A.M.–3 P.M.
Dinner:	Monday–Saturday, 5:30–10 P.M.

Atmosphere / setting: Hardwood floors, high ceilings, open kitchen, exposed ductwork, and takeout counter—your basic modern cafe, set in a Westside office building.

House specialties: Very good antipasto buffet at lunch; fettuccine with mascarpone and lemon sauce; grilled lamb chops with country herbs and oyster mushrooms; vanilla custard with caramel or chocolate sauce.

Other recommendations: Potato soup with broccoli, chicken, and herbs; linguine primavera with rock shrimp; appealing pizzas.

Summary & comments: From the team who gave the city Locanda Veneta, Ca'Brea, and Ca'del Sole, Il Moro serves aromatic, satisfying Italian country cooking at Olive Garden prices. A stylish, fun newcomer.

Il Pastaio

<table>
<tr><td colspan="2">Italian
★★★
Inexp/Mod</td></tr>
</table>

Zone 3   Golden Triangle
400 North Canon Drive, Beverly Hills
(310) 205-5444

Zone 6   San Gabriel Valley
141 South Lake Avenue, Pasadena
(818) 795-4006

	Italian
	★★★
	Inexp/Mod
Quality 84	Value A

Reservations:	Accepted
When to go:	Any time
Entree range:	$8–12.50
Payment:	Major credit cards
Service rating:	★★★★
Friendliness rating:	★★★★
Parking:	Valet available for dinner
Bar:	Beer and wine in Beverly Hills; full service in Pasadena
Wine selection:	Pretty good
Dress:	Casual
Disabled access:	Yes
Customers:	Neighborhood regulars
Lunch:	*Pasadena:* Monday–Friday, 11:30 A.M.–2:30 P.M.
Lunch/Dinner:	*Beverly Hills:* Monday–Saturday, 11:30 A.M.–11 P.M.
Dinner:	*Pasadena:* Monday–Thursday, 5:30–9:30 P.M., Friday and Saturday, 5:30–11 P.M.; *Beverly Hills:* Sunday, 5–10 P.M.

Atmosphere / setting: Stylish and informal, with open kitchens, polished light woods, and hip halogen lighting. The Beverly Hills location is smaller and more cramped.

House specialties: Smoked salmon salad with capers and crispy leeks; venison carpaccio with celery; duck-liver pâté and truffle oil; pappardelle with duck ragu; spaghetti with seafood and a light tomato sauce; apple tart.

Other recommendations: Arancine di riso, fried rice cones stuffed with beef ragu; smoked swordfish carpaccio with fennel and orange salad; crespelle (crêpes) filled with wild mushrooms, fontina, and truffle sauce.

Summary & comments: Celestino Drago, of Drago fame, and his chef brother, Giacomino Drago, have partnered in these two winning trattorias. Salads, appetizers, carpaccios, pastas, and risottos are the only offerings, and they are uniformly excellent. A richly satisfying salad-and-risotto meal will cost less than an entree at most other restaurants of this caliber.

Il Ristorante di Giorgio Baldi

Italian	
★ ★ ★	
Moderate	
Quality 82	Value C

Zone 1   Westside
114 West Channel Road, Santa Monica
(310) 573-1660

Reservations:	Advised
When to go:	Any time
Entree range:	$12.50–20
Payment:	VISA, MC, DC
Service rating:	★ ★
Friendliness rating:	★ ★ ★
Parking:	Valet available
Bar:	Beer and wine
Wine selection:	Italians
Dress:	Casual chic
Disabled access:	Yes
Customers:	Well-heeled locals
Dinner:	Tuesday–Sunday, 6–10 P.M.

Atmosphere / setting: If it were only sitting on the sand, instead of a block or so from the beach, this would be the perfect beach-house restaurant: white-washed walls, white wooden chairs, blue-and-white silkscreens on the walls, cool tile floor, open kitchen, and Italian beach-boy waiters with tans and dazzling smiles.

House specialties: Prosciutto with melon or figs; hot seafood salad in olive oil and lemon sauce; caciucco, a heady seafood soup in a tomato-herb broth; grigliata mista, a mixed grill of seafood; fresh-fruit tarts.

Other recommendations: Various risotto, with seafood or mushrooms; grilled salmon in lemon sauce.

Summary & comments: A curious business problem inspired Giorgio Baldi to change the name and phone number of his restaurant, but everything else remains unchanged. The setting, service, and seafood-based cuisine will convince you that you're dining in Forte dei Marmi, the Tuscan beach town that Baldi hails from.

ITA-CHO

Zone 5   Central City
6775 Santa Monica Boulevard,
    Hollywood
(213) 871-0236

Japanese	
★★★½	
Inexpensive	
Quality 88	Value A

Reservations:	Accepted
When to go:	Any time
Entree range:	Grazing dishes are $3.50–7
Payment:	VISA, MC, AMEX
Service rating:	★★★
Friendliness rating:	★★★
Parking:	Self
Bar:	Beer and saké
Wine selection:	Excellent saké list
Dress:	Casual
Disabled access:	Yes
Customers:	In-the-know Japanese food lovers
Dinner:	Monday–Saturday, 6:30–11 P.M.

Atmosphere / setting: A most unpromising-looking spot next to an adult video store in a dingy Hollywood minimall. Inside are a few plain tables and a counter.

House specialties: Richer than usual miso soup; extraordinarily succulent yellowtail braised with teriyaki; agedashi tofu, delicate fried tofu cubes in an irresistible soy-ginger-scallion sauce; buta kakuni, butter-tender pork simmered for two days in saké and soy.

Other recommendations: Perfect sashimi; nasu ebisoboro, peeled Japanese eggplant in a thick sweet-wine sauce with ground shrimp; broiled freshwater eel with a cucumber-vinegar salad; steamed whitefish with napa cabbage and chrysanthemum leaves and a red-maple-radish dipping sauce.

Summary & comments: This authentic koryori-ya-style restaurant serves a bevy of jewel-like little cooked dishes, each more wonderful than the next. If you think Japanese food is sushi or tempura, ignore the dreary location and hurry into Ita-Cho for an education in the joys of savory, high-quality, affordable Japanese home cooking.

The Ivy

Zone 3   Golden Triangle
113 North Robertson Boulevard,
    West Hollywood
(310) 274-8303

New American
★★★
Very Expensive
Quality 80   Value F

Reservations:	Advised
When to go:	Lunchtime is horribly expensive
Entree range:	$22–35
Payment:	Major credit cards
Service rating:	★★★
Friendliness rating:	★
Parking:	Valet available
Bar:	Full service
Wine selection:	Choice and pricey
Dress:	Casual to upscale, as long as it's expensive
Disabled access:	Yes
Customers:	Impossibly beautiful people drawn from Hollywood, fashion, design, and other such fields
Lunch/Dinner:	Every day, 11:30 A.M.–10 P.M.

Atmosphere / setting: A luxuriously ramshackle country cottage that Martha Stewart would swoon for, with clumps of garden roses, thick hand-painted crockery, plump, worn upholstery, a decrepit picket fence, and a brick patio that's probably the prettiest in town.

House specialties: Justly famous crab cakes; crisp Caesar salad; fried chicken; grilled tuna; fabulous tarte tatin.

Other recommendations: Monstrous hamburgers; homey meat loaf; crab salad; fresh berry pies; any other of the exceptional desserts.

Summary & comments: If you aren't a regular or a famous face, steel yourself for some major attitude—not to mention some serious sticker shock. The setting may be all aw-shucks country charm, but the vibe is pure power dining. Though it's painfully overpriced, the updated American food is generously served and usually quite good, and the desserts are among the best anywhere.

The Ivy at the Shore

Zone 1 Westside	New American
1541 Ocean Avenue, Santa Monica	★★★
(310) 393-3113	Expensive
	Quality 80 Value D

Reservations: Advised
When to go: Any time
Entree range: $22–32
Payment: Major credit cards
Service rating: ★★★
Friendliness rating: ★★★
Parking: Valet available
Bar: Full service
Wine selection: Good, pricey
Dress: Expensively casual
Disabled access: Yes
Customers: Models, beautiful beach people,
                             well-known actors
Lunch/Dinner: Every day, 11:30 A.M.–10:30 P.M.

Atmosphere/setting: A festive, handsome tropical decor updated with some serious contemporary art and a display of vintage Hawaiian shirts. With its roomy seating and amusing people-watching, the bar is great fun.

House specialties: Same as at The Ivy: crab cakes; Caesar salad; meat loaf; Maui onion rings; fried chicken; all the desserts, especially tarte tatin.

Other recommendations: Zippy tropical drinks; Cajun pizza; daily fresh fish specials.

Summary & comments: The attitude is more welcoming but the scene is still significant at this beachy offshoot of The Ivy. It's known for its leggy, beautiful women, its crab cakes, and its entertaining bar scene.

Jackson's

<table>
<tr><td></td><td>New American</td></tr>
<tr><td>Zone 3   Golden Triangle</td><td>★★★</td></tr>
<tr><td>8908 Beverly Boulevard,
  West Hollywood</td><td>Expensive</td></tr>
<tr><td>(310) 550-8142</td><td>Quality 83   Value C</td></tr>
</table>

Reservations:	Advised
When to go:	Any time
Entree range:	$18–21
Payment:	Major credit cards
Service rating:	★★★★
Friendliness rating:	★★★★
Parking:	Valet available
Bar:	Full service
Wine selection:	Good
Dress:	Upscale
Disabled access:	Yes
Customers:	Showbiz people; lots of tan, sculpted bodies
Lunch:	Monday–Friday, 11:30 A.M.–2:15 P.M.
Dinner:	Monday–Saturday, 6–10:30 P.M.; Sunday, 5:30–9 P.M.

Atmosphere / setting: A Wild West decor, softened for an audience that's hardly rough and ready: distressed leather banquettes, rough wood, old photos of nineteenth-century pioneer types, pleasant rear enclosed patio, and requisite open kitchen.

House specialties: Fat filet of beef tenderloin topped with a gorgeous crisp tapestry of potato; roasted rabbit with polenta gnocchi; banana–peanut butter tart.

Other recommendations: Exceptional salmon; crab-leek ravioli; fruit soup with ice cream.

Summary & comments: Chuckwagon fare for Range Rover pioneers is the order of the day at this new hot spot, a labor of love for Alan Jackson, son of talk-radio star Michael Jackson. The setting is as good-looking as the diners, and the service is much better than at the typical pretentious Hollywood hangout.

JASMINE TREE

Zone 1   Westside
11057 Santa Monica Boulevard,
    West L.A.
(310) 444-7171

Chinese	
★★½	
Inexpensive	
Quality 79	Value B

Reservations:	Accepted for large parties
When to go:	Any time
Entree range:	$7.95–12.50
Payment:	Major credit cards
Service rating:	★★
Friendliness rating:	★★★
Parking:	Self
Bar:	Beer and wine
Wine selection:	Limited
Dress:	Casual
Disabled access:	Yes
Customers:	Neighborhood locals
Lunch/Dinner:	Monday–Saturday, 11:30 A.M.–10 P.M.;
	Sunday, noon–9:30 P.M.

Atmosphere / setting: An attractive second-story pod-mall restaurant overlooking Santa Monica Boulevard, with comfortable tables and greenery.

House specialties: Seafood sizzling hot plate; lamb Hunan style; hot braised lobster or whole fish, with a delicious Shanghai-style brown sauce; baby bok choy with Chinese mushrooms; sautéed fresh asparagus in season.

Other recommendations: Cold smoked fish plate; pork chop Peking style; Peking duck; sautéed spinach.

Summary & comments: This quiet, pleasant restaurant serves food that's well above the typical neighborhood-Chinese norm. A worthy taste of Monterey Park for Westsiders who don't want to drive far.

Jitlada

Zone 5 Central City	**Thai**
5233 West Sunset Boulevard,	★★★
Hollywood	Inexpensive
(213) 667-9809	Quality 85 Value B

Reservations:	Accepted
When to go:	Any time
Entree range:	$6–14
Payment:	VISA, MC
Service rating:	★★
Friendliness rating:	★★
Parking:	Self
Bar:	Beer and wine
Wine selection:	Limited
Dress:	Casual
Disabled access:	Yes
Customers:	Local Thais, an L.A. cross-section
Lunch:	Tuesday–Sunday, 11:30 A.M.–3 P.M.
Dinner:	Tuesday–Sunday, 5–10 P.M.

Atmosphere / setting: Outside is a typically dreary East Hollywood mini-mall; inside are two pleasantly dark and handsome rooms, with real tablecloths and Thai art.

House specialties: Flawless Thai spring rolls; poh-taek soup with lemongrass and seafood; sautéed shrimp with red curry paste and fresh-cut green beans; spinach "of flame," with black-bean sauce and cashews.

Other recommendations: Even the normally trite classics are outstanding: mee krob; beef pa nang, with Thai curry paste and coconut milk; pad thai noodles; barbecued chicken.

Summary & comments: Forget all those neighborhood Thai cafes with gummy mee krob and bitter curries, and hurry to Jitlada for the most authentic, delicious Thai food in town. Flavors sizzle and sing, ingredients are fresh, and unusual offerings are plentiful. Be warned that hot really is hot here.

Jitlada West

<table>
<tr><td></td><td>Thai</td></tr>
<tr><td></td><td>★★★</td></tr>
<tr><td></td><td>Inexpensive</td></tr>
<tr><td></td><td>Quality 81   Value B</td></tr>
</table>

Zone 7   San Fernando Valley East
11622 Ventura Boulevard, Studio City
(818) 506-9355

Reservations:	Accepted
When to go:	Any time
Entree range:	$5–12
Payment:	VISA, MC, AMEX
Service rating:	★★
Friendliness rating:	★★★
Parking:	Self
Bar:	Beer and wine
Wine selection:	Limited
Dress:	Casual
Disabled access:	Yes
Customers:	Locals
Lunch/Dinner:	Sunday–Thursday, 11:30 A.M.–10 P.M.;
	Friday and Saturday, 11:30 A.M.–11 P.M.

Atmosphere/setting: A bright, sunny, upscale Thai restaurant, with large windows and soft pastels.

House specialties: Thai sausage salad; crispy Bangkok duck; fried catfish with coconut cream; stir-fried asparagus with cashews and bacon.

Other recommendations: Yum yai salad, with cucumbers, carrots, shrimp, chicken, and tomatoes; fried squid; barbecued chicken.

Summary & comments: East Valleyites couldn't ask any more of a local Thai restaurant. Jitlada West (no longer associated with Hollywood's Jitlada) serves first-rate Thai classics in a welcoming setting.

JOE'S

Zone 1   Westside
1023 Abbot Kinney Boulevard, Venice
(310) 399-5811

	New American
	★★★
	Moderate
	Quality 83 Value B

Reservations:	Advised
When to go:	Lunch is a great bargain
Entree range:	$14–17
Payment:	VISA, MC, AMEX
Service rating:	★★★
Friendliness rating:	★★★
Parking:	Valet available at dinner
Bar:	Beer and wine
Wine selection:	Decent
Dress:	Casual chic
Disabled access:	Yes
Customers:	Stylish locals
Lunch:	Tuesday–Sunday, 11:30 A.M.–2:30 P.M.
Dinner:	Tuesday–Sunday, 6–11 P.M.

Atmosphere / setting: A narrow, awkward Venice storefront—charming to some, cramped to others—with a simple, modern, white decor.

House specialties: Tuna tartare with lemon and cucumbers; scallops with risotto and a sprinkling of crispy fried carrots; wonderful roasted monkfish marinated in pesto with succotash; roast beef with artichokes and mashed potatoes; excellent tarte tatin.

Other recommendations: Arugula salad with pancetta and little ovalina cheeses; grilled shrimp on creamy polenta with crispy leeks.

Summary & comments: Joe Miller took over the space that once housed Rockenwagner, and within moments word had spread of his intelligent, utterly delicious modern American cooking, his good cheer, and his very reasonable prices. Consequently, tables are hard to come by, so reserve early.

JULiENNE

Zone 6   San Gabriel Valley
2649 Mission Street, San Marino
(818) 441-2299

New American
★★★
Moderate

Quality 83   Value C

Reservations:	Not accepted
When to go:	Lunch
Entree range:	$6–13
Payment:	VISA, MC
Service rating:	★★★
Friendliness rating:	★★★
Parking:	Self
Bar:	None
Wine selection:	Bring your own
Dress:	Casual
Disabled access:	Yes
Customers:	Well-groomed Pasadena lady lunchers
Breakfast/Lunch:	Monday–Friday, 7 A.M.–5 P.M.;
	Saturday, 8 A.M.–5 P.M.

Atmosphere / setting: One of the prettiest lunch spots around: a painstaking re-creation of a bistro in a French village, with time-burnished wood, a long zinc counter, old-fashioned tile, and a tree-lined patio under a colonnade.

House specialties: Menu changes daily. Excellent possibilites may include braised Alsatian lamb shank; salmon with red onion crust and spicy crème fraiche; broccoli quiche; lemon soufflé.

Other recommendations: Other examples include many salads, especially the delicious Caesar adaptations; spicy Thai beef salad; vegetable lasagne; brown butter tart with fresh berries.

Summary & comments: Owner Sue Campoy first came to fame as one of the region's best caterers, and this breakfast-and-lunch cafe and gourmet-to-go shop grew out of her success. Her cooking is homey yet luxurious, and the desserts will make you swoon.

Kachina Grill

Zone 5 Central City	Southwestern
Wells Fargo Center,	★★½
333 South Hope Street, Downtown	Inexp/Mod
(213) 625-0956	Quality 79 Value C

Reservations:	Accepted
When to go:	Dinner is quieter than lunch
Entree range:	$9–17
Payment:	Major credit cards
Service rating:	★★★
Friendliness rating:	★★★★
Parking:	Validated at night
Bar:	Full service
Wine selection:	Decent
Dress:	Mostly business, casual is fine
Disabled access:	Yes
Customers:	Downtown office workers
Lunch/Dinner:	Monday–Friday, 11:30 A.M.–9 P.M.
Dinner:	Saturday, 5–9 P.M.

Atmosphere/setting: A noisy, hectic, modern-Southwestern dining room flanked by an open kitchen and a long bar; outside is a sprawling second-story patio with views of surrounding high-rises.

House specialties: Light, multicolored tortilla chips and fresh salsa; excellent margaritas; chili relleno with blue-cornmeal coating and papaya salsa; delicious sweet-corn pudding; shrimp soft tacos; orange-honey crème brûlée.

Other recommendations: Daily fresh fish, particularly grilled salmon, perhaps with a green-chili pesto; tasty tostada-type salads; salmon burrito with goat cheese; chocolate-pecan pie.

Summary & comments: Jammed at lunch and festive at happy hour, the Kachina Grill is a welcome addition to the relatively limited high-rise restaurant scene. Stick with the least complicated dishes.

Katsu

Japanese	
★★★½	
Moderate	
Quality 86	Value C

Zone 5   Central City
1972 Hillhurst Avenue, Los Feliz
(213) 665-1891

Reservations:	Accepted
When to go:	Any time
Entree range:	$10–15; about $30 for sushi dinner
Payment:	Major credit cards
Service rating:	★★★★
Friendliness rating:	★★★★
Parking:	Valet available
Bar:	Beer and saké
Wine selection:	Good sakés
Dress:	Casual chic
Disabled access:	Yes
Customers:	Upscale sushi lovers
Lunch:	Monday–Friday, noon–2 P.M.
Dinner:	Monday–Thursday, 6–10 P.M.;
	Friday and Saturday, 6–11 P.M.

Atmosphere / setting: Minimalist in the artful extreme, with a few carefully placed stones by the front door, intriguing paintings, works-of-art plates, and a sushi bar.

House specialties: Some of the best sushi and sashimi you'll ever eat: salmon skin rolls; hamachi (yellowtail); uni (sea urchin); maguro and toro tuna; and much more.

Other recommendations: Very fine teriyaki and tempura meals; bento box lunches.

Summary & comments: Still as cutting-edge and hip as it was when it opened in the early '80s, Katsu remains home to meticulously prepared sushi and sashimi of exceptional flavor and freshness.

Katsu 3rd

Zone 3 Golden Triangle	Japanese
8636 West 3rd Street, West Hollywood	★★★
(310) 273-3605	Moderate
	Quality 84 Value C

Reservations:	Accepted
When to go:	Any time
Entree range:	$11–15; $3–7 per order of sushi
Payment:	VISA, MC, AMEX
Service rating:	★★★
Friendliness rating:	★★★
Parking:	Valet available
Bar:	Beer and wine
Wine selection:	Saké and some wines
Dress:	Casual chic
Disabled access:	Yes
Customers:	Stylish, black-clad sushi lovers
Lunch:	Monday–Friday, 11:30 A.M.–2:30 P.M.
Dinner:	Monday–Saturday, 6–10 P.M.

Atmosphere / setting: Cool and austere, with smooth white walls and little decoration.

House specialties: A full range of sushi and sashimi, of excellent quality and preparation.

Other recommendations: Daily-changing broiled fish specials; better-than-the-norm teriyaki and tempura meals.

Summary & comments: After the success of Katsu in Los Feliz, chef Katsu branched out here and served more unusual cooked dishes in the koryori-ya vein, but the public didn't go for it. Now Katsu 3rd is merely another excellent sushi restaurant, hewing closely to the standards set by its parent restaurant.

Koutoubia

Zone 1 · Westside
2116 Westwood Boulevard, Westwood
(310) 475-0729

Reservations:	Accepted
When to go:	Any time
Entree range:	$12.50–19.50
Payment:	VISA, MC, AMEX
Service rating:	★★★★
Friendliness rating:	★★★★
Parking:	Self
Bar:	Full service
Wine selection:	Quite nice
Dress:	Casual
Disabled access:	Yes
Customers:	Everyone
Dinner:	Tuesday–Thursday and Sunday, 6–10 P.M.;
	Friday and Saturday, 6–11 P.M.

Atmosphere / setting: Lush and romantic, in typical Moroccan fashion, with fabric-tented walls and plush pillows on which to recline during your meal.

House specialties: Steaming chicken b'stilla, a savory-sweet pie filled with chicken, egg, and almond, with a dusting of powdered sugar and cinnamon; couscous with fresh vegetables and merguez sausage; crisp-skinned roast squab with saffron rice and almonds.

Other recommendations: Moroccan-style lamb shank with artichokes; vegetarian couscous with walnuts and raisins; marinated vegetables, particularly the carrots and the tomato-onion-cucumber blend.

Summary & comments: The food is the draw—not gimmicks and floor shows—at this venerable restaurant, a pampering, romantic adventure with wonderful food and graceful, gentle service.

Kuala Lumpur

Zone 6   San Gabriel Valley
132 West Colorado Boulevard, Pasadena
(818) 577-5175

Malaysian	
★★½	
Inexpensive	
Quality 79	Value B

Reservations:	Accepted
When to go:	Any time
Entree range:	$8–12
Payment:	VISA, MC
Service rating:	★★★
Friendliness rating:	★★★
Parking:	Self
Bar:	Beer and wine
Wine selection:	Decent
Dress:	Casual
Disabled access:	Yes
Customers:	Savvy Eastsiders
Lunch:	Tuesday–Friday, 11:30 A.M.–2:30 P.M.;
	Saturday and Sunday, noon–4 P.M.
Dinner:	Tuesday–Thursday and Sunday, 5:30–10:30 P.M.;
	Friday and Saturday, 5:30–10:30 P.M.

Atmosphere / setting: Hidden away from the Old Town trendies, Kuala Lumpur is a graceful gem with high ceilings, fresh flowers, and a contemporary flair.

House specialties: Puteri rolls, bite-size Malaysian egg rolls stuffed with shrimp, pork, jicama, and carrots; "night market" noodles, fresh noodles stir-fried with garlic, a complex soy sauce, shrimp, chicken, cabbage, and choy sum; Malaysian beef, chicken, vegetarian, or shrimp curry with kaffir leaf, lemongrass, and garlic.

Other recommendations: Curry laska, rice noodles with chicken, shrimp, tofu, vegetables, and a light coconut-curry sauce.

Summary & comments: The food of Malaysia brings together Chinese and Indian influences, and this marriage works beautifully here. Flavors are hot and clear, with a lovely balance of sweet, hot, savory, and salty.

La Cabanita

Zone 6   San Gabriel Valley
3447 North Verdugo Road, Montrose
(818) 957-2711

Mexican	
★★★	
Inexpensive	
Quality 82	Value A

Reservations:	No
When to go:	Very early or late for dinner; mobbed from 6–8 P.M.
Entree range:	$6.75–8.75
Payment:	VISA, MC, AMEX
Service rating:	★★
Friendliness rating:	★★★★
Parking:	Self
Bar:	Beer and wine
Wine selection:	Limited
Dress:	Casual
Disabled access:	Yes
Customers:	Locals
Open:	Saturday and Sunday, 8 A.M.–10 P.M.
Lunch/Dinner:	Monday–Friday, 10 A.M.–10 P.M.

Atmosphere/setting: A humble two-room storefront filled with glass-topped tables, red vinyl chairs, and stucco walls hung with bright Mexican textiles.

House specialties: Guacamole; robust salsas; the incredibly rich taco norteno, stuffed with beef, avocado, cheese, and pico de gallo; sopes compuestos, three cornmeal boats topped with lettuce, dry white cheese, crema fresca, and either chicken, chorizo, or picadillo.

Other recommendations: Taco de rajas con crema, stuffed with poblano chili, cream sauce, and beans; sweetish chicken mole; pork chops in pasilla chili sauce; soupy, delicious beans.

Summary & comments: La Cabanita's fame hasn't spread far beyond the confines of quiet Montrose, which is a good thing given the paucity of tables. With apologies to the fiercely protective locals, it's high time for the word to get out about the consistently wonderful cooking at this friendly, if sometimes overwhelmed, family restaurant.

Lake Spring Cuisine

Zone 6   San Gabriel Valley
219 East Garvey Avenue, Monterey Park
(818) 280-3571

	Chinese
	★★★½
	Inexpensive
	Quality 85 Value B

Reservations:	Accepted
When to go:	Any time
Entree range:	$7.25–11.50
Payment:	VISA, MC
Service rating:	★★★
Friendliness rating:	★★
Parking:	Self
Bar:	Beer and wine
Wine selection:	Limited
Dress:	Casual
Disabled access:	Yes
Customers:	Chinese food cognoscenti
Lunch:	Every day, 11:30 A.M.–3 P.M.
Dinner:	Every night, 5–9:30 P.M.

Atmosphere / setting: Two small, subdued, tasteful dining rooms with carpeting and table linens.

House specialties: Two cold appetizers, Shanghai-style wine-marinated chicken and ching chiang cured pork; noisette pork pump, a hunk of the tenderest, sweetest pork imaginable; jade shrimp.

Other recommendations: Cured pork with bamboo shoot casserole; shredded pork with bean curd sheets and vegetable; fresh scallops in garlic sauce.

Summary & comments: Shanghaiese food is the speciality at Lake Spring, and this complex, robustly seasoned cuisine is prepared with more flair and finesse here than anywhere else. The melt-in-your-mouth noisette pork "pump" (sounds awful, tastes heavenly) alone is worth a drive across town.

La Loggia

Zone 7 San Fernando Valley East	Italian
11814 Ventura Boulevard, Studio City	★★½
(818) 985-9222	Moderate
	Quality 79 Value B

Reservations:	Accepted
When to go:	Any time
Entree range:	$7.75–16.95
Payment:	Major credit cards
Service rating:	★★
Friendliness rating:	★★★
Parking:	Valet available
Bar:	Beer and wine
Wine selection:	Decent
Dress:	Casual
Disabled access:	Yes
Customers:	Locals
Lunch:	Monday–Friday, 11:30 A.M.–2:30 P.M.
Dinner:	Monday–Thursday, 5:30–10:30 P.M.;
	Friday and Saturday, 5:30–11 P.M.;
	Sunday, 5–10 P.M.

Atmosphere / setting: A simple, square, very noisy room with cane chairs, white linens, pale woods, and an open kitchen.

House specialties: Portobello mushrooms with sautéed spinach and port wine; sautéed duck and chicken cakes (polpettini) on a bed of onion confit; pork chop stuffed with zucchini, mushrooms, herbs, and polenta cakes in a yellow plum sauce.

Other recommendations: Gnocchi with a meat-herb sauce; linguine with lobster, other seafood, whole roasted garlic, and spicy tomato sauce.

Summary & comments: Studio City is blessed with not one but two fine trattorias, located right across the street from each other: La Loggia and Il Mito. Il Mito stole a little of La Loggia's thunder when it opened to great acclaim, but La Loggia remains as popular as ever, and it's still doing a bang-up job serving garlic-and-herb-laden Italian favorites (though some are overly complicated).

LA LUNA

Zone 5   Central City
113 North Larchmont Boulevard,
    Hancock Park
(213) 962-2130

Italian	
★★½	
Moderate	
Quality 79	Value C

Reservations:	Accepted
When to go:	Any time
Entree range:	$8–20
Payment:	Major credit cards
Service rating:	★★★
Friendliness rating:	★★★
Parking:	Self
Bar:	Beer and wine
Wine selection:	Excellent—many affordable Italians and Californians
Dress:	Casual
Disabled access:	Yes
Customers:	Hancock Park locals
Lunch:	Monday–Saturday, 11:30 A.M.–3 P.M.
Dinner:	Monday–Saturday, 5:30–10 P.M.; Sunday, 5–10 P.M.

Atmosphere / setting: Located on Hancock Park's quaint shopping street, La Luna has a front room with rough plaster walls, white linens, and a polished concrete floor; an open kitchen with a dining counter; and, in back, a charming room with exposed brick and an old wall fountain.

House specialties: Assorted grilled vegetables with smoked cheese; spaghetti with wild mushrooms, garlic, and white wine; risotto with quail and a saffron sauce; a very good antipasto buffet at lunch.

Other recommendations: Classic thin-crust pizzas, topped with prosciutto and tomato or duck sausage and mushrooms; excellent house bread; homemade gelati.

Summary & comments: Although Hancock Park is a wealthy, refined neighborhood, it's never had much in the way of restaurants—until La Luna came along. Now that Le Petit Greek is also on Larchmont, locals are blessed with two terrific neighborhood restaurants. La Luna is quietly chic, with a skilled chef from Abruzzi who keeps the regulars very happy.

LANGER'S

Zone 5   Central City
704 South Alvarado Street, Downtown
(213) 483-8050

Delicatessen	
★★½	
Inexpensive	
Quality 80	Value B

Reservations: Not accepted
When to go: Breakfast or lunch
Entree range: $6–8 for sandwiches, $9–14 for entrees
Payment: VISA, MC
Service rating: ★★
Friendliness rating: ★★
Parking: Self
Bar: Beer and wine
Wine selection: Limited
Dress: Casual
Disabled access: Yes
Customers: Businesspeople, multiethnic locals
Breakfast/Lunch: Monday–Saturday, 8 A.M.–4 P.M.

Atmosphere / setting: As faded as the neighborhood, but welcoming nonetheless, with roomy booths and a long coffee shop–style counter. Lunch gets mobbed.

House specialties: Pastrami about a dozen ways, particularly in hot sandwiches, with sauerkraut, with Swiss cheese and Russian dressing, or in a French dip; corned beef sandwiches.

Other recommendations: Very good chicken soup; smoked fish plates; coffee cake.

Summary & comments: Metrorail construction and the decline of the neighborhood nearly killed Langer's, the beloved home of superb pastrami and perfect rye bread. But now the new Metrorail stops right near Langer's front door, and sandwich-starved downtowners have given Langer's a new lease on life. Let's hope it lasts.

La Parrilla

	Mexican
	★★★
	Inexpensive
	Quality 81 Value B

Zone 5   Central City
2126 Cesar Chavez Avenue,
   Boyle Heights
(213) 262-3434

Zone 8   San Fernando Valley West
19265 Roscoe Boulevard, Northridge
(818) 993-7773

Zone 8   San Fernando Valley West
19601 Ventura Boulevard, Tarzana
(818) 708-7422

Reservations:	Accepted
When to go:	Any time
Entree range:	$6–10
Payment:	Major credit cards
Service rating:	★★★★
Friendliness rating:	★★★★
Parking:	Self
Bar:	Beer and wine in Boyle Heights, otherwise full bar
Wine selection:	Limited
Dress:	Casual
Disabled access:	Yes
Customers:	Cross-section
Open:	Every day, 8 A.M.–11:30 P.M. in Boyle Heights; other branches lunch and dinner only

Atmosphere / setting: Festive and pretty; the original Boyle Heights location is cheered with hand-painted tiles and hanging earthenware bowls; the
Northridge branch is the largest, with a similarly colorful atmosphere and lots of
cozy booths and nooks.

House specialties: Handmade tortillas; sizzling, smoky, charcoal-grilled
carne asada, chicken, chorizo, spare ribs, and more; pork in chipotle sauce; seafood
grill for two.

Other recommendations: Shrimp in a seductive garlic sauce; fresh tamales
and pozole; chicken en pipian, with a pumpkin-seed sauce.

Summary & comments: Years ago, La Parrilla showed L.A.'s non-Mexican
population that Mexican food was much more complex and wonderful than
taco-enchilada combinations. Now there are three branches, all great fun, all
serving delicious grilled meats and high-quality, authentic Mexican dishes.

La Pergola

	Italian
	★★½
Zone 7 San Fernando Valley East	Moderate
15005 Ventura Boulevard,	
Sherman Oaks	Quality 77 Value C
(818) 905-8402	

Reservations:	Accepted
When to go:	Any time
Entree range:	$12–18.50
Payment:	VISA, MC, AMEX
Service rating:	★★★
Friendliness rating:	★★★
Parking:	Valet available
Bar:	Full service
Wine selection:	Good
Dress:	Casual chic
Disabled access:	Yes
Customers:	Sherman Oaks locals
Lunch:	Monday–Friday, 11 A.M.–2:30 P.M.
Dinner:	Sunday–Thursday, 5–10 P.M.;
	Friday and Saturday, 5–10:30 P.M.

Atmosphere / setting: A sweet, romantic place most notable for its huge adjacent garden, where all the restaurant's produce is grown. A few tables fill a patio near the garden.

House specialties: Panzerotti filled with fresh vegetables, topped with marinara; angel hair with the freshest daily vegetables, perhaps peas, tomatoes, squash blossoms, and broccoli; simple grilled fish, notably salmon, trout, and tuna; fresh figs.

Other recommendations: Green salads from the garden; bruschetta with garden tomatoes; chicken breast with artichoke hearts.

Summary & comments: One of the very few restaurants in the region to grow its own produce (Parkway Grill is another), La Pergola is a vegetable lover's paradise, featuring salads, pastas, pizzas, and other dishes made with beauties from the 6,000-square-foot garden. The cooking is less memorable than the garden, but it works just fine.

La Plancha Grill

Zone 5   Central City
2814 West 9th Street, Downtown
(213) 383-1449

Nicaraguan	
★★½	
Inexpensive	
Quality 78	Value A

Reservations:	Accepted
When to go:	Any time
Entree range:	$6.25–10.95
Payment:	VISA, MC
Service rating:	★★
Friendliness rating:	★★★★
Parking:	Self
Bar:	Beer and wine
Wine selection:	Limited
Dress:	Casual
Disabled access:	Yes
Customers:	Locals, adventurous diners
Lunch / Dinner:	Every day, 11 A.M.–9 P.M.

Atmosphere / setting: La Plancha recently reopened in the space previously called La Plancha Pupuseria, next door to the larger restaurant space it once filled. The 50-seat room is basic, with roomy booths and Latin music on the stereo.

House specialties: Wonderful pupusas, hand-patted masa pancakes stuffed with chicharron (fried pork), cheese, and meat; lomito asado, a Nicaraguan dish of achiote-marinated pork tenderloin, served with rice and fried plantains; nacatamals, jumbo Nicaraguan tamales stuffed with meat and prunes.

Other recommendations: Shrimp with special sauce and Mexican cotija cheese; whole fish in garlic sauce.

Summary & comments: Milton Molino's restaurant is back downtown after a stint in Highland Park. Although Nicaraguan food is the specialty, the best thing here are the excellent Salvadoran pupusas, especially the chicharron variety. The Nicaraguan specialties are delicious, too, though meat dishes can be tough.

La Serenata de Garibaldi

Zone 5   Central City
1842 East 1st Street, East L.A.
(213) 265-2887

Mexican	
★★★½	
Moderate	
Quality 87	Value B

Reservations:	Advised
When to go:	Any time
Entree range:	$9.25–17.50
Payment:	Major credit cards
Service rating:	★★★
Friendliness rating:	★★★★
Parking:	In back
Bar:	Beer and wine
Wine selection:	Limited; good Mexican beers
Dress:	Casual
Disabled access:	Yes
Customers:	Downtown business at lunch; everyone at dinner
Lunch/Dinner:	Tuesday–Saturday, 11 A.M.–10:30 P.M.;
	Sunday, 10 A.M.–10 P.M.

Atmosphere / setting: Don't let the grimy East L.A. block of storefronts put you off—inside is a handsome room with contemporary art, good lighting, and glass-topped tables decorated with Mexican textiles.

House specialties: At lunch, shrimp gorditas (stuffed masa pockets) and fish enchiladas; at dinner, giant shrimp al mojo de ajo (garlic sauce); fisherman's soup; whole snapper or other fresh fish in chipotle (smoked chili) sauce or fresh spinach sauce.

Other recommendations: Shrimp cocktails; any of the daily-changing soups; chicken in mole sauce; flan.

Summary & comments: Word has gradually leaked out about this extraordinary Mexican seafood restaurant, and now Lexus-driving Westsiders dine here as often as East L.A. locals. The fish is impeccable, the sauces and soups boast great finesse, and the atmosphere is welcoming. Worth a trip.

Lawry's The Prime Rib

Zone 3 Golden Triangle	American
100 North La Cienega Boulevard, West Hollywood	★★★
(310) 652-2827	Moderate
	Quality 81 Value C

Reservations:	Accepted
When to go:	Any time
Entree range:	$18–25, including salad
Payment:	Major credit cards
Service rating:	★★★
Friendliness rating:	★★★
Parking:	Valet available
Bar:	Full service
Wine selection:	Decent
Dress:	Casual to upscale
Disabled access:	Yes
Customers:	Families, birthday partiers, large groups of Japanese tourists
Dinner:	Monday–Thursday, 5–10 P.M.; Friday and Saturday, 5–11 P.M.; Sunday, 4–10 P.M.

Atmosphere / setting: It moved across the street, but it looks pretty much the same—a huge, open dining hall with large banquettes, bright lighting, waitresses with silly hats, and gleaming carts encasing great hunks of prime rib.

House specialties: Prime rib, prime rib, and prime rib. It comes in four sizes, ranging from the relatively dainty California cut to the macho Diamond Jim Brady cut.

Other recommendations: Delicious (and fat-choked) creamed spinach; the other sides are forgettable.

Summary & comments: When nothing but a big ol' slab of red meat will do, head for this shrine to the best prime rib in town—it's always juicy, salty, and perfectly tender. The Disneyesque dining experience is a bit hokey, and the rest of the food is ordinary, but the meat is memorable.

Le Chardonnay

Zone 3   Golden Triangle
8284 Melrose Avenue, West Hollywood
(213) 655-8880

<table>
<tr><td>French</td></tr>
<tr><td>★★★</td></tr>
<tr><td>Expensive</td></tr>
<tr><td>Quality 83   Value C</td></tr>
</table>

Reservations:	Advised
When to go:	Dinnertime is the most glittering
Entree range:	$18.75–28
Payment:	Major credit cards
Service rating:	★★★★
Friendliness rating:	★★★★
Parking:	Valet available
Bar:	Full service
Wine selection:	Fine, rather pricey French
Dress:	Upscale
Disabled access:	Yes
Customers:	Handsome and elegant
Lunch:	Tuesday–Friday, noon–2 P.M.
Dinner:	Tuesday–Saturday, 6–10 P.M.

Atmosphere / setting: A gorgeous replica of one of Paris's great bistros, Vagenende. The art nouveau woodwork glows, the lights and mirrors glitter, and the great rotisserie spits turn; only the authentic bistro noise level keeps this from being the most romantic setting in town.

House specialties: Menu changes daily, but the acclaimed rotisserie chicken with fries is always offered. Rack of lamb (with garlic and herbs) and Peking-style duck (with honey and ginger sauce) are often on the spit as well.

Other recommendations: Possibilities include several lovely salads, perhaps red leaf and endive with Roquefort, bacon, and garlic croutons; light grilled fish dishes; medallions of venison with surprisingly good pineapple fritters; crème brûlée; apple fritters.

Summary & comments: Everyone looks beautiful in this stunning bistro, though most of them would look beautiful in McDonald's, too. The cuisine is a winning blend of French bistro classics and lighter, looser California cooking, and the food is consistently good.

LE DOME

Zone 3   Golden Triangle
8720 Sunset Boulevard,
   West Hollywood
(310) 659-6919

French
★★★
Mod/Exp

Quality 83   Value D

Reservations:	Advised
When to go:	Lunch if you're meeting your agent; dinner if you're meeting your lover
Entree range:	$16.50–24.75
Payment:	Major credit cards
Service rating:	★★★
Friendliness rating:	★★★
Parking:	Valet available
Bar:	Full service
Wine selection:	Extensive
Dress:	Hollywood chic to business
Disabled access:	Yes
Customers:	Agents, music biz, celebrities, pretty people
Lunch/Dinner:	Monday–Friday, noon–11:45 P.M.
Dinner:	Saturday, 6:30–11:45 P.M.

Atmosphere / setting: More bistro than *grand restaurant,* but definitely not a casual cafe: warm lighting, glowing woodwork, thick linens, dramatic flowers. The bar does a big business.

House specialties: Fresh fish soup; endive, mache, and beet salad; snails Burgundy-style; ahi sashimi; boudin noir sausages with apples and mashed potatoes; osso buco with fresh fettuccine; caramelized apple tart.

Other recommendations: Sea bass ceviche; rabbit sautéed with mushrooms, pearl onions, and tarragon sauce; grilled free-range chicken with mustard sauce.

Summary & comments: Given its enduring status as *the* power-lunch spot in town for the music and showbiz industry, you'd expect the food to be an afterthought. But year in and year out, Le Dome's kitchens continue to turn out skillful bistro standards that would hold their own in France.

PETIT BISTRO

Zone 3   Golden Triangle
631 North La Cienega Boulevard,
    West Hollywood
(310) 289-9797

<table>
<tr><td colspan="2">French</td></tr>
<tr><td colspan="2">★★★</td></tr>
<tr><td colspan="2">Inexpensive</td></tr>
<tr><td>Quality 83</td><td>Value B</td></tr>
</table>

Reservations:	Advised
When to go:	Early to avoid crowds
Entree range:	$6.50–12.95
Payment:	VISA, MC, AMEX
Service rating:	★★★
Friendliness rating:	★★★
Parking:	Valet available
Bar:	Full service
Wine selection:	Good French choices
Dress:	Casual
Disabled access:	Yes, but close quarters
Customers:	French expatriates, models, all sorts of stylish people
Lunch:	Monday–Friday, 11:30 A.M.–3 P.M.
Dinner:	Every night, 5:30 P.M.–1 A.M.

Atmosphere / setting: Pure Paris. The windows are beveled and leaded glass, the butcher-paper-covered tables are piled atop each other, the walls are lined with mirrors and marvelous old cognac and wine posters, the waiters are French, and the Bordeaux flows freely.

House specialties: Steamed mussels mariniere; duck mousse pâté; crisp, thin french fries; duck legs confit with coco beans and apples; calves' liver lyonnaise.

Other recommendations: Green salad with goat cheese and endive; gnocchi with Greek olives and merguez sausage; braised lamb shank with couscous and Vichy carrots; profiteroles au chocolat; pot de chocolat.

Summary & comments: French restaurants haven't fared well in L.A. in recent years, but this deeply authentic French bistro is jam-packed, thanks to the straightforward but terrific bistro food, the low prices, and the robust joie de vivre.

184

Le Petit Greek

Zone 5   Central City
127 North Larchmont Boulevard,
    Hancock Park
(213) 464-5160

Zone 5   Central City
Beverly Connection,
    100 North La Cienega Boulevard, 2nd Fl.
(310) 657-5932

	Greek
	★★★
	Moderate
	Quality 80 Value B

Reservations:	Accepted
When to go:	Any time
Entree range:	$12–18.50, with salad
Payment:	Major credit cards
Service rating:	★★★★
Friendliness rating:	★★★★
Parking:	Self
Bar:	Beer and wine
Wine selection:	Fair
Dress:	Casual
Disabled access:	Yes
Customers:	Locals
Lunch:	Monday–Saturday, 11:30 A.M.–3 P.M.
Dinner:	Tuesday–Sunday, 5:30–10 P.M.; Sunday, 5–9 P.M.

Atmosphere / setting: A cheerful taverna setting, with whitewashed rafters, a tile floor, colorful tablecloths, and greenery.

House specialties: Exceptionally fresh, handmade pita; taramosalata, a whipped red caviar dip; Greek village salad; tender lamb shank braised with red wine, tomato, and herbs; lemon potatoes; homemade baklava and rice pudding.

Other recommendations: Spinach or cheese filo pies; daily fresh fish, broiled with lemon and herbs; savory gyro sandwiches; moussaka.

Summary & comments: Sister establishments of Le Petit Greek bed and breakfast inn on Santorini, these cheerful, personal restaurants serve high-quality Greek classics without the dancing and plate-smashing gimmicks. The Larchmont branch is a perfect neighborhood restaurant.

Lincoln Bay Cafe

Zone 1 Westside	American
1928 Lincoln Boulevard,	★★½
Santa Monica	Moderate
(310) 396-4039	Quality 79 Value B

Reservations:	Accepted
When to go:	Any time
Entree range:	$9–16.75
Payment:	VISA, MC, AMEX
Service rating:	★★★
Friendliness rating:	★★★★
Parking:	Self
Bar:	Beer and wine
Wine selection:	Small but choice and affordable
Dress:	Casual
Disabled access:	Yes
Customers:	In-the-know locals
Dinner:	Tuesday–Sunday, 5:30–10 P.M.

Atmosphere / setting: A modest white storefront in an auto-repair-shop neighborhood, with a crisp, open decor.

House specialties: Big Al's gumbo, a first-rate classic gumbo; smoked turkey salad with roasted pecans; Southern-fried catfish with spicy cilantro sauce; pecan diamonds.

Other recommendations: Menu changes regularly; good choices might be asparagus with tomato-herb vinaigrette; pork chops with sweet pecan yams; seared salmon with lemon-pesto vinaigrette; apple crisp.

Summary & comments: Owner/chef Eddie Herbert came to fame as chef of the now-defunct Southern restaurant, the Ritz; now he's on his own, combining some terrific New Orleans staples with a friendly, eclectic, affordable menu that perfectly suits this south Santa Monica neighborhood.

LOCANDA VENETA

Zone 3   Golden Triangle
8638 West 3rd Street, West Hollywood
(310) 274-1893

Italian	
★★★½	
Moderate	
Quality 87	Value C

Reservations:	Essential
When to go:	Any time
Entree range:	$10–22
Payment:	Major credit cards
Service rating:	★★★★
Friendliness rating:	★★★
Parking:	Valet available
Bar:	Beer and wine
Wine selection:	Italian
Dress:	Casual chic
Disabled access:	Yes
Customers:	Cedars-Sinai doctors, celebrities, foodies
Lunch:	Monday–Friday, 11:30 A.M.–2:30 P.M.
Dinner:	Monday–Thursday, 5:30–10:30 P.M.

Atmosphere / setting: A small, authentically Italian trattoria, with packed-together tables, light wood, an open kitchen, and casement windows open to 3rd Street.

House specialties: Menu changes seasonally; excellent possible choices include fresh house-made mozzarella with a Venetian ratatouille; risotto with porcini and asparagus; a huge veal chop with herbs and a vegetable-marsala sauce; equally huge grilled langoustines brushed with olive oil and herbs; crema (a rich custard) with caramel sauce.

Other recommendations: Lobster ravioli in a saffron sauce; grilled fresh fish, perhaps branzino; pear tart.

Summary & comments: Before there was Ca'Brea, Il Moro, and Ca'del Sole, there was Locanda Veneta, a charming trattoria serving Antonio Tommasi's superb Venetian cuisine. Tommasi and partner Jean-Louis De Mori are busy restaurant moguls now, but they make sure that the standards stay high in this L.A. Italian trendsetter.

L'Opera

	Italian
	★★★
	Moderate
	Quality 83 Value C

Zone 2   South Bay
101 Pine Avenue, Long Beach
(310) 491-0066

Reservations:	Accepted
When to go:	Any time
Entree range:	$10–22
Payment:	Major credit cards
Service rating:	★★★
Friendliness rating:	★★★
Parking:	Valet available
Bar:	Full service
Wine selection:	Good
Dress:	Casual chic to upscale
Disabled access:	Yes
Customers:	Businesspeople, date-nighters
Lunch/Dinner:	Monday–Thursday, 11:30 A.M.–11 P.M.;
	Friday, 11:30 A.M.–midnight;
	Saturday, 5 P.M.–midnight; Sunday, 5–10 P.M.

Atmosphere / setting: Set in a grandiose former bank, with high ceilings, imposing columns, and opulent woodwork, modernized with chic halogen lighting and a glass-walled kitchen. Taped Italian-language lessons play in the restrooms.

House specialties: Crispy fried calamari; green salad with feta, strawberries, and almonds; mezzaluna pasta stuffed with lobster; beef filet topped with radicchio and peppercorns in a balsamic sauce; tiramisu.

Other recommendations: Artichoke panzerotti stuffed with duck; daily-changing carpaccio and fresh fish specials; chocolate box filled with fresh fruits and zabaglione.

Summary & comments: An exceptionally handsome contemporary Italian restaurant in Long Beach's renovated Old Town area, L'Opera has a special-occasion feel, with luxurious antipasti and pastas to match. The desserts are exceptional.

L'ORANGERIE

	French
Zone 3 Golden Triangle	★★★★★
903 North La Cienega Boulevard,	Very Expensive
West Hollywood	
(310) 652-9770	Quality 97 Value D

Reservations:	Advised
When to go:	Any time
Entree range:	$25–45
Payment:	Major credit cards
Service rating:	★★★★★
Friendliness rating:	★★★★★
Parking:	Valet available
Bar:	Full service
Wine selection:	Very fine, very expensive
Dress:	Upscale (tie)
Disabled access:	Yes
Customers:	Special-occasion celebrants and the very wealthy
Dinner:	Tuesday–Sunday, 6:30–11 P.M.

Atmosphere / setting: Seriously pretty and romantic in the best Parisian fashion: stunning flower displays, tall French windows, luxe banquettes, handsome young French waiters, the finest crystal and china. The best seats are in the large faux patio surrounded by twinkling white lights.

House specialties: Eggs scrambled with caviar and served in their shell; feuillantine of langoustines with sesame seeds and a curry sauce of masterful subtlety; Maine lobster fricassee with roasted potatoes and garlic; a dreamy thin, pizza-size caramelized apple tart; a vanilla-bean crème brûlée that puts all others to shame.

Other recommendations: Salad of duck foie gras with asparagus and green beans; luxurious duck foie gras with spices and melted figs; extraordinary daurade cooked in a salt crust; honey-roasted squab marinated in spices.

Entertainment & amenities: Subtle piano music Wednesday–Saturday.

Summary & comments: Fancy French may be out of fashion in casual L.A., but L'Orangerie continues to hew to the most serious Parisian standards. Chef Jean-Claude Parachini, trained at L'Ambroisie among others, produces a cuisine of striking opulence, subtlety, and flavor; every other detail, from the quality of each wine glass to the French-style service, lives up to the stunningly high price tag.

Honors / awards: One of America's top five restaurants in *Condé Nast Traveler's* 1995 "America's Best Restaurants."

Louis XIV

Zone 5   Central City
606 North La Brea Avenue,
(213) 934-5102

French

★★½

Moderate

Quality 79   Value B

Reservations:	Advised
When to go:	Later is cooler
Entree range:	$8.50–17
Payment:	Major credit cards
Service rating:	★
Friendliness rating:	★★
Parking:	Valet available
Bar:	Beer and wine
Wine selection:	Good, simple French choices
Dress:	High-style casual
Disabled access:	Yes
Customers:	Models, Euroslackers, club-goers
Dinner:	Monday–Saturday, 6 P.M.–midnight

Atmosphere / setting: Loads of rustic charm: mottled, sponge-painted walls, heavy wooden tables set with old candelabra, a romantic loft, and a pounding noise level.

House specialties: A classic French mixed green salad with goat cheese; steak pommes frites; grilled salmon with fried baby onions; raspberry or banana tarts.

Other recommendations: Tomato-basil salad; filet mignon bordelaise; chocolate mousse.

Summary & comments: The scene and the negligent, attitude-laden service can get on one's nerves, but they don't completely ruin the considerable charm of this atmospheric bistro with very tasty, straightforward French bistro fare. Come early if you just want a good steak frites, later if you want to make the scene.

Lula

Zone 1   Westside
2720 Main Street, Santa Monica
(310) 392-5711

Reservations:	Accepted
When to go:	Any time
Entree range:	$8–11
Payment:	Major credit cards
Service rating:	★★
Friendliness rating:	★★★
Parking:	Self
Bar:	Full service
Wine selection:	Fair
Dress:	Casual
Disabled access:	Yes
Customers:	Beachy locals
Brunch:	Saturday and Sunday, 10 A.M.–3 P.M.
Lunch/Dinner:	Monday–Thursday, 11:30 A.M.–10 P.M.;
	Friday, 11:30 A.M.–11 P.M.
Dinner:	Saturday, 5:30–11 P.M.; Sunday, 5–10 P.M.

Atmosphere/setting: A casual, colorful, beachy cafe on Main Street's stylish shopping and restaurant row, with windows open to the beach air and a pleasant back patio.

House specialties: Zesty, powerful margaritas; light, fresh chips; lovely fresh tamales, especially the blue-corn chicken tamale with a red chili sauce; chocolate bread pudding.

Other recommendations: Corn pudding with roasted tomato chipotle sauce; huevos rancheros for brunch; tacos al carbon, filled with carnitas, chicken adobado, or grilled fish; espresso brownies.

Summary & comments: In the Border Grill vein, Gerri Gilliland's tribute to Mexican cook Lula Betran works well as a lively, affordable spot for fresh, authentic Mexican food. Some of the entrees are a bit bland, but plenty of good tastes abound, especially if you succumb to the fine margaritas.

LUNARIA

Zone 3   Golden Triangle
10351 Santa Monica Boulevard,
   Century City
(310) 282-8870

French	
★★★½	
Moderate	
Quality 89	Value C

Reservations:	Accepted
When to go:	Any time
Entree range:	$11–22
Payment:	Major credit cards
Service rating:	★★★★
Friendliness rating:	★★★★
Parking:	Valet available
Bar:	Full service
Wine selection:	Very good
Dress:	Upscale
Disabled access:	Yes
Customers:	Well-dressed, middle-aged professionals
Lunch:	Monday–Friday, 11:30 A.M.–2:30 P.M.
Dinner:	Tuesday–Thursday, 5:30–10 P.M.;
	Friday and Saturday, 5:30–10:30 P.M.

Atmosphere / setting: A stylish modern bistro: a sleek bar, an oyster bar, a glass-walled kitchen, a sunken dining area with large tables and comfy woven armchairs, and, on the walls, a display of impressive watercolors by the owner's grandfather.

House specialties: Menu changes daily, but popular regulars include cold soup with tomato, cucumber, basil, and salmon; tomato confit tart; braised Chilean sea bass on a potato-fennel puree; chocolate tart with fresh pistachio sauce.

Other recommendations: Roasted lamb rib-eye and ribs with shallot and balsamic vinegar; braised orange roughy au pistou; glazed banana linzer torte.

Entertainment & amenities: High-quality live jazz in the bar, 8:30 P.M. weeknights, 9:30 P.M. weekends.

Summary & comments: In the early '80s, Bernard Jacoupy made downtown's Bernard's into the city's finest French restaurant. His current restaurant aspires to be more a superb Provencal bistro than a grand restaurant, and it succeeds fully. The lively, sophisticated setting and excellent jazz make the food taste even better.

The Main Course

American
★★½
Inexpensive
Quality 78   Value A

Zone 1   Westside
10509 West Pico Boulevard,
    Rancho Park
(310) 475-7564

Reservations:	Not accepted
When to go:	Any time
Entree range:	$5–9
Payment:	VISA, MC, DC
Service rating:	★★
Friendliness rating:	★★★
Parking:	Self
Bar:	None
Wine selection:	Bring your own
Dress:	Casual
Disabled access:	Yes
Customers:	Neighborhood locals
Lunch/Dinner:	Monday–Saturday, 11 A.M.–9 P.M.

Atmosphere / setting: A true hole-in-the-wall, with a small counter, a handful of table seats, and a friendly, neighborhood feel.

House specialties: Vegetarian split pea soup; fresh roasted turkey; meat loaf; fat-free mashed potatoes; homemade apple-peach or apple-blueberry pies.

Other recommendations: Chinese chicken salad; Hungarian beef goulash; roasted lemon chicken with steamed vegetables.

Summary & comments: Simple, satisfying, wonderfully affordable Mom's home cooking—made with no pork and a minimum of fat and sugar—has brought this tiny cafe a loyal neighborhood following. The owner makes everything from scratch himself.

The Mandarin

	Chinese
	★★★½
Zone 3 Golden Triangle	Moderate
430 North Camden Drive, Beverly Hills	
(213) 272-0267	Quality 85 Value D

Reservations: Accepted
When to go: Any time
Entree range: $12–15
Payment: Major credit cards
Service rating: ★★★★
Friendliness rating: ★★★★
Parking: Valet available
Bar: Full service
Wine selection: Good
Dress: Casual to upscale
Disabled access: Yes
Customers: Prosperous Beverly Hills locals
Lunch/Dinner: Sunday–Thursday, 11:30 A.M.–10 P.M.;
                       Friday and Saturday, 11:30 A.M.–10:30 P.M.

Atmosphere / setting: A soft, glowing, elegant restaurant, with a new, more casual noodle cafe in one of the old banquet rooms.

House specialties: Minced chicken in lettuce cups; delicate steamed buns and dumplings; fried shrimp in puffy batter; outstanding Peking duck (order in advance); crispy beef with crushed peanuts and spinach.

Other recommendations: Chinese chicken salad; double pan-fried noodles; shrimp sautéed with yellow chives; orange-peel beef; steamed eggplant with garlic, soy, and sesame oil.

Summary & comments: Philip Chiang isn't giving the food away at the swank Beverly Hills restaurant founded by his mother—prices are high and portions are small. But each dish is a gem, prepared with a finesse that almost justifies the prices. The newish noodle cafe within the restaurant, offering excellent fried rice, noodle, and dumpling dishes, is a relative bargain.

Mandarin Deli/Mandarin Noodle House

	Chinese
	★★½
	Inexpensive
Zone 5 Central City	
356 East 2nd Street, Little Tokyo	Quality 79 Value A
(213) 617-0231	

Zone 6   San Gabriel Valley
701 West Garvey Avenue, Monterey Park
(818) 570-9795

Zone 8   San Fernando Valley West
9305 Reseda Boulevard, Northridge
(818) 993-0122

Reservations:	Not accepted
When to go:	Any time
Entree range:	$4–7
Payment:	VISA, MC; no credit cards in Monterey Park
Service rating:	★★; ★ in Monterey Park
Friendliness rating:	★★★;★ in Monterey Park
Parking:	Self
Bar:	None
Wine selection:	None
Dress:	Casual
Disabled access:	Limited
Customers:	All sorts
Lunch/Dinner:	Sunday–Thursday, 11 A.M.–9:30 P.M.;
	Friday and Saturday, 11 A.M.–10 P.M.;
	hours may vary between branches

Atmosphere / setting: The Mandarin Noodle House in Monterey Park is a chipped-Formica dive; the others are newer and more comfortable, with booth seating and better service.

House specialties: Juicy pan-fried dumplings; irresistible onion pancakes, a layered, pan-fried bread studded with scallions; noodles with special pork sauce; cold noodles in spicy sesame sauce; special family noodles, thick, hand-cut noodles in a rich broth with vegetables and pork.

Other recommendations: Steamed fish dumplings; excellent won ton soup; beef tendon noodles.

Summary & comments: First-rate, dirt-cheap noodles and dumplings, served in settings ranging from the down-and-dirty (Monterey Park) to the almost-elegant (Little Tokyo). There's also a Chinatown branch, but it cannot be recommended.

Maple Drive

	New American
Zone 3 Golden Triangle	★★★½
345 North Maple Drive, Beverly Hills	Expensive
(310) 274-9800	
	Quality 84 Value C

Reservations:	Advised
When to go:	Any time
Entree range:	$16–28
Payment:	Major credit cards
Service rating:	★★★★
Friendliness rating:	★★★★
Parking:	Valet available
Bar:	Full service
Wine selection:	Very good
Dress:	Hollywood chic
Disabled access:	Yes
Customers:	Entertainment business
Lunch:	Monday–Friday, 11:30 A.M.–2:30 P.M.
Dinner:	Monday–Thursday, 6–10 P.M.;
	Friday and Saturday, 6–11 P.M.

Atmosphere / setting: Modern and rambling, with a bird's-eye-maple bar, a couple of lovely patios, a gleaming baby grand piano, an oyster bar, and a back entrance for celebs who just want to sit in a booth and have a quiet meal.

House specialties: Menu changes daily. Commonly seen winners include the "Kick-Ass" chili with cornbread; Caesar salad; yellowtail and tuna tartare with Japanese cole slaw; famous meat loaf with spinach and mashed potatoes; grilled swordfish with four peppercorns, Maui onion, and garlic.

Other recommendations: Various oysters on ice; homemade turkey sausage with mashed sweet potatoes; hot apple tart with cinnamon ice cream.

Entertainment & amenities: Live jazz every night at 7 P.M. Dudley Moore occasionally plays piano.

Summary & comments: With Dudley Moore and producer-director Tony Bill as owners and a glittering lineup of famous investors, it's no surprise that Maple Drive serves as a commissary for the film community. Leonard Schwartz's updated American food is very easy on the taste buds, if not on the wallet, and the setting is chic but comfortable.

Mario's Peruvian

Zone 5   Central City
5786 Melrose Avenue, Hollywood
(213) 466-4181

Peruvian
★★★
Inexpensive
Quality 80   Value B

Reservations:	Accepted
When to go:	Any time
Entree range:	$6.75–10.75
Payment:	VISA, MC
Service rating:	★★
Friendliness rating:	★★
Parking:	Self
Bar:	None
Wine selection:	Bring your own
Dress:	Casual
Disabled access:	Yes
Customers:	Locals
Lunch/Dinner:	Sunday–Thursday, 11:30 A.M.–8 P.M.;
	Friday and Saturday, 11:30 A.M.–9:30 P.M.

Atmosphere / setting: A simple minimall storefront cafe with bright lighting and infectious Peruvian music.

House specialties: Cold squid salad with Peruvian olives, tomatoes, and onion; parihuela (a wonderful fish chowder); saltado de mariscos (stir-fried shrimp, squid, onions, and tomatoes); papas à la huancaina (a famed Peruvian potato salad).

Other recommendations: Several good ceviches; french fries (the potato is a native of Peru); steamed mussels with pickled onion.

Summary & comments: The robust good cooking of Peru, particularly seafood, is the draw at this modest cafe. Flavors are forthright and delicious, portions are large, and prices are low.

MAROUCH

Zone 5   Central City
4905 Santa Monica Boulevard,
    Hollywood
(213) 662-9325

	Middle Eastern
	★★★
	Inexpensive
	Quality 83 Value B

Reservations:	Accepted for 4 or more
When to go:	Any time
Entree range:	$7.50–10
Payment:	VISA, MC
Service rating:	★★
Friendliness rating:	★★★
Parking:	Self
Bar:	Beer and wine
Wine selection:	Limited
Dress:	Casual
Disabled access:	Yes
Customers:	Lebanese and other Middle Easterners, various food-lovers
Lunch/Dinner:	Tuesday–Sunday, 11 A.M.–11 P.M.

Atmosphere / setting: A lively cafe notable mostly for its slowly rotating schwarma spits (one each for lamb, beef, and chicken) and rotisserie spits holding whole chickens.

House specialties: Enormous platters of assorted mezze (appetizers), some with as many as 20 dishes; outstanding schwarma; moughrabiye (a tender, incredibly delicious stew of chicken, beef, and chickpeas over couscous).

Other recommendations: Baba ganouj; whole chickens with garlic sauce; various baklavas.

Summary & comments: One of L.A.'s ethnic treasures, Marouch serves an almost overwhelming variety of Lebanese and other Middle Eastern dishes, each more delicious than the next. Visit with a group so you can revel in the endless mezze assortments.

Marrakesh

Zone 7 San Fernando Valley East	Moroccan
13003 Ventura Boulevard, Studio City	★★½
(818) 788-6354	Moderate
	Quality 78 Value C

Reservations:	Advised
When to go:	Any time
Entree range:	$16.50–22 for complete meal
Payment:	Major credit cards
Service rating:	★★★★
Friendliness rating:	★★★★
Parking:	Valet available
Bar:	Full service
Wine selection:	Decent
Dress:	Casually upscale
Disabled access:	Yes
Customers:	Birthday partiers
Dinner:	Sunday–Thursday, 5–10 P.M.;
	Friday and Saturday, 5–11 P.M.

Atmosphere / setting: A series of languid, tented rooms with low tables, seating on plush pillows, attentive service, and belly dancing on request.

House specialties: Fixed-price dinners that include very good platters of marinated vegetables; savory-sweet b'stilla, a wonderful chicken-almond pie; ultra-sweet baklava; generous fresh fruit.

Other recommendations: The couscous with tender lamb or the slowly simmered rabbit are the best entree choices; chicken can be dry.

Summary & comments: Although the food isn't quite up to Koutoubia's standards, it's still pretty tasty (particularly the b'stilla), and an evening at Marrakesh is always an enjoyable experience.

Matsuhisa

Zone 3 Golden Triangle	Japanese
129 North La Cienega Boulevard,	★★★★½
Beverly Hills	Very Expensive
(310) 659-9639	Quality 95 Value C

Reservations:	Advised
When to go:	Any time
Entree range:	Roughly $13–15 for smallish seafood dishes; figure on $50 per person, maybe more
Payment:	Major credit cards
Service rating:	★★★★
Friendliness rating:	★★★★
Parking:	Valet available
Bar:	Beer and wine
Wine selection:	Good sakés
Dress:	Casual chic
Disabled access:	Yes
Customers:	Showbiz, dedicated foodies
Lunch:	Monday–Friday, 11:45 A.M.–2:15 P.M.
Dinner:	Every night, 5:45–10:15 P.M.

Atmosphere / setting: Quite modest, given the quality of the food and the restaurant's considerable fame: two rooms, with a sushi counter, a crowding of small, simple tables, soft lighting, and amusing cameo-style shadow paintings of diners on the walls.

House specialties: Sublime miso-flavored black cod; tuna sashimi salad, just-seared tuna fanned around a mesclun salad with a thick, spicy sauce; shrimp in a powerful, complex pepper sauce; baby abalone with asparagus and shiitakes in a light, spicy sauce; squid "pasta" (cut like noodles) with garlic sauce.

Other recommendations: Flawless sashimi; tempura sea urchin in a shiso leaf; halibut cheeks with pepper sauce; exceptional sushi hand rolls; crispy fried soft-shell crab with black-bean sauce.

Summary & comments: For several years now, food-loving Angelenos have felt superior about being home to this extraordinary restaurant, surely the only one of its kind in the United States. But now that owner / chef Nobu Matsuhisa has opened the ultra-chic Nobu in Manhattan to great fanfare, we don't feel so special any more. Nonetheless, Matsuhisa remains a culinary experience that wows almost everyone, except for the faint of wallet. Get your waiter's advice in ordering a symphony of small seafood dishes, or, best of all, ask for chef Matsuhisa to create a meal of the day's best dishes. The modest setting won't prepare you for the staggering price, but the quality and inventiveness of the food are worth it.

MEXICA

Zone 5   Central City
7313 Beverly Boulevard
(213) 933-7385

	Mexican
	★★★
	Moderate
	Quality 82 Value B

Reservations:	Accepted
When to go:	Any time
Entree range:	$8.25–17.50
Payment:	VISA, MC, AMEX
Service rating:	★★★
Friendliness rating:	★★★
Parking:	Self, in back
Bar:	Beer and sangria
Wine selection:	Sangria only
Dress:	Casual and black
Disabled access:	Yes
Customers:	The coffeehouse crowd
Lunch:	Monday–Friday, noon–2:30 P.M.
Dinner:	Sunday–Thursday, 5–10 P.M.;
	Friday and Saturday, 5–11 P.M.

Atmosphere / setting: A cool old-L.A. room (this used to be the Chinese Kitchen, a '30s relic), with high, exposed ceilings, roomy booths, a neon wall clock, and moody Mexican art, from masks to colorful murals.

House specialties: Tiny quesadillas filled with zucchini flowers; cochinita pibil; wonderful green-corn tamales; an earthy, outstanding mole poblano; Mexican-style walnut crêpes with caramel.

Other recommendations: Cactus salad; smoky grilled shrimp with peppers and onions; chicken enchiladas with tomatillo sauce; good flan.

Summary & comments: Authentic Mexican cafe food meets an artistic setting and clientele in this friendly restaurant across the street from the eternally mobbed El Coyote. Instead of El Coyote's kick-ass margaritas and gloopy, sodden Cal-Mex food, you get Mexican beer and the fresh, clear, appealing flavors of corn, chilis, meats, and salsas.

Michael's

Zone 1 Westside	New American
1147 3rd Street, Santa Monica	★★★½
(310) 451-0843	Expensive
	Quality 88 Value C

Reservations:	Advised
When to go:	Lunch on fair days is lovely
Entree range:	$15–29
Payment:	Major credit cards
Service rating:	★★★★
Friendliness rating:	★★★★
Parking:	Valet available
Bar:	Full service
Wine selection:	Excellent
Dress:	Stylish
Disabled access:	Yes
Customers:	Well-groomed Westsiders
Lunch:	Tuesday–Friday, 11:30 A.M.–2:30 P.M.
Dinner:	Monday–Saturday, 5:30–10:30 P.M.

Atmosphere / setting: A California dream. Inside are white walls and extraordinary paintings by some of California's finest artists; outside is the walled patio, rife with flowers and cooled by ocean air.

House specialties: Menu changes frequently. Possibilities include fresh shad roe in season; fettuccine with Norwegian salmon and double-blanched garlic; Carpinteria squab with New York state foie gras and raspberry-vinegar sauce; tarte tatin.

Other recommendations: Excellent salads made from locally grown organic greens; daily fresh fish and Maine lobster specials.

Summary & comments: Once considered the ultimate California restaurant, Michael's fame has waned. But the patio is as beautiful as ever, the wine list is still a marvel, and the food, while not as memorable (or expensive), remains a fine example of the modern French-American hybrid, emphasizing quality regional ingredients.

Milano's Italian Kitchen

	Italian
	★★½
	Inexpensive
	Quality 78 Value A

Zone 1   Westside
1056 Westwood Boulevard, Westwood
(310) 443-5401

Zone 6   San Gabriel Valley
525 North Brand Boulevard, Glendale
(818) 244-1150

Zone 8   San Fernando Valley West
21550 Oxnard Street, Woodland Hills
(818) 340-8400

Reservations:	Accepted
When to go:	Any time
Entree range:	$7–10
Payment:	Major credit cards
Service rating:	★★
Friendliness rating:	★★★
Parking:	Self
Bar:	Full service
Wine selection:	Modest but appealing
Dress:	Casual
Disabled access:	Yes
Customers:	After-work locals, families
Lunch/Dinner:	Monday–Thursday, 11 A.M.–10 P.M.; Friday and Saturday, 11 A.M.–11 P.M.
Dinner:	Sunday, 3–10 P.M.

Atmosphere/setting: An Italian bar and grill setting, with wooden booths, an open kitchen, and honor-system jugs of wine on the tables.

House specialties: Meal-size bruschetta with fresh tomato; rigatoni with chicken, roasted peppers, olives, and spinach; pappardelle with chicken, sun-dried tomatoes, and roasted eggplant; sorbettos.

Other recommendations: Grilled chicken or sausage sandwiches; generous pizzas.

Summary & comments: Milano's winning formula of tasty, generously served and affordable Italian cafe classics and house wines has hit a nerve—it's up to three branches, and more may be on the way. A good family spot.

Mi Piace

	Italian
Zone 6 San Gabriel Valley	★★★
25 East Colorado Boulevard, Pasadena	Inexpensive
(818) 795-3131	
	Quality 80 Value B

Reservations:	Advised
When to go:	Weekends are mobbed
Entree range:	$7–15.95
Payment:	Major credit cards
Service rating:	★★
Friendliness rating:	★★
Parking:	Valet availabe
Bar:	Beer and wine
Wine selection:	Good
Dress:	Casual
Disabled access:	Yes
Customers:	Stylish date-night Old Town crowd
Open:	Sunday–Thursday, 9 A.M.–11:30 P.M.;
	Friday and Saturday, 9 A.M.–1 A.M.

Atmosphere / setting: A high-tech storefront in the middle of Old Town, with high ceilings, walls of glass, crisp white linens, and prized sidewalk tables.

House specialties: Insalata Caprese with fresh bufula mozzarella; capellini primavera with garlic, basil, and olive oil; pollo Mi Piace, chicken breast sautéed with bell pepper, mushrooms, and garlic–white wine sauce; light Italian cheesecake topped with pears.

Other recommendations: Risotto with crayfish, shrimp, and crispy ginger; veal saltimbocca with Parma prosciutto and sage sauce.

Summary & comments: The most popular restaurant in booming Old Town, Mi Piace has undergone some chef and menu changes, but the quality should remain high. The desserts from neighboring (and affiliated) Pasadena Baking Company are superb.

Mi Ranchito

	Mexican
	★★½
Zone 4 City South	Inexpensive
8694 West Washington Boulevard, Culver City	
(310) 837-1461	Quality 78 Value A

Reservations:	Not accepted
When to go:	Any time
Entree range:	$6–8.50
Payment:	VISA, MC
Service rating:	★★
Friendliness rating:	★★★
Parking:	Self
Bar:	Full service
Wine selection:	Limited
Dress:	Casual
Disabled access:	Yes
Customers:	Locals
Lunch / Dinner:	Monday–Thursday, 11 A.M.–9 P.M.; Friday and Saturday, 10 A.M.–10 P.M.; Sunday, 10 A.M.–9 P.M.

Atmosphere / setting: A tacky, family-run Mexican storefront, livened with a Latin-music jukebox that would fit right in on Rosarita Beach.

House specialties: Camarones al mojo de ajo (shrimp with garlic); stuffed red snapper; fish and shellfish caldos (stews); seductive moles.

Other recommendations: Fiery huevos endiablados for breakfast; chilequiles; pozole (pork and hominy soup).

Summary & comments: A cherished part of quiet Culver City for a couple of decades, Mi Ranchito is a good neighborhood Mexican cafe specializing in Veracruz seafood dishes. Be adventurous and pass on the combinations in favor of the seafood.

Mishima

Zone 1 Westside	Japanese
11301 Olympic Boulevard,	★★½
No. 210, West L.A.	Inexpensive
(310) 473-5297	Quality 77 Value B

Reservations:	Not accepted
When to go:	Any time
Entree range:	$6–8
Payment:	VISA, MC, AMEX
Service rating:	★★
Friendliness rating:	★★
Parking:	Self
Bar:	None
Wine selection:	None
Dress:	Casual
Disabled access:	Yes
Customers:	Westsiders, Japanese
Lunch/Dinner:	Every day, 11:30 A.M.–9 P.M.

Atmosphere / setting: On the second floor of an upscale pod mall, with signed photos of celebrities offering the main decorative touch.

House specialties: Fat udon noodles topped with grilled beef and egg; various soba and ramen noodles dishes.

Other recommendations: Chirashi sushi, sushi rice with sashimi and noodles.

Summary & comments: One of the many authentic Japanese-style noodle houses in West L.A., Mishima is also one of the most popular, with a constant crush of noodle junkies.

Mon Kee

		Chinese
		★★★
Zone 5 Central City		Moderate
679 North Spring Street, Chinatown		
(213) 628-6717		Quality 84 Value B

Reservations:	Accepted
When to go:	Any time
Entree range:	$7.25–15.50
Payment:	Major credit cards
Service rating:	★★
Friendliness rating:	★★
Parking:	Valet available
Bar:	None
Wine selection:	Bring your own
Dress:	Casual
Disabled access:	Yes
Customers:	Cross-section
Lunch / Dinner:	Sunday–Thursday, 11:30 A.M.–9:45 P.M.;
	Friday and Saturday, 11:30 A.M.–10:15 P.M.

Atmosphere / setting: A classic Formica and fluorescent Chinese diner setting, ornamented with great platters of steaming seafood.

House specialties: Neptune seafood soup; crab in black-bean sauce; excellent crispy whole shrimp with special salt; black cod with asparagus and rich, robust black-bean sauce.

Other recommendations: Stir-fried scallops with ginger and green onion; steamed whole tilapia or catfish with special soy sauce; fresh squid with garlic, pepper, and onion.

Summary & comments: Trendies who have moved on to the San Gabriel Valley seafood emporiums may have forgotten Mon Kee, but that makes more room for the lucky regulars, who don't have to wait as long to eat this first-rate Chinese seafood. Mon Kee is still terrific.

MR. STOX

	New American/Continental
Zone 9 Orange County North	★★★
1105 East Katella Avenue, Anaheim	Moderate
(714) 634-2994	
	Quality 80 Value C

Reservations:	Accepted
When to go:	When you're in Anaheim
Entree range:	$12–25
Payment:	Major credit cards
Service rating:	★★★★
Friendliness rating:	★★★★
Parking:	Valet available
Bar:	Full service
Wine selection:	Outstanding and affordable
Dress:	Suburban dress-up
Disabled access:	Yes
Customers:	Wine lovers, loyal locals, upscale tourists
Lunch:	Monday–Friday, 11:30 A.M.–2:30 P.M.
Dinner:	Every night, 5:30–10 P.M.

Atmosphere / setting: An old-fashioned romantic in the shadow of Disneyland, with enveloping booths and soft music.

House specialties: Maryland back-fin crab cakes; osso buco in a sweet vermouth sauce with vegetables; various special soufflés.

Other recommendations: Breads baked fresh in-house; mesquite-grilled striped bass on a ragout of onions, olives, spinach, and potatoes; nightly special fresh fish.

Summary & comments: If you're a wine lover, a trip to Mr. Stox is a must, both for the wonderful, fairly priced cellar and for the enthusiasm of owner/oenophile Ron Marshall. The Anaheim-California cuisine isn't as memorable as the wine list, but it does Anaheim right proud.

MUSE

Zone 5   Central City
7360 Beverly Boulevard
(213) 934-4400

New American
★★★
Moderate

Quality 83   Value C

Reservations:	Accepted
When to go:	Any time
Entree range:	$11–22
Payment:	VISA, MC, AMEX
Service rating:	★★★★
Friendliness rating:	★★★★
Parking:	Valet available
Bar:	Full service
Wine selection:	Fair
Dress:	Casual chic, business
Disabled access:	Yes
Customers:	Interesting mix of couples and Hollywood businesspeople
Dinner:	Tuesday–Thursday, 6–10:30 P.M.; Friday and Saturday, 6–11:30 P.M.

Atmosphere / setting: Starkly modern yet still comfortable and quiet enough for conversation, with good modern art and a huge aquarium over the bar. A great space.

House specialties: Thai eggroll; Chinese dumplings; delicious homemade rigatoni with chicken, tomatoes, and Thai spices; classic flourless chocolate cake.

Other recommendations: A fine Caesar salad; pan-seared salmon with a well-balanced ginger-soy glaze; coconut bread pudding.

Summary & comments: In the '80s, Muse seemed like the quintessential '80s restaurant, a showpiece of minimalist style and eclectic cooking. The amazing thing is that today, well into the '90s, it doesn't seem the least bit dated. The interior is still wonderful, the vibe is cool but not annoyingly trendy, and the cooking is consistently good.

Musso & Frank

Zone 5   Central City
6667 Hollywood Boulevard,
    Hollywood
(213) 467-7788

American
★★
Moderate

Quality 72   Value D

Reservations:	Accepted
When to go:	Any time
Entree range:	$8.50–24
Payment:	Major credit cards
Service rating:	★★
Friendliness rating:	★
Parking:	Self
Bar:	Full service
Wine selection:	Fair
Dress:	Casual to business
Disabled access:	Yes
Customers:	Tourists to screenwriters
Lunch/Dinner:	Tuesday–Saturday, 11 A.M.–11 P.M.

Atmosphere / setting: A great bar, rich with a patina from decades of smoke, Scotch and Hollywood blarney, and a classic American bar-and-grill room with scarred wooden booths, a long grill counter, and curmudgeonly waiters.

House specialties: Flannel cakes (thin, delicate, plate-size pancakes); chicken pot pie; grilled lamb chops and filet mignon.

Other recommendations: Proper old-fashioned cocktails.

Summary & comments: A 1919 landmark that has played a significant part in Hollywood legend and lore, Musso's reeks with old-L.A. charm. The atmosphere alone is well worth a visit; though the simplest steaks and chops are decent, most of the food is dreary.

Nam Kang

Zone 5   Central City
3055 West 7th Street, Koreatown
(213) 380-6606

	Korean
	★ ★ ★
	Inexpensive
	Quality 83 Value B

Reservations:	Not accepted
When to go:	Any time
Entree range:	$8–10
Payment:	VISA, MC
Service rating:	★ ★
Friendliness rating:	★ ★ ★
Parking:	Self
Bar:	None
Wine selection:	None
Dress:	Casual
Disabled access:	Limited
Customers:	Koreans
Lunch/Dinner:	Every day, 11:30 A.M.–9:30 P.M.

Atmosphere / setting: A rudimentary, rather shabby restaurant, with a decorative fish tank and grills on some tables.

House specialties: An exceptional, daily-changing selection of panchan, or small side dishes, from various puckery kimchees to oysters in chili sauce to fried whitefish to spinach with sesame oil; wonderful bibimbap, a spicy, savory mix of meat and vegetables with rice.

Other recommendations: Grilled bulgogi (marinated beef grilled at the table); a milder, brothy kimchee.

Summary & comments: Creature comforts are few and English is scarce, but the food more than makes up for any inconveniences. Nam Kang's selection of panchan, the myriad small dishes that accompany a Korean meal, surpasses most any other local restaurant. Heaven for kimchee lovers.

Nawab of India

Indian
★★★
Inexpensive

Quality 80   Value A

Zone 1   Westside
1621 Wilshire Boulevard, Santa Monica
(310) 829-1106

Reservations:	Accepted
When to go:	Any time
Entree range:	$7.50–11
Payment:	Major credit cards
Service rating:	★★★
Friendliness rating:	★★★
Parking:	Self
Bar:	Beer and wine
Wine selection:	Limited
Dress:	Casual
Disabled access:	Yes
Customers:	Locals
Lunch:	Monday–Friday, 11:30 A.M.–2:30 P.M.; Saturday and Sunday, noon–3 P.M.
Dinner:	Sunday–Thursday, 5:30–10:30 P.M.; Friday and Saturday, 5:30–11 P.M.

Atmosphere / setting: A serene room that once housed a sushi bar. Flowers and good table linens add warmth.

House specialties: Excellent onion kulcha, garlic naan, and other Indian breads; chicken chat, a cold salad of tandoor-roasted chicken, tomatoes, and cucumber; tandoori eggplant sautéed with onions and tomatoes.

Other recommendations: Stir-fried chicken curry; tasty kebabs.

Summary & comments: Lighter-than-usual Indian food—notable for crisp, clean flavors and careful preparations—has won this gentle Westsider a loyal following.

Neptune's Net

Seafood

★★

Inexpensive

Quality 75   Value A

Zone 1   Westside
42505 Pacific Coast Highway, Malibu
(310) 457-3095

Reservations:	Not accepted
When to go:	Sunny summer afternoons
Entree range:	$4–6.85; live seafood sold by the pound
Payment:	VISA, MC
Service rating:	★
Friendliness rating:	★★
Parking:	Self
Bar:	Beer and wine
Wine selection:	Limited
Dress:	Casual
Disabled access:	Yes
Customers:	Beach-goers, bikers, surfers
Open:	Monday–Thursday, 9 A.M.–8 P.M.; Friday and Saturday, 9 A.M.–9 P.M.; Sunday, 9 A.M.–8:30 P.M.

Atmosphere / setting: A funky beach shack near County Line, with self-service, plastic utensils, and rustic outdoor tables.

House specialties: Great clam chowder; sweet steamed shrimp and crab; corn on the cob.

Other recommendations: For splurgers, lobster sold by the pound, simply steamed and served on a paper plate.

Summary & comments: When you've had enough of $28 plates of salmon with wasabi vinaigrette, head for this classic seafood shack for a liberating California-dream dining experience: plain, cheap seafood and chowder eaten in the sun among a zany L.A. cross-section, across the street from the great blue Pacific.

Nicola

Zone 5 Central City	International
Sanwa Bank Building,	★★★
601 South Figueroa Street, Downtown	Moderate
(213) 485-0927	Quality 83 Value C

Reservations:	Accepted
When to go:	Any time
Entree range:	$11–17
Payment:	Major credit cards
Service rating:	★★★★
Friendliness rating:	★★★★
Parking:	Valet at night, validated in day
Bar:	Full service
Wine selection:	Good
Dress:	Business to casual
Disabled access:	Yes
Customers:	Upscale downtowners
Lunch:	Monday–Friday, 11:30 A.M.–2 P.M.
Dinner:	Tuesday–Saturday, 5:30–9 P.M.

Atmosphere / setting: Self-consciously architectural—cold to some, exciting to others—with hard, angular chairs, strange wire-fabric light fixtures, and an open feeling.

House specialties: Nicola oysters on bed of spinach with walnuts and garlic; risotto with artichokes, prosciutto, and Parmesan; ginger cream napoleon.

Other recommendations: Vegetarian spring roll with tangerine sweet-and-sour; grilled chicken breast with Boston lettuce, oranges, jicama, and sesame-apple dressing; seared rib-eye steak.

Entertainment & amenities: Piano at lunch, guitar at happy hour.

Summary & comments: Nicola's stark architectural setting and multicultural menu aren't for everyone, but the cooking is accomplished, and the service, led by genial owner Larry Nicola, is friendly and smart.

Noodle World

Zone 6 San Gabriel Valley	Asian
46 West Valley Boulevard, Alhambra	★★
(818) 293-8800	Inexpensive
	Quality 78 Value A

Reservations:	Not accepted
When to go:	Good for a late snack
Entree range:	$3–5 for noodles
Payment:	No credit cards
Service rating:	★
Friendliness rating:	★
Parking:	Self
Bar:	None
Wine selection:	None
Dress:	Casual
Disabled access:	Yes
Customers:	An Asian melange
Open:	Every day, 10:30 A.M.–1 A.M.

Atmosphere / setting: A big, bright cafe setting.

House specialties: Noodle dishes from almost every Asian country except Japan: Thailand (pad thai), Vietnam (pho), China (chow mein), Malaysia, and Singapore.

Summary & comments: A fun, lively new restaurant that serves noodles and only noodles, from some of the best noodle-making countries in the world.

Ocean Avenue Seafood

Zone 1   Westside
1401 Ocean Avenue, Santa Monica
(310) 394-5669

Seafood	
★★★	
Moderate	
Quality 83	Value C

Reservations:	Advised
When to go:	Any time
Entree range:	$14.25–23.50
Payment:	Major credit cards
Service rating:	★★★
Friendliness rating:	★★★★
Parking:	Valet available
Bar:	Full service
Wine selection:	Excellent
Dress:	Casual chic
Disabled access:	Yes
Customers:	Good-looking Westsiders
Lunch / Dinner:	Every day, 11:30 A.M.–10 P.M.

Atmosphere / setting: A swell location in eyeshot of the Pacific, with an equally swell outdoor patio complete with an oyster bar. Inside is a large, busy, pretty space.

House specialties: Dungeness crab cakes with ginger-horseradish dip; sake-kasu (Chilean sea bass with seaweed salad); wok-fried whole Idaho catfish; braised Mediterranean-style striped bass with lemon couscous.

Other recommendations: Seared rare ahi with lemon-ginger marinade; white king salmon with grilled vegetable salad; rustic apple tart.

Summary & comments: First-rate, always fresh seafood is cooked usually to perfection in this attractive beach restaurant, a sister to downtown's even better Water Grill. The dishes are inventive but intelligent, and the place is very well managed.

Ocean Seafood

Zone 5 Central City	Chinese / Seafood
747 North Broadway, Chinatown	★★★½
(213) 687-3088	Moderate
	Quality 85 Value C

Reservations:	Accepted at dinner
When to go:	Dim sum is particularly memorable
Entree range:	$7.50–15
Payment:	Major credit cards
Service rating:	★★★
Friendliness rating:	★★
Parking:	Valet available
Bar:	Full service
Wine selection:	Limited
Dress:	Casual to business
Disabled access:	Yes
Customers:	Downtowners, Chinese families, everyone
Open:	Every day, 8 A.M.–10 P.M.

Atmosphere / setting: A capacious, moderately glitzy second-story seafood emporium on the site of the former Miriwa, with fish tanks and large round tables for groups.

House specialties: The dim sum is exceptional, with an unusual array of seafood noodle and dumpling dishes: fabulous shrimp and scallop dumplings; fresh, flavorful vegetable dumplings; savory crystal shrimp har gow; slippery shrimp rice noodle.

Other recommendations: A beautiful, well-prepared roster of Cantonese seafood classics: deep-fried whole fish, steamed fresh shrimp, crab with black bean and chili.

Summary & comments: This large, slick, Hong Kong–style seafood house procures first-rate seafood and prepares it with delicacy and finesse, letting the flavors of the fish and shellfish come through. The dim sum is one of the best in town.

OCEAN STAR

Zone 6 San Gabriel Valley	Chinese / Seafood
145 North Atlantic Boulevard,	★★★★
Monterey Park	Moderate
(818) 308-2128	Quality 91 Value B

Reservations:	Accepted for large parties
When to go:	Any time
Entree range:	$6.50–15
Payment:	VISA, MC
Service rating:	★★★★
Friendliness rating:	★★★
Parking:	In garage
Bar:	Full service
Wine selection:	Limited
Dress:	Casual to business
Disabled access:	Yes
Customers:	Large parties: families, businesspeople, social groups, mostly Chinese
Open:	Monday–Friday, 10 A.M.–10 P.M.; Saturday and Sunday, 9 A.M.–10 P.M.

Atmosphere / setting: Quite grand and handsome: dramatic marble foyer, tuxedoed captains, private rooms draped in luxurious fabrics, and an endless dining hall with mirrors, polished woodwork, recessed fish tanks, and flexible dividers to separate wedding parties and banquets.

House specialties: Boiled shrimp with soy-chili dipping sauce; prawns with spicy salt; Alaskan king crabs the size of Buicks; pan-fried squid with ginger and green onions; whole steamed fish with various sauces; sautéed snow-pea sprouts.

Other recommendations: Rock cod with black bean and chili; huge scallops served in their shells; daily special vegetables.

Summary & comments: Seafood doesn't get any fresher or more delicious than at this swank Hong Kong–style restaurant. Shrimp, lobster, and other ocean goodies are plucked out of spotless tanks, cooked in moments, and paired with sauces and spices of impeccable flavor and complexity. This should be your first stop on a tour of L.A.'s marvelous "new" Chinatown.

Old Town Bakery

Zone 6 San Gabriel Valley	American
166 West Colorado Boulevard,	★★★
Pasadena	Inexpensive
(818) 792-7943	Quality 80 Value B

Reservations:	Not accepted
When to go:	Weekend days are mobbed
Entree range:	$7–10
Payment:	VISA, MC, AMEX
Service rating:	★
Friendliness rating:	★★
Parking:	Self
Bar:	None
Wine selection:	None
Dress:	Casual
Disabled access:	Yes
Customers:	Families, couples, all sorts
Open:	Every day, 7:30 A.M.–11 P.M.

Atmosphere / setting: A long, narrow space with bakery counters along one side and tables along the other. The best tables are outside on the lovely patio, complete with gurgling fountain and lots of greenery.

House specialties: Wonderful breakfasts, including savory chicken sausages, hearty pancakes, and spicy home fries; some of the best desserts in town, from the glistening tarte tatin to the sumptuous Milky Way cake to the suave pear–sour cream crumble. Even the cookies are memorable.

Other recommendations: Classic burgers; a tasty low-fat chicken–white corn chili; generous salads.

Summary & comments: Amy Pressman's dreamy American desserts put the Old Town Bakery on L.A.'s culinary map (her breads are less successful), and now her cafe fare is drawing even more loyal fans. The mystery is why the service is so inept.

Original Pantry Cafe

Zone 5   Central City
877 South Figueroa Street, Downtown
(213) 972-9279

American
★★
Inexpensive
Quality 74   Value A

Reservations:	Not accepted
When to go:	Any time
Entree range:	$4.50–10
Payment:	No credit cards
Service rating:	★★★
Friendliness rating:	★★
Parking:	Across street
Bar:	None
Wine selection:	None
Dress:	Casual
Disabled access:	Yes
Customers:	A great urban mix, from suited businesspeople to college students to down-and-outers
Open:	Every day, 24 hours

Atmosphere / setting: A plain, worn bar-and-grill setting, with vinyl booths, a long diner counter, crotchety old waiters, and grease-encrusted paintings of dubious quality.

House specialties: Stacks of substantial pancakes; generous pork and lamb chops; decent, cheap steaks; fine hash browns.

Other recommendations: Regular specials, like short ribs, chicken-rice soup, and roast beef hash with gravy; hamburgers.

Summary & comments: Any time, day or night, the Pantry will serve you a solid meal and a boatload of old L.A. atmosphere at a very low price. A beloved landmark.

Original Sonora Cafe

Zone 5 Central City	Southwestern
180 South La Brea Avenue	★★★
(213) 857-1800	Moderate
	Quality 81 Value D

Reservations:	Accepted
When to go:	Any time
Entree range:	$11–23
Payment:	Major credit cards
Service rating:	★★★
Friendliness rating:	★★★
Parking:	Valet available
Bar:	Full service
Wine selection:	Fair
Dress:	Casual to upscale
Disabled access:	Yes
Customers:	Chiliheads, chic local businesspeople
Lunch:	Monday–Saturday, 11:30 A.M.–2:30 P.M.
Dinner:	Sunday–Thursday, 5–10 P.M.;
	Friday and Saturday, 5–11 P.M.

Atmosphere / setting: The barren space that once held City has been transformed into a theatrical, extravagant restaurant with oversized fireplaces, swooping Flying Nun indoor umbrellas, rich fabrics, and glowing lighting.

House specialties: Tortilla soup with roasted tomatoes; sweet green corn tamales with mole sauce; delicious duck-confit tamale with guajillo chili sauce; New Mexican blue corn enchiladas stuffed with chicken and topped with a smoked poblano sauce.

Other recommendations: Chili-charred ahi; Gulf shrimp and angel hair in a spicy garlic pasilla sauce; elegant tropical fruit taco.

Summary & comments: After surviving years of relative isolation in a downtown office building, this modern-Southwestern stalwart has gone high-profile in a chic La Brea setting. The setting may have changed, but the food remains the same—an occasionally gimmicky but mostly successful NewMex/ CalMex hybrid.

Osteria Nonni

Zone 5   Central City
3219 Glendale Boulevard, Atwater
(213) 666-7133

Italian	
★★½	
Inexpensive	
Quality 79	Value B

Reservations: Accepted
When to go: Any time
Entree range: $6.50–12.50
Payment: VISA, MC, AMEX
Service rating: ★★
Friendliness rating: ★★★
Parking: Self
Bar: Beer and wine
Wine selection: Modest but good
Dress: Casual
Disabled access: Yes
Customers: Atwater/Silverlake intellectual types
Lunch: Tuesday–Friday, 11:30 A.M.–2:45 P.M.
Dinner: Every night, 5:30–10 P.M.

Atmosphere / setting: A glass-walled modern storefront with an open kitchen, plain wooden tables, and exposed ductwork.

House specialties: First-rate, very Italian pizzas, from the checca with fresh tomatoes, basil, and garlic to the funghi e carciofi (mushrooms and artichokes); focaccia sandwiches; roast chicken with herbed roasted garlic puree.

Other recommendations: The simple green salad; spinach-ricotta ravioli with butter and sage.

Summary & comments: Pasquale Morra has left his happy mark across town, first as the creator of Angeli's perfect pizzas, then as founder of this hip cafe (run by his relatives) in a futsy old neighborhood, and now as proprietor of Beverly Hills's Da'Pasquale. The pizzas here are seriously addictive, and the rest of the simple menu offers modest Italian home cooking tò a neighborhood that desperately needed it.

Out Take Cafe

	California
	★★½
	Inexpensive
	Quality 78 Value A

Zone 7   San Fernando Valley East
12159 Ventura Boulevard, Studio City
(818) 760-1111

Reservations:	Accepted
When to go:	Any time
Entree range:	$6.95–10.95
Payment:	VISA, MC, AMEX
Service rating:	★★★
Friendliness rating:	★★★
Parking:	Self
Bar:	Beer and wine
Wine selection:	Fair
Dress:	Casual
Disabled access:	Yes
Customers:	Locals
Lunch/Dinner:	Monday–Friday, 11:30 A.M.–9:30 P.M.;
	Saturday and Sunday, noon–9:30 P.M.

Atmosphere / setting: A narrow storefront with plate-glass windows to the street, crowded banquettes, and simple art on the wall.

House specialties: Homemade borscht; potato vareniki, marvelous dumplings sautéed until crisp outside, paired with sweet caramelized onions; steamed mussels in lemongrass soup.

Other recommendations: The green salad, only $1 if you order an entree; buckwheat pasta with mushrooms; lamb shank with celeriac puree; pecan or lemon meringue pies.

Summary & comments: What sets this place apart from every other neighborhood cafe on Ventura is the owner's Ukrainian roots, which are happily in evidence in the wonderful borscht and potato vareniki. The rest of the food—rustic French and Italian, with some Asian touches from the Asian chef—is quite fine neighborhood bistro fare, at low prices.

Parkway Grill

New American	
★★★★	
Moderate	
Quality 90	Value C

Zone 6   San Gabriel Valley
510 South Arroyo Parkway, Pasadena
(818) 795-1001

Reservations:	Advised
When to go:	Any time
Entree range:	$9.50–22
Payment:	Major credit cards
Service rating:	★★★★
Friendliness rating:	★★★★
Parking:	Valet available
Bar:	Full service
Wine selection:	Very good Californians
Dress:	Casual chic to upscale
Disabled access:	Yes
Customers:	Upscale Eastsiders
Brunch:	Sunday, 11 A.M.–2:30 P.M.
Lunch:	Monday–Friday, 11:30 A.M.–2:30 P.M.
Dinner:	Monday, 5:30–10 P.M.;
	Tuesday–Thursday, 5:30–10 P.M.;
	Friday and Saturday, 5–11 P.M.;
	Sunday, 5–10 P.M., late supper to 11 P.M.

Atmosphere / setting: A handsome contemporary bar-and-grill setting, with brick walls, exposed wooden rafters, a gleaming open kitchen, and an opulent carved wooden bar. The dining room gets noisy.

House specialties: A suave cocoa crêpe stuffed with lobster in a lobster bisque sauce; whole fried catfish with ginger, scallions, and lime-soy sauce; succulent roasted Chinese crispy duck with shoestring yams.

Other recommendations: Wood-fired California pizzas; roasted chili pasilla stuffed with smoked chicken, corn, cilantro, and mozzarella; daily pasta specials; a sweet, nostalgic s'mores dessert.

Entertainment & amenities: Piano music in the bar.

Summary & comments: The trends of California cuisine have come and gone, and the Parkway Grill has proved to be one of its lasting successes. The setting radiates modern American bonhomie, the lively menu reflects our Latino-Anglo-Asian culture, and the cooking is creative, tasty, and sometimes quite inspired. Chef Hugo Molina gets the best ingredients and grows much of the restaurant's produce on a neighboring organic urban farm.

Honors / awards: Ranked in *Condé Nast Traveler's* "America's Best Restaurants."

224

Pascal

	French
Zone 9　Orange County North	★★★★
Plaza Newport,	Mod / Exp
1000 North Bristol Avenue,	
Newport Beach	Quality 93　　Value C
(714) 752-0107	

Reservations:	Advised
When to go:	Any time
Entree range:	$17.50–22.50
Payment:	All major cards
Service rating:	★★★★
Friendliness rating:	★★★★
Parking:	Self
Bar:	Beer and wine
Wine selection:	Good
Dress:	Casual-chic to upscale
Disabled access:	Yes
Customers:	Quiet, happy Francophiles
Lunch:	Monday–Friday, 11:30 A.M.–2:30 P.M.
Dinner:	Monday–Saturday, 6–10 P.M.

Atmosphere / setting: You'll completely forget the strip-mall setting once you're settled among the Provençal fabrics, antiques, whitewashed brick, and abundant fresh flowers.

House specialties: Menu changes seasonally. Outstanding choices have included cheese and herb raviolis in a pesto broth; Provençal fish soup, heady and divine; the famed sea bass with thyme, perhaps paired with a champagne sauce; swordfish steak Niçoise; poached pear with chocolate sauce; some of the best cheeses in Southern California.

Other recommendations: Other fine examples have included lamb salad with apple-walnut dressing; sautéed sweetbreads with shallot confit; rabbit with mustard sauce; fat scallops with a frisse-cabernet sauce; suave lemon tart.

Summary & comments: Orange County's best French restaurant is also one of the state's best French restaurants. Owner / chef Pascal Olhats is a dedicated, serious chef who makes his food sing with Provençal spirit. Flavors are clear, strong, and seductive—a perfect match for the warm, romantic setting. Don't miss the new epicerie and wine shop next door, packed with irresistible pâtés, salads, and prepared dishes.

PATINA

Zone 5 Central City	French
5955 Melrose Avenue, Hollywood	★★★★★
(213) 467-1108	Expensive
	Quality 98 Value B

Reservations:	Advised
When to go:	Any time
Entree range:	$22–25
Payment:	Major credit cards
Service rating:	★★★★★
Friendliness rating:	★★★★★
Parking:	Valet available
Bar:	Full service
Wine selection:	Prime and expensive
Dress:	Upscale
Disabled access:	Yes
Customers:	Business and studio execs, upscale folks
Lunch:	Tuesday–Friday, 11:30 A.M.–2 P.M.
Dinner:	Sunday–Thursday, 6–9:30 P.M.;
	Friday, 6–10:30 P.M.; Saturday, 5:30–10:30 P.M.

Atmosphere / setting: To the right, a small, chic bar with limited table seating; to the left, a subdued dining room with a cool, architectural feel. If Patina were a suit, it would be an Armani.

House specialties: Menu changes seasonally. Exceptional choices have included corn blinis with osetra caviar and crème fraiche; sweet Santa Barbara shrimp with ethereal mashed potatoes and potato-truffle chips; gratin of lamb; quartet of crème brûlées: chocolate, vanilla, corn, and gallangha.

Other recommendations: Cock's comb with curly cabbage, pearl onion, and Pinot sauce; seared striped bass with white bean mousse and apple-smoked bacon; and virtually every other dish on the menu.

Summary & comments: Los Angeles's best restaurant is neither grandly opulent nor kiss-kiss showbizzy. What sets Patina apart is the sublime cooking of Joachim Splichal, whose inventiveness is tempered with intelligence. Although French in inspiration and execution, Splichal's food is right at home in L.A., combining elegance with homey warmth. His way with potatoes first brought him fame, but Splichal and his crew are equally adept with fish, mushrooms, polenta, lobster, rabbit, vegetables, and pasta. Christine Splichal adds warmth and vivacity to the rather austere setting, and she keeps the service humming. To those who doubt L.A.'s standing in the food world—hurry over to Patina and find out for yourself.

Honors / awards: Highly ranked in *Condé Nast Traveler's* 1995 "America's Best Restaurants."

Pedals

Zone 1   Westside
Shutters on the Beach,
  1 Pico Boulevard, Santa Monica
(310) 587-1707

American
★★★
Moderate

Quality 79   Value C

Reservations:	Accepted
When to go:	Sunny beach days
Entree range:	$10–17
Payment:	Major credit cards
Service rating:	★★★
Friendliness rating:	★★★
Parking:	Valet available
Bar:	Full service
Wine selection:	Decent
Dress:	Casual
Disabled access:	Yes
Customers:	Hotel guests, increasing number of locals
Open:	Every day, 6:30 A.M.–11 P.M.

Atmosphere / setting: An attractive modern-Mediterranean room with an open kitchen and lots of tilework. The real draw is the beach on the other side of the windows and the bike path thick with cyclists, skaters, and runners.

House specialties: Simple Cal-Italian cafe fare: crab ravioli with tomato-herb sauce, focaccia sandwiches; grilled swordfish or skirt steak.

Other recommendations: At breakfast, tasty baked goods, jumbo lattes, and asparagus-herb omelets; various pizzas.

Summary & comments: Beachfront cafes are rare in L.A., which is why Pedals is worthy of notice. The food is perfectly fine cafe stuff and the atmosphere is kicked back, but the real draw is sprawling Santa Monica beach right outside.

PINOT

<table>
<tr><td></td><td>French</td></tr>
<tr><td>Zone 7   San Fernando Valley East</td><td>★★★★</td></tr>
<tr><td>12969 Ventura Boulevard, Studio City</td><td>Moderate</td></tr>
<tr><td>(818) 990-0500</td><td></td></tr>
<tr><td></td><td>Quality 91   Value C</td></tr>
</table>

Reservations:	Advised
When to go:	Any time
Entree range:	$16.95–22.50
Payment:	Major credit cards
Service rating:	★★★★★
Friendliness rating:	★★★★★
Parking:	Valet available
Bar:	Full service
Wine selection:	Good
Dress:	Hollywood casual to upscale
Disabled access:	Yes
Customers:	Producers, actors, agents, working Hollywood
Lunch:	Monday–Friday, 11:30 A.M.–2 P.M.
Dinner:	Monday–Thursday, 6–10 P.M.;
	Friday and Saturday, 5:30–10:30 P.M.;
	Sunday, 5:30–10 P.M.

Atmosphere / setting: Pinot positively glows: warm yellow walls, white-washed rafters, highly polished dark wood cabinets and hutches, eighteenth- and nineteenth-century etchings and lithographs, framed displays of old postcards. It feels just like a stylish sixth arrondissement bistro.

House specialties: Oven-baked onion soup; caramelized onion tart with marinated salmon, cream, "and a few calories"; succulent farm chicken with crisp fries; rich braised oxtail with porcini mashed potatoes and garlic sauce; warm chocolate tart with coffee-nougatine sauce.

Other recommendations: All the plats du jour, such as the roasted garlic rabbit on Mondays and the bouillabaisse on Fridays; warm Pinot-smoked white-fish; daily-changing spa menu. Pastas, particularly stuffed ones, can be too heavy.

Summary & comments: First considered an offshoot of Patina, this partner-ship project of Joachim and Christine Splichal and chef Octavio Becerra now stands on its own very sturdy feet. The service is crackerjack, the setting as Parisian as can be, and the hearty bistro dishes are the real thing and then some. Hollywood comes here to eat well and relax, far from the who-sits-where scene at Drai's and Morton's.

The Players

Zone 3 Golden Triangle	Hungarian/American
9513 Little Santa Monica Boulevard, Beverly Hills	★★★
(310) 278-6669	Moderate
	Quality 80 Value C

Reservations:	Accepted
When to go:	Any time
Entree range:	$10–20
Payment:	VISA, MC, AMEX
Service rating:	★★★
Friendliness rating:	★★★
Parking:	Valet available at night
Bar:	Full service
Wine selection:	Fine
Dress:	Casual
Disabled access:	Yes
Customers:	A solid, middle-aged Beverly Hills crowd
Lunch/Dinner:	Monday–Thursday, 11:30 A.M.–10 P.M.; Friday and Saturday, 11:30 A.M.–11 P.M.; Sunday, 11 A.M.–10 P.M.

Atmosphere/setting: Several charming rooms (and an outdoor patio) done in a French bistro style, adorned with old photos of such legends as Groucho Marx.

House specialties: Chicken paprika; savory, warming veal goulash; spaetzle; wonderful chocolate cake.

Other recommendations: A great selection of chopped salads at lunch; penne with mushrooms, broccoli, and ricotta; homemade sorbets.

Summary & comments: In the '30s and '40s, Mama Weiss's Csarda was a beloved Rodeo Drive restaurant that served homey old-country food to showbiz heavies. Now her son has opened this tribute to his mother and the good ol' days, and the surprise is that the place is not a foolish attempt to reclaim old glories. The Hungarian dishes are wonderful, the rest of the Cal-American food is also good, and the setting is relaxed and inviting.

Plum Tree Inn

	Chinese
	★★★
	Inexpensive
	Quality 79 Value C

Zone 1   Westside
12400 Wilshire Boulevard, West L.A.
(310) 826-8008

Zone 5   Central City
937 North Hill Street, Chinatown
(213) 613-1819

Zone 8   San Fernando Valley West
20461 Ventura Boulevard, Woodland Hills
(818) 348-4490

Reservations:	Accepted
When to go:	Any time
Entree range:	$8.25–15
Payment:	VISA, MC, AMEX
Service rating:	★★★
Friendliness rating:	★★★
Parking:	Self
Bar:	Full service; beer and wine in West L.A.
Wine selection:	Decent
Dress:	Casual
Disabled access:	Yes
Customers:	Businesspeople and families
Dinner:	Sunday–Thursday, 11 A.M.–10 P.M.;
	Friday and Saturday, 11 A.M.–11 P.M.;
	hours may vary by branch

Atmosphere / setting: Slick and elegant in a brassy way, with comfortable seating and pleasant lighting.

House specialties: Dumplings; rich Hunanese lamb; crispy and tangy orange beef; kung pao chicken.

Other recommendations: Peking duck; various noodle dishes; sautéed vegetables.

Summary & comments: This much-loved Chinese chain combines tasty, fairly authentic Chinese cooking with service that goes beyond the rushed-Chinese norm. More branches continue to open.

POSTO

Italian
★★★½
Mod/Exp

Quality 87   Value C

Zone 7   San Fernando Valley East
14928 Ventura Boulevard,
  Sherman Oaks
(818) 784-4400

Reservations:	Advised
When to go:	Any time
Entree range:	$15–27
Payment:	Major credit cards
Service rating:	★★★★
Friendliness rating:	★★★★
Parking:	Valet available
Bar:	Full service
Wine selection:	Excellent
Dress:	Casual chic to upscale
Disabled access:	Yes
Customers:	Well-heeled, middle-aged hill dwellers
Dinner:	Every night, 5:30–10:30 P.M.

Atmosphere / setting: An upscale modern trattoria that's always busy and always noisy.

House specialties: Frico, addictive fried Parmesan chips; skewers of pancetta-wrapped snails with polenta and garlicky spinach; any of the regularly changing risotti, perhaps with seafood or sweet and hot peppers; excellent tiramisu.

Other recommendations: Osso buco with gnocchetti; grilled lamb chops with herbs; agnolotti with ricotta and sage; the multicourse tasting menu.

Summary & comments: As at its sister establishment, Valentino, Posto does best with tasting menus. Ask for the chef to surprise you, and you'll be rewarded with beautiful little dishes that are far more inventive and delicious than the menu's standard items—which are still pretty terrific. Pastas and risotti are particularly wonderful, as well as reasonably priced.

PREGO

Zone 3   Golden Triangle
362 North Camden Drive,
  Beverly Hills
(310) 277-7346

Italian	
★★★	
Moderate	
Quality 80	Value B

Reservations:	Accepted
When to go:	Late lunch is pleasant
Entree range:	$9.75–20
Payment:	Major credit cards
Service rating:	★★★
Friendliness rating:	★★★★
Parking:	Valet available at dinner
Bar:	Full service
Wine selection:	Good Italians
Dress:	Casual chic
Disabled access:	Yes
Customers:	Beverly Hills shoppers and businesspeople
Lunch/Dinner:	Monday–Thursday, 11:30 A.M.–11:30 P.M.;
	Friday and Saturday, 11:30 A.M.–midnight
Dinner:	Sunday, 5:30–11:30 P.M.

Atmosphere / setting: Open kitchen, wood-burning pizza oven, white linens on the tables, and a busy bar—a classic trattoria, lively and informal but comfortable enough for Beverly Hills.

House specialties: Bruschetta Toscana, with tomatoes, mozzarella, and prosciutto; agnolotti filled with lobster and ricotta in a lemon-lobster sauce; fettuccine with wild mushrooms and Parmesan.

Other recommendations: Any of the crisp-crusted pizzas; spinach salad with pancetta, mushrooms, and onions; capellini alla checca.

Summary & comments: Part of an upscale chain, Prego deserves credit for its consistently satisfying collection of modern-Italian standards, from carpacci to pasta to pizza. A cheerful, feel-good place that's a good value by Beverly Hills standards.

Primi

Zone 1   Westside
10543 West Pico Boulevard,
    Rancho Park
(310) 475-9235

Italian	
★★★½	
Moderate	
Quality 85	Value C

Reservations:	Advised
When to go:	Any time
Entree range:	$12–22
Payment:	VISA, MC, AMEX
Service rating:	★★★★
Friendliness rating:	★★★★
Parking:	Valet available
Bar:	Full service
Wine selection:	Excellent roster of Italians
Dress:	Casual chic to upscale
Disabled access:	Yes
Customers:	Handsome Westsiders, including many in the industry
Lunch:	Monday–Friday, 11:30 A.M.–2 P.M.
Dinner:	Monday–Saturday, 5:30–10:30 P.M.

Atmosphere / setting: Contemporary but hardly stark and minimalist. An artist sponge-painted the walls in several rich hues; a modern sculpture is a focal point of the dining room, as are some good paintings.

House specialties: An outstanding Caesar salad; all the risotti, perhaps with lamb and Barolo wine or porcini and Parmesan; duckling crêpe with Cremona mustard.

Other recommendations: Black garganelli pasta with shrimp; chicken sausages with beans and tomato; roast rabbit with sweet peppers; tiramisu.

Summary & comments: This more casual offshoot of Valentino began ten years ago as a grazing spot but later broadened its culinary repertoire. The grazing dishes, however—particularly the antipasti, soups, and risotti—remain the most memorable from the generally excellent menu. Consistent and well run.

Real Food Daily

	American / Vegetarian
	★★½
	Inexpensive
	Quality 77 Value A

Zone 1   Westside
514 Santa Monica Boulevard,
    Santa Monica
(310) 451-7544

Reservations:	Not accepted
When to go:	When you're feeling unhealthy
Entree range:	$5–9.75
Payment:	VISA, MC, AMEX
Service rating:	★★
Friendliness rating:	★★★
Parking:	Self
Bar:	None
Wine selection:	None
Dress:	Birkenstocks
Disabled access:	Yes
Customers:	Virtuous vegans and the health-conscious
Lunch / Dinner:	Monday–Saturday, 11:30 A.M.–10 P.M.

Atmosphere / setting: A homey, coffee shop–style storefront, with a counter and green wooden tables.

House specialties: Kukicha tea; eggless Caesar salad with soy Parmesan; quinoa salad with corn and peas; various commendable entree combinations of beans and vegetables; a good sugarless pear-apple crisp.

Other recommendations: Vegetable sushi made with brown rice; tasty lentil-walnut pâté; polenta with a vegetable puree sauce; carob macaroons.

Summary & comments: No animal products pass through the kitchen of this newish vegan restaurant—no fish, no cheese, not even eggs. But that doesn't stop the food from being appetizing and tasty. Health-conscious Santa Monicans immediately embraced this friendly spot, which has quickly become a leader of L.A.'s health-conscious restaurants.

Reed's

Zone 2 South Bay	New American
2640 North Sepulveda Boulevard,	★★★
Manhattan Beach	Moderate
(310) 546-3299	Quality 83 Value B

Reservations:	Advised
When to go:	Any time
Entree range:	$9–18
Payment:	Major credit cards
Service rating:	★★★
Friendliness rating:	★★★
Parking:	Self
Bar:	Beer and wine
Wine selection:	Good
Dress:	Casual chic to upscale
Disabled access:	Yes
Customers:	Stylish South Bay foodies
Lunch:	Monday–Friday, 11:30 A.M.–2:30 P.M.
Lunch/Dinner:	Monday–Saturday, 5:30–10:30 P.M.

Atmosphere/setting: More stylish than the strip-mall site would suggest, with blonde-wood walls, tall windows, and dramatic food-related paintings.

House specialties: Menu changed regularly. Possibilities are rock shrimp cakes; smoked salmon ravioli; pork tenderloin with mashed potatoes; tarte tatin.

Other recommendations: Tuna tartare; potato-basil cannelloni with sautéed scallops; chicken pot pie; lemon tart.

Summary & comments: The site that once held John Sedlar's pioneering St. Estephe has been given new life by the team of Joe Miller (of the excellent Joe's in Venice) and chef Brandon Reed. Reed's cooking is the sort of updated American fare that's done so well in San Francisco, served at reasonable prices to a South Bay crowd that's hungry for a smart restaurant.

The Reel Inn

Zone 1   Westside
18661 Pacific Coast Highway, Malibu
(310) 456-8221

Seafood	
★★	
Inexpensive	
Quality 77	Value A

Reservations:	Not accepted
When to go:	Sunny summer afternoons
Entree range:	$7.95–14.95
Payment:	VISA, MC
Service rating:	★
Friendliness rating:	★★
Parking:	Self
Bar:	Beer and wine
Wine selection:	Limited
Dress:	Casual
Disabled access:	Yes
Customers:	Surfers, beachcombers, PCH-driving tourists
Lunch/Dinner:	Sunday–Thursday, 11 A.M.–9:30 P.M.;
	Friday and Saturday, 11 A.M.–10:30 P.M.

Atmosphere/setting: A salty beach-adjacent seafood shack with an order counter and plain wooden tables.

House specialties: Chowders, from a tomato-fish chowder to Sunday's clam chowder; delicious grilled-fish tacos; grilled shrimp; grilled swordfish.

Other recommendations: For splurgers, fresh Dungeness crab or 1.5-pound lobsters, simply steamed.

Summary & comments: The Reel Inn is just the sort of place you'd hope to find on a drive up the coast: an order-at-the-counter seafood shack serving unfussy grilled seafood on paper plates. The other branch in Santa Monica lacks the beachy appeal.

Regent Beverly Wilshire Dining Room

	New American
	★★★★
	Very Expensive

Zone 3   Golden Triangle
9500 Wilshire Boulevard, Beverly Hills
(310) 275-5200

Quality 90   Value D

Reservations:	Accepted
When to go:	To celebrate, to luxuriate, to dance
Entree range:	$23–35
Payment:	Major credit cards
Service rating:	★★★★★
Friendliness rating:	★★★★★
Parking:	Valet available
Bar:	Full service
Wine selection:	Premium producers, premium prices
Dress:	Upscale (tie)
Disabled access:	Yes
Customers:	Couples celebrating 20th or 40th anniversaries; businesspeople
Open:	Monday–Saturday, 7 A.M.–10:30 P.M.; Sunday, 10:30 A.M.–10 P.M.

Atmosphere / setting: Seriously handsome. The open, split-level space is given formality with satinwood and mahogany woodwork, striped silk Scalamandre curtains, classical wall murals, upholstered Biedermeier and Regency furniture, and a small dance floor; a glass-walled kitchen adds a bit of modern informality.

House specialties: Menu changes daily. Fine possibilities include open-faced lobster tortilla with roasted corn and tomato salsa; salmon medallions coated with Chinese mustard; roasted saddle of lamb with sweet pepper and goat cheese cannelloni; house-made sorbets.

Other recommendations: Hand-carved smoked Scottish salmon; potato-crusted Chilean sea bass with jumbo asparagus; wood-fired filet mignon.

Entertainment & amenities: Dancing, Thursday–Saturday after 8 P.M.

Summary & comments: Although it is now best known as the place that took up the dinner-dancing mantle after L'Escoffier closed, the Regent's dining room also deserves acclaim for its savvy, well-balanced contemporary American cooking and its top-drawer service. The bar across the rear lobby is pretty swell, too.

Honors / awards: Highly rated in *Condé Nast Traveler's* "America's Best Restaurants."

Remi

Zone 1   Westside
1451 Third Street Promenade,
   Santa Monica
(310) 393-6545

	Italian
	★★★½
	Mod/Exp
Quality 86	Value D

Reservations:	Advised
When to go:	For a late lunch
Entree range:	$13–25
Payment:	Major credit cards
Service rating:	★★★★
Friendliness rating:	★★★★
Parking:	Valet available
Bar:	Full service
Wine selection:	Great grappa collection
Dress:	Casual chic to upscale
Disabled access:	Yes
Customers:	Tanned, fit Westsiders
Lunch:	Monday–Saturday, 11:30 A.M.–3 P.M.; Sunday, noon–3:30 P.M.
Dinner:	Sunday–Thursday, 5:30–10:30 P.M.; Friday and Saturday, 5:30–11 P.M.

Atmosphere / setting: A great-looking place created by famed designer Adam Tihany: crisp, nautical navy-and-white-striped fabrics, gleaming ship-quality woodwork, and crossed Venetian-style oars overhead; patio seating fronts the Promenade.

House specialties: Dreamy crespelle (crêpes) with ricotta and spinach; linguine with shellfish, fresh tomato, and herbed olive oil; excellent calves' liver with caramelized onions and fresh polenta.

Other recommendations: Grilled quail wrapped in bacon; grilled salmon with spinach and bacon vinaigrette; good tiramisu.

Summary & comments: When the crush of humanity on the Third Street Promenade gets too oppresive, retreat to this handsome Venetian restaurant, home to both style and substance. Cigar lovers should call for the schedule of smokers' dinners.

Rex Il Ristorante

Zone 5 Central City	Italian
617 South Olive Street, Downtown	★★★★
(213) 627-2300	Exp/Very Exp
	Quality 93 Value D

Reservations:	Advised
When to go:	When you're feeling flush
Entree range:	$18–28
Payment:	Major credit cards
Service rating:	★★★★★
Friendliness rating:	★★★★
Parking:	Valet available
Bar:	Full service
Wine selection:	All the Italian heavy hitters
Dress:	Upscale (tie)
Disabled access:	Yes
Customers:	Downtown's elite, visiting Italians
Lunch:	Thursday and Friday, noon–3:30 P.M.
Dinner:	Monday–Saturday, 6–10 P.M.

Atmosphere / setting: A former haberdashery in one of L.A.'s architectural jewels, the Oviatt Building, Rex is one of the most beautiful restaurants in the country. A gleaming, glowing, art deco vision of an ocean-liner dining room, the two-story space is appointed with original Lalique light fixtures and mirrors, flawless woodwork, and well-spaced tables set with silver and crystal.

House specialties: Menu changes regularly; excellent possibilities include a squab salad with pumpkin, squash, raisins, and cornfield lettuce; timeless tagliolini with tomato sauce and basil; breaded veal chop with French beans; panna cotta.

Other recommendations: Seafood salad; ravioli with ricotta and spinach; whole-wheat tagliatelle with lamb ragu; baked sea bass layered with potato.

Entertainment & amenities: Dance floor; pianist/singers are sometimes pretty lounge-lizardy.

Summary & comments: Newer, trendier restaurants have stolen much of Rex's thunder, but the quality hasn't slipped a bit. Now under the direction of Odette Fada, the kitchen presents hearty, homey Italian dishes in an exceedingly elegant fashion, and the dining room continues to enchant. The upstairs bar is beloved by romantics and beleaguered smokers alike.

Rincon Chileno

Zone 5   Central City
4352 Melrose Avenue, Hollywood
(213) 666-6075

Chilean
★★½
Inexpensive
Quality 77   Value B

Reservations:	Accepted
When to go:	Any time
Entree range:	$6.95–12.95
Payment:	Major credit cards
Service rating:	★★★
Friendliness rating:	★★★
Parking:	Self
Bar:	Beer and wine
Wine selection:	Very good Chilean bottles
Dress:	Casual
Disabled access:	Yes
Customers:	Cross-section
Lunch/Dinner:	Tuesday–Thursday and Sunday,
	11:30 A.M.–10 P.M.;
	Friday and Saturday, 11:30 A.M.–11 P.M.

Atmosphere / setting: On a grungy block in East Hollywood, this tiny storefront has a handful of tables and lots of good cheer.

House specialties: Chilean bouillabaisse, spicy and wonderful; humitas, a creamy tamale with salad; pastel de choclo, a sweet-savory tart filled with chicken, beef, onion, and corn.

Other recommendations: Unusual Chilean seafood dishes.

Summary & comments: For years this humble restaurant has stayed true to its roots, serving authentic Chilean dishes untempered by local tastes. Many of these good tastes are available "to go" from the neighboring deli, which also sells some terrific, bargain-basement Chilean wines.

Ritrovo

Zone 8   San Fernando Valley West
1125 Lindero Canyon Road,
    Westlake Village
(818) 889-0191

Italian	
★★½	
Moderate	
Quality 79	Value C

Reservations:	Accepted
When to go:	Any time
Entree range:	$8.25–16
Payment:	VISA, MC, AMEX
Service rating:	★★★
Friendliness rating:	★★★
Parking:	Self
Bar:	Beer and wine
Wine selection:	Decent
Dress:	Casual
Disabled access:	Yes
Customers:	Well-heeled suburbanites
Breakfast/Lunch:	Monday–Friday, 7 A.M.–2:30 P.M.;
	Saturday, 10 A.M.–2:30 P.M.
Dinner:	Monday–Thursday, 5:30–10 P.M.;
	Friday and Saturday, 5:30–11 P.M.;
	Sunday, 5–10 P.M.

Atmosphere / setting: The generic minimall setting is improved with sponge-painted walls, an open kitchen, Italian music, and thickly accented Italian waiters.

House specialties: Wonderful mushroom soup; fettuccine bolognese with slippery house-made noodles; grilled pressed chicken with spinach and checca; chocolate-filled beignets.

Other recommendations: The antipasti buffet at lunch; thin-crust pizzas with classic toppings.

Summary & comments: Ritrovo does an admirable job of making you forget you're in a faceless suburban mini-mall, thanks to its authentic Italian warmth and very respectable cooking.

ROCKENWAGNER

Zone 1   Westside
2435 Main Street, Santa Monica
(310) 399-6504

French / New American
★★★★
Expensive

Quality 94   Value C

Reservations:	Advised
When to go:	Any time
Entree range:	$17.50–22.50
Payment:	Major credit cards
Service rating:	★★★★
Friendliness rating:	★★★★
Parking:	Valet available
Bar:	Full service
Wine selection:	Good
Dress:	Casual chic to upscale
Disabled access:	Yes
Customers:	Prosperous artists, writers, and creative types
Brunch:	Saturday–Sunday, 9 A.M.–2:30 P.M.
Lunch:	Tuesday–Friday, 11:30 A.M.–2:30 P.M.
Dinner:	Monday–Friday, 6–10 P.M.;
	Saturday, 5:30–10 P.M.

Atmosphere / setting: A dynamic space in a building designed by Frank Gehry. Soaring ceilings, subtle space dividers, upholstered booths, and a separate bakery in front evoke a town square feeling.

House specialties: Menu changes seasonally. Memorable dishes include crab soufflé with fresh papaya and lobster-butter sauce; short stack of smoked salmon, potato chips, crème fraiche, and caviar; tian of lamb with spinach, mushrooms, and tomato concassé; beef tenderloin with goat cheese mashed potatoes.

Other recommendations: At brunch, German apple pancakes or the pretzel burger; at the Tuesday night drop-in Stammtisch dinners, various Bavarian snacks; warm chocolate tart with hazelnut parfait.

Summary & comments: Hans Rockenwagner is one of the most exciting talents in town, and now his food is being served in an equally exciting space that represents the best sort of L.A. modernism. The boyishly handsome German-born chef fuses the generous good flavors of his home country with his rigorous French training and a free-wheeling L.A. sensibility to produce a smart, superbly delicious cuisine.

Romeo Cucina

	Italian
	★★½
Zone 10 Orange County South	Inexpensive
249 Broadway, Laguna Beach	
(714) 497-6627	Quality 79 Value B

Reservations:	Accepted
When to go:	Any time
Entree range:	$7–15
Payment:	Major credit cards
Service rating:	★★★
Friendliness rating:	★★★
Parking:	Self
Bar:	Full service
Wine selection:	Good Italians
Dress:	Casual
Disabled access:	Yes
Customers:	Chic locals
Lunch:	Tuesday–Sunday, 11:30 A.M.–2:30 P.M.
Dinner:	Sunday–Thursday, 5–10 P.M.;
	Friday and Saturday, 5–11 P.M.

Atmosphere / setting: A wonderful, carefully considered interior design, sort of Tuscan art nouveau in style, with gleaming terra cotta floors, rustic blonde-wood chairs, and a tiny patio.

House specialties: House salad with mint; generous, messy linguine with seafood, tomatoes, and olives; good thin-crust pizzas, like the one topped with wild mushrooms; tagliatelle with a meat-tomato ragu; polletto, a whole game hen, split and grilled.

Other recommendations: Grilled vegetable assortment; charred tuna salad; grilled salmon or other fresh fish; osso buco.

Summary & comments: Like Laguna itself, Romeo Cucina is casually great-looking, romantic, and self-assured. It's an ideal spot for a pizza and a glass of wine at the bar or a lively dinner with friends among the beautiful people.

Rosalind's

<table>
<tr><td></td><td>West African</td></tr>
</table>

Zone 5   Central City
1044 South Fairfax Avenue
(213) 936-2486

West African
★★½
Inexpensive

Quality 78   Value B

Reservations:	Accepted
When to go:	Any time
Entree range:	$10–12.50
Payment:	VISA, MC, AMEX
Service rating:	★★
Friendliness rating:	★★★
Parking:	Self
Bar:	Full service
Wine selection:	Limited
Dress:	Casual
Disabled access:	Yes
Customers:	Expatriate Africans, local adventurers
Lunch/Dinner:	Every day, 11:30 A.M.–midnight

Atmosphere / setting: A large, comfortable place in a ragtag but friendly neighborhood, with dim lighting and a pan-African decor.

House specialties: Special tibs, an Ethiopian hot pot with filet mignon; yedoro wot, a savory chicken stew with boiled egg; groundnut stew, a delicious blend of peanuts, beef, chicken, and spices.

Other recommendations: Dishes from around West Africa, including Nigerian-style spinach and snapper; Liberian-style cabbage-collards with beef and chicken; and a Senegalese dish of broiled chicken smothered in a lemon-onion sauce.

Entertainment & amenities: Live African music on weekends.

Summary & comments: Originally known as an Ethiopian restaurant, Rosalind's has broadened its scope to offer a tasty sampling from across West Africa. Don't miss the spongy, strange but wonderful injera bread served with the Ethiopian dishes. A fun place that's good to try with a group.

Roscoe's House of Chicken and Waffles

	American
	★★½
	Inexpensive
	Quality 76 Value A

Zone 4   City South
106 West Manchester Avenue, South-Cen[
(213) 752-6211

Zone 5   Central City
1514 North Gower Street, Hollywood
(213) 466-7453

Zone 6   San Gabriel Valley
830 North Lake Avenue, Pasadena
(818) 791-4890

Reservations:	Not accepted
When to go:	When you're starving
Entree range:	$5–9
Payment:	Major credit cards
Service rating:	★★
Friendliness rating:	★★★
Parking:	Self
Bar:	Beer and wine
Wine selection:	Limited
Dress:	Casual
Disabled access:	Yes
Customers:	A wonderful mix
Open:	Sunday–Thursday, 8:30 A.M.–11:45 P.M.; Friday and Saturday, 8:30 A.M.–4 A.M.; South-Central and Pasadena branches close earlier

Atmosphere / setting: Bright, busy cafes with wooden tables and greenery.

House specialties: Crisp-skinned, delicious fried chicken served with cinnamon-flecked waffles and syrup; smothered chicken livers; tasty greens.

Other recommendations: For breakfast, waffles without the chicken. Unless you're really hungry.

Summary & comments: The name says it all: juicy fried chicken is paired with sweet, fluffy waffles in a strangely wonderful marriage that will have your cholesterol and blood-sugar levels slugging it out. The rest of the gut-busting Southern food is pretty good, too. The Hollywood branch is great for night owls.

R-23

	Japanese
	★ ★ ★
	Moderate
	Quality 84 Value B

Reservations:	Accepted
When to go:	Lunch is busy, dinner quiet
Entree range:	$10–22
Payment:	VISA, MC, DC
Service rating:	★ ★ ★
Friendliness rating:	★ ★ ★ ★
Parking:	Self
Bar:	Beer and saké
Wine selection:	Good sakés
Dress:	Casual
Disabled access:	Yes
Customers:	Loft artists, garment-district workers
Lunch:	Monday–Friday, noon–2 P.M.
Dinner:	Monday–Saturday, 6–10:30 P.M.

Atmosphere / setting: Set in an artistic neighborhood in downtown's warehouse district, R-23 is spare and pure: unadorned brick walls, wood floors, plain tables, and minimalist seating.

House specialties: Sushi of noteworthy quality and simplicity, from rich, subtle toro to not-for-everyone sea urchin and sea eel.

Other recommendations: Sushi's the main draw, but there's also a well-prepared roster of traditional Japanese dishes, from yakitori to tempura.

Summary & comments: Sushi freaks manage to find this out-of-the-way downtowner, thanks to the flawless fish prepared by a rogue band of former Katsu chefs. The atmospheric comforts are few, the culinary rewards many.

Ruth's Chris Steak House

<table>
<tr><td></td><td>Steakhouse</td></tr>
<tr><td>Zone 3   Golden Triangle</td><td>★★★</td></tr>
<tr><td>224 South Beverly Drive, Beverly Hills</td><td>Expensive</td></tr>
<tr><td>(310) 859-8744</td><td>Quality 84   Value D</td></tr>
</table>

Reservations:	Accepted
When to go:	Any time
Entree range:	$17–34
Payment:	Major credit cards
Service rating:	★★★
Friendliness rating:	★★
Parking:	Valet available
Bar:	Full service
Wine selection:	Appropriate bold reds
Dress:	Casual to upscale
Disabled access:	Yes
Customers:	Meat eaters of all stripes
Dinner:	Monday–Thursday, 5–10 P.M.;
	Friday and Saturday, 5–10:30 P.M.;
	Sunday, 5–9:30 P.M.

Atmosphere / setting: More elegant and less brawny than the typical steakhouse—but the aproned waiters carrying six plates of steak at once lend the appropriate meaty feeling.

House specialties: Sizzling filet, New York strip, and porterhouse steaks, topped with pats of melting butter; shoestring fries; whiskey bread pudding.

Other recommendations: Perfect broiled lamb and veal chops; creamed spinach; simple grilled fresh fish.

Summary & comments: Part of the New Orleans–based chain, Ruth's Chris serves one of the best steaks in town, along with some respectable side dishes. If the thought of butter-topped meat starts your heart to palpitating, take comfort that the fresh fish is satisfying, too.

Saddle Peak Lodge

	American
Zone 8 San Fernando Valley West	★★★★
419 Cold Canyon Road, Calabasas	Expensive
(818) 222-3888	
	Quality 90 Value C

Reservations:	Advised
When to go:	Just before dusk, to revel in the mountains, or Sunday brunch
Entree range:	$17.50–27.50
Payment:	VISA, MC, AMEX
Service rating:	★★★★
Friendliness rating:	★★★★
Parking:	Valet available
Bar:	Full service
Wine selection:	Good
Dress:	Like a country squire
Disabled access:	Yes
Customers:	Everyone
Brunch:	Sunday, 11 A.M.–2 P.M.
Dinner:	Wednesday–Saturday, 6 P.M.–midnight; Sunday, 5–10 P.M.

Atmosphere / setting: This former lodge and alleged bordello is set back in the Santa Monica Mountains far from the West Valley subdivisions. Tables on the rambling patio are highly prized at Sunday brunch; inside are several dining rooms, adorned with fireplaces, game heads, library bookshelves, and loads of romance.

House specialties: Game in many guises: delicious venison with Burgundy-poached pear and potato pancakes; pheasant under glass; California quail broiled with juniper berry sauce; chocolate taco with white chocolate mousse.

Other recommendations: Excellent salads; salmon cooked in a paper bag with a julienne of vegetables; grilled Lake Superior whitefish with fresh spinach; apricot soufflé.

Summary & comments: Proof that Southern California is home to more than starlets and strip malls, the Saddle Peak is a country hunting lodge that even animal lovers have a hard time resisting (if you can't handle elk heads watching you eat, request a table in the library room). High-quality ingredients, skillful cooking, and a respect for honest, albeit upscale, American cooking, round out a dining experience that is well worth a considerable drive.

Sanamluang Cafe

Zone 5   Central City
5176 Hollywood Boulevard, Hollywood
(213) 660-8006

Zone 7   San Fernando Valley East
12980 Sherman Way, North Hollywood
(818) 764-1180

<table>
<tr><td>Thai</td></tr>
<tr><td>★★½</td></tr>
<tr><td>Inexpensive</td></tr>
<tr><td>Quality 80   Value A</td></tr>
</table>

Reservations:	Not accepted
When to go:	Great for late-night snack
Entree range:	$4–5.50
Payment:	No cards
Service rating:	★★
Friendliness rating:	★
Parking:	Self
Bar:	None
Wine selection:	None
Dress:	Casual
Disabled access:	Yes
Customers:	Thais, late-nighters of all stripes
Open:	Every day, 10 A.M.–4 A.M.;
	Hollywood, until 5 A.M.

Atmosphere / setting: All Formica and fluorescent, these all-hours cafes typify the bare-bones Asian diner.

House specialties: Rahd na (rice noodles with squid, shrimp, Chinese broccoli, pork stomach, baby corn, chicken, even a fried egg); wonderful chicken soup with rice noodles, bean sprouts, and fried garlic; General's Noodle (egg noodles with roast duck, barbecued pork, shrimp, scallions, and chopped peanut).

Other recommendations: Non-noodle dishes are good, too: fried rice biscuits, roast duck salad with hot lime dressing, many rice-based dishes.

Summary & comments: These Thai joints are beloved for many reasons: their dozens of noodle dishes, each more delicious than the next; their salads and other snacks; their give-away prices; and their ultra-late hours.

Seafood Strip

Zone 6   San Gabriel Valley
140 West Valley Boulevard,
   No. 212, San Gabriel
(818) 288-9899

Chinese
★★★
Inexp/Mod

Quality 81   Value C

Reservations:	Accepted
When to go:	Any time
Entree range:	$6.95–17.95
Payment:	VISA, MC
Service rating:	★★★
Friendliness rating:	★★★
Parking:	Self
Bar:	Beer and wine
Wine selection:	Limited
Dress:	Casual
Disabled access:	Yes
Customers:	Chinese, Chinese Americans
Lunch:	Every day, 11 A.M.–3 P.M.
Dinner:	Every night, 5 P.M.–3 A.M.

Atmosphere / setting: A shiny, sparkly restaurant with lots of dining rooms and private rooms, bubbling fish tanks, and black-suited waiters and captains.

House specialties: Pristine Japanese-style sashimi; chicken with wine in chafing pot; steamed cod in dry bean, topped with a salty, crunchy crumble of dry soybeans; beautiful whole fish.

Other recommendations: Various chafing-pot stews; shrimp with salty pepper; steamed crab with rice cake; pan-fried crab Taiwanese style.

Summary & comments: Seafood Strip sets itself apart from the many other seafood restaurants in the South San Gabriel Valley by hewing to the richer, spicier Taiwanese style instead of the lighter Cantonese. There's also a Japanese influence in the excellent sashimi and the karaoke bar. Note the late hours.

17th Street Cafe

Zone 1   Westside
1610 Montana Avenue,
   Santa Monica
(310) 453-2771

American
★★★
Inexpensive

Quality 80   Value B

Reservations:	Accepted at dinner
When to go:	Any time
Entree range:	$9–15
Payment:	MC, VISA, D
Service rating:	★★★
Friendliness rating:	★★★
Parking:	Self
Bar:	Beer and wine
Wine selection:	Decent
Dress:	Casual
Disabled access:	Yes
Customers:	Relaxed, upscale locals
Breakfast/Lunch:	Monday–Saturday, 8 A.M.–3 P.M.; Sunday, 9 A.M.–3 P.M.
Dinner:	Sunday–Thursday, 5:30–9:30 P.M.; Friday and Saturday, 5:30–10 P.M.

Atmosphere/setting: Plain and simple: hardwood floors, modern art, table linens.

House specialties: Better-than-the-norm Chinese chicken salad; chopped grilled vegetable salad; grilled salmon on a bed of mashed potatoes.

Other recommendations: At breakfast, breakfast pasta, scrambled with eggs; yogurt pancakes.

Summary & comments: A first-rate neighborhood cafe run by a friendly family and filled with loyal regulars. Home cooking for those who eat out a lot.

72 Market Street

New American
★★★
Expensive

Quality 84   Value D

Zone 1   Westside
72 Market Street, Venice
(310) 392-8720

Reservations:	Advised
When to go:	Any time
Entree range:	$18–24
Payment:	Major credit cards
Service rating:	★★★
Friendliness rating:	★★★
Parking:	Valet available
Bar:	Full service
Wine selection:	Interesting
Dress:	Casual chic to high-style
Disabled access:	Yes
Customers:	Westside baby boomers, artistic types
Lunch:	Monday–Friday, 11:30 A.M.–2:30 P.M.
Dinner:	Monday–Thursday, 6–10 P.M.;
	Friday and Saturday, 6–11 P.M.;
	Sunday, 5:30–9 P.M.

Atmosphere / setting: Still visually exciting after many years on this quiet Venice side street, 72 Market contrasts its homey food with a modern, architectural space that's fun to be in.

House specialties: Flawless oysters, either on the half shell or broiled with pesto; "kick-ass" chili; a thick slab of Market Street meat loaf with spinach and mashed potatoes.

Other recommendations: Caesar salad with shrimp croutons; roast duck with sweet pear-mint sauce and wild rice; crispy seared salmon; crème brûlée.

Entertainment & amenities: Piano music Thursday–Sunday.

Summary & comments: The cooking got rocky for awhile at this bastion of contemporary Americana owned by Tony Bill and Dudley Moore, but brand-new chef Roland Gibert brings talent and great promise to his post. The feel-good food is matched with a feel-good vibe provided by the dramatic architecture, lively bar scene, good piano music, and artistic clientele. By the time you read this, Gibert may have moved the cuisine up a few points.

Shabu Shabu House

Zone 5 Central City	Japanese
127 Japanese Village Plaza Mall,	★★½
off 2nd Street, Little Tokyo	Inexpensive
(213) 680-3890	Quality 80 Value B

Reservations:	Not accepted
When to go:	Any time
Entree range:	$10–16.50 for complete meal
Payment:	VISA, MC
Service rating:	★★
Friendliness rating:	★★★
Parking:	Self
Bar:	Beer and saké
Wine selection:	Sakés
Dress:	Casual
Disabled access:	Yes
Customers:	Local office workers
Lunch:	Tuesday–Sunday, 11:30 A.M.–2:30 P.M.
Dinner:	Tuesday–Sunday, 5:30–10 P.M.

Atmosphere / setting: A small, cute, and clean little cafe with horseshoe-shaped counters.

House specialties: Shabu shabu is the extent of the menu, except for a few accompaniments like rice. You're given thin slices of beef and vegetables, which you cook yourself in a savory bubbling broth.

Other recommendations: Iced coffee with cream and sugar syrup.

Summary & comments: A fun, cook-it-yourself adventure serving wonderful shabu shabu, featuring first-rate ingredients and a rich broth.

Shahrezad

Zone 1   Westside
1422 Westwood Boulevard, Westwood
(310) 470-3242

Zone 8   San Fernando Valley West
17547 Ventura Boulevard, Encino
(818) 906-1616

Middle Eastern	
★★½	
Inexpensive	
Quality 79	Value B

Reservations:	Accepted
When to go:	Any time
Entree range:	$6.95–14.95
Payment:	Major credit cards
Service rating:	★★★
Friendliness rating:	★★★
Parking:	Self
Bar:	Beer and wine
Wine selection:	Limited
Dress:	Casual
Disabled access:	Yes
Customers:	Iranian businesspeople; all sorts
Lunch/Dinner:	*Westwood:* Sunday–Thursday, 11:30 A.M.–9 P.M.;
	Friday and Saturday, 11:30 A.M.–4 A.M.;
	Encino: every day, 11:30 A.M.–10:30 P.M.

Atmosphere/setting: Cheerful, comfortable restaurants with more elegance than the typical neighborhood ethnic joint.

House specialties: Excellent kebabs; stews combining meat and fruit, like the fesenjan, with chicken and a walnut-pomegranate paste; mast o'khiar, a dipping sauce of yogurt, cucumber, herbs, walnuts, and raisins.

Other recommendations: Eggplant "delight"; lamb tahchin, yogurt-and-saffron-marinated lamb with polo rice and a yogurt-egg-rice mixture.

Entertainment & amenities: The Westwood branch offers Middle Eastern piano music most nights.

Summary & comments: First-rate Iranian food—kebabs, rice dishes, savory-sweet stews—has brought this mini-chain a loyal following. The Flame, a related restaurant next to the Westwood branch, is home to a wonderful wood-burning oven that turns out great tanuri bread.

Shenandoah Cafe

	American
	★★½
Zone 2 South Bay	Inexp / Mod
4722 East 2nd Street, Long Beach	
(310) 434-3469	Quality 79 Value B

Reservations:	Accepted
When to go:	When you long for Aunt Bea
Entree range:	$11–21 for complete meal
Payment:	VISA, MC, AMEX
Service rating:	★★★
Friendliness rating:	★★★★
Parking:	Self
Bar:	Beer and wine
Wine selection:	Decent
Dress:	Casual
Disabled access:	Yes
Customers:	Families, couples, locals
Lunch:	Monday–Friday, 11:30 A.M.–2:30 P.M.
Dinner:	Monday–Thursday, 5–10 P.M.;
	Friday, 5–11 P.M.; Saturday, 4:30–11 P.M.;
	Sunday, 4:30–10 P.M.

Atmosphere / setting: Done up like New Orleans parlors, the dining rooms reek of small-town, Southern charm. Waitresses wear gingham in keeping with the spirit.

House specialties: Sweet, irresistible apple fritters, served instead of bread; Cajun prime rib; the excellent riverwalk steak, thinly sliced and served with a mustard-caper sauce; beer-battered shrimp; suave cheesecakes.

Other recommendations: Boneless fried chicken breasts; blackened fish of the day; brownie sundaes.

Summary & comments: Well-prepared, deeply satisfying recipes from America's community and ladies' club cookbooks are showcased in this nostalgic, warm-and-fuzzy Long Beach institution. It's just the place when you've got the *Leave It to Beaver* blues.

Shiro

Zone 6   San Gabriel Valley
1505 Mission Street, South Pasadena
(818) 799-4774

Reservations:	Advised
When to go:	Any time
Entree range:	$13.50–19.50
Payment:	VISA, MC, AMEX
Service rating:	★★★
Friendliness rating:	★★★
Parking:	Self
Bar:	Beer and wine
Wine selection:	Good, affordable
Dress:	Casual chic
Disabled access:	Yes
Customers:	In-the-know Eastsiders of all types
Dinner:	Tuesday–Thursday, 6–9 P.M.;
	Friday and Saturday, 6–10 P.M.;
	Sunday, 5:45–9:15 P.M.

Atmosphere / setting: A square, stylishly plain room with a high, exposed ceiling, an open kitchen, and contemporary paintings.

House specialties: Chinese ravioli stuffed with shrimp-salmon mousse; whole sizzling catfish with ponzu sauce; Mexican shrimp and Canadian scallops with saffron sauce; wonton with blackberries, poached pear, and orange custard.

Other recommendations: Tuna sashimi salad; broiled snapper marinated in basil and garlic; chicken with rosemary-mustard sauce; raspberry crème brûlée.

Summary & comments: . Owner / chef Hideo "Shiro" Yamashiro has resisted the temptation to expand—and it is surely a considerable temptation, since his restaurant has been full every night since it opened several years ago. Shiro knows that expanding would mean losing some control over his kitchen, which would mean the end of his cuisine's remarkable consistency and excellence. Every single dish on this intelligent French-American-Asian menu is superb; seafood is a particular specialty. Worth a trip to sleepy South Pasadena.

Sofi Estiatorian

Zone 3   Golden Triangle
8030 West 3rd Street, West Hollywood
(213) 651-0346

Greek	
★ ★ ★	
Moderate	
Quality 84	Value B

Reservations:	Accepted
When to go:	On warm days for the patio
Entree range:	$12–17
Payment:	Major credit cards
Service rating:	★ ★ ★
Friendliness rating:	★ ★ ★ ★
Parking:	Valet available
Bar:	Beer and wine
Wine selection:	Good retsinas
Dress:	Casual chic
Disabled access:	Yes
Customers:	Grecophiles
Lunch:	Monday–Saturday, noon–2:30 P.M.
Dinner:	Every night, 5:30–11 P.M.

Atmosphere / setting: A homelike yet refined taverna setting, enlivened with recorded Greek music and given interest with carefully displayed Greek art and artifacts. In fair weather the trellised patio is a dream.

House specialties: Pikilia, a sampling of wonderful appetizers, including keftedes (delicious fried meatballs) and chtapodi (marinated octopus); superb moussaka; roasted leg of lamb with garlic and oregano and Greek-style baked potatoes.

Other recommendations: Choriatiki, a salad with tomatoes, cucumbers, peppers, onions, feta, marinated olives and oregano; garidopita, shrimp phyllo pies.

Summary & comments: Let others carry on at the Greek restaurants where plate smashing takes precedence over food, while you head for Sofi, the city's best taverna. Greek-born Sofi Konstantinidis trained as a doctor, but she decided to follow her real bliss, cooking, which she learned at her grandmother's knee. Her food is consistently excellent; when it's eaten on the patio on a summer evening, you'll feel like you're in Greece.

SPAGO

Zone 3   Golden Triangle
1114 Horn Avenue, West Hollywood
(310) 652-4025

New American
★★★½
Expensive
Quality 89   Value D

Reservations:	Advised
When to go:	Early—prime time is saved, for regulars and the famous
Entree range:	$14–28
Payment:	VISA, MC, CB, DC
Service rating:	★★★★
Friendliness rating:	★★
Parking:	Valet available
Bar:	Full service
Wine selection:	Very good
Dress:	Casual chic to agent Armani
Disabled access:	Yes
Customers:	Hollywood A-list and tourists alike
Dinner:	Sunday–Thursday, 6–10:30 P.M.; Friday and Saturday, 6–11:30 P.M.

Atmosphere / setting: Perched above the Sunset Strip, Spago set the tone for the zillions of modern California-style restaurants that followed: open kitchen, wood-burning pizza oven, baseball-hatted cooks, modern art, unfussy decor, and a palpable buzz.

House specialties: Menu changes daily. You can usually count on a field-greens salad against which all others are measured; seared foie gras in various guises, perhaps with sweet-potato chips and plum chutney; duck-sausage pizza with tomatoes, basil, and shiitakes; and the "Jewish" pizza, with smoked salmon and crème fraiche.

Other recommendations: Good examples have included roasted whole fish with warm eggplant ragout; roasted salmon with roasted vegetable vinaigrette; grilled prime New York steak; flawless crème brûlées.

Summary & comments: So-called California cuisine may have been born at Chez Panisse and Michael's, but Spago imprinted it onto the nation's consciousness. Now there's a Puck pizza in every supermarket freezer case and a Wolfgang Puck Express headed for a mall near you. And yet, somehow, Spago hasn't suffered from Puck's overexposure, remaining as celebrity-packed as ever—often at the expense of the unknown diner, who has, on occasion, been treated like pond scum. The food still sparkles with modern American inventiveness and respect for good produce, and the experience still delivers a stereotypical L.A. scene.

Splashes

Zone 10 Orange County South	Mediterranean
Surf & Sand Hotel,	★★★½
1555 South Pacific Coast Highway,	Moderate
Laguna Beach	Quality 84 Value C
(714) 497-4477	

Reservations:	Accepted
When to go:	When the weather's fine
Entree range:	$15–22
Payment:	Major credit cards
Service rating:	★★★★
Friendliness rating:	★★★★
Parking:	Valet available
Bar:	Full service
Wine selection:	Good
Dress:	Casual-chic
Disabled access:	Yes
Customers:	Upscale tourists, tanned locals
Breakfast:	Monday–Saturday, 7–11 A.M.
Brunch:	Sunday, 10 A.M.–4:30 P.M.
Lunch:	Monday–Saturday, 11:30 A.M.–4:30 P.M.
Dinner:	Sunday–Thursday, 5–10 P.M.;
	Friday and Saturday, 5–11 P.M.

Atmosphere / setting: A dream location fronting the ocean, matched with a dreamy interior decor: an opulent stone floor, blonde woods, lazy ceiling fans, dramatic flower arrangements, a fireplace, and lots of little windows bringing the sparkling ocean inside.

House specialties: Menu changes daily. Good recurring choices include granola at breakfast; excellent sandwiches at lunch, like the grilled portobello mushroom and arugula or the Moroccan spiced chicken salad; and superb lamb osso buco at dinner.

Other recommendations: Dishes are Mediterranean in style, strong on grilled fresh fish. Expect such flavors and ingredients as pesto, goat cheese, saffron, and couscous, typically used with skill and flair.

Summary & comments: There's no better location on the water for lunch or a twilight dinner than this handsome hotel restaurant sitting atop the sand. For the most part, the luxuriously rustic Mediterranean-style cooking works in harmony with the oceanfront setting and great-looking interior design. Come when you can sit and languish awhile.

Super Antojitos

Zone 9   Orange County North
1702 North Bristol Street, Santa Ana
(714) 835-3619

Zone 9   Orange County North
2510 South Bristol Street, Santa Ana
(714) 957-0994

Zone 9   Orange County North
580 West 19th Street, Santa Ana
(714) 645-0481

Reservations:	Not accepted
When to go:	Any time
Entree range:	$5–10
Payment:	No credit cards
Service rating:	★★
Friendliness rating:	★★★
Parking:	Self
Bar:	Beer and wine
Wine selection:	Limited
Dress:	Casual
Disabled access:	Yes
Customers:	Blue-collar workers, locals, families
Open:	Monday–Friday, 9 A.M.–10 P.M.; Saturday and Sunday, 7 A.M.–10 P.M.; some branches open later

Atmosphere / setting: It looks like another fast-food taco joint, but inside is an actual restaurant, with counter service at lunch, table service at dinner, and a TV tuned to sports all the time. The South Bristol branch has tile floors, ceiling fans, and the same TV.

House specialties: First-rate posole—the pork tender, the broth spicy; menudo on weekends; excellent chili verde with tender chunks of pork; barbecued meats, such as birria (made here with lamb) and al pastor, savory (chewy marinated pork).

Other recommendations: Fresh tortillas; tasty breakfasts; good tortas for lunch; barbacoa (barbecued beef with cumin and garlic).

Summary & comments: This small chain serves simple Sonoran-style food that's notably fresh, tasty, and inexpensive, in homey, roadhouse-style cafes. Neighborhood joints like this are one of Southern California's great assets.

Sushi Nozawa

Zone 7   San Fernando Valley East
11288 Ventura Boulevard, Studio City
(818) 508-7017

Japanese
★★★½
Moderate
Quality 88   Value C

Reservations:	Not accepted
When to go:	Any time
Entree range:	$3.50–10, a la carte; sashimi for two, $15–20
Payment:	VISA, MC
Service rating:	★★★
Friendliness rating:	★★
Parking:	Self
Bar:	Beer and saké
Wine selection:	Sakés
Dress:	Casual
Disabled access:	Yes
Customers:	Serious sushi lovers
Lunch:	Monday–Friday, noon–2 P.M.
Dinner:	Monday–Saturday, 6–10 P.M.

Atmosphere / setting: A traditional Japanese pod-mall restaurant with a traditional sushi counter.

House specialties: Whatever chef Nozawa has fresh that day, put together in whatever way he feels is best: sushi, sashimi, hand rolls, and such.

Other recommendations: Let him call the shots.

Summary & comments: Chef Nozawa doesn't buy it if it isn't of perfect freshness, so don't get your heart set on a particular fish. Besides, you're best off following the advice of the sign behind the bar: "Today's Special—Trust Me." Ask the master to make the chef's choice, and let an extraordinary sushi meal unfold. He'll guide you along the way, telling you about each fish you're tasting and instructing you on the proper way to eat it.

Talesai

<table>
<tr><td></td><td>Thai</td></tr>
<tr><td>Zone 3   Golden Triangle</td><td>★★★</td></tr>
<tr><td>9043 Sunset Boulevard,</td><td>Moderate</td></tr>
<tr><td>West Hollywood</td><td></td></tr>
<tr><td>(310) 275-9724</td><td>Quality 85   Value C</td></tr>
</table>

Zone 7   San Fernando Valley East
11744 Ventura Boulevard, Studio City
(818) 753-1001

Reservations:	Accepted
When to go:	Any time
Entree range:	$8–17
Payment:	Major credit cards
Service rating:	★★★★
Friendliness rating:	★★★★
Parking:	Valet available
Bar:	Full service
Wine selection:	Good
Dress:	Casual chic
Disabled access:	Yes
Customers:	Music industry, Hollywood
Lunch:	Monday–Friday, 11:30 A.M.–2:30 P.M.
Dinner:	*Studio City:* every night, 5:30–10:30 P.M.;
	West Hollywood: Monday–Saturday,
	5:30–11:30 P.M.

Atmosphere / setting: Modern and minimalist in a seductive way, with a curvy bar and counter, well-displayed contemporary art, stylish china, and heavy bronze chopsticks and flatware. The Sunset restaurant is much smaller.

House specialties: Hidden Treasures, precious little cups filled with bits of seafood cooked with coconut sauce, chili, and Thai basil; special pad thai, which really is more special than the norm; gourmet vegetables.

Other recommendations: Steamed tiger prawns with garlic sauce; Vietnamese rolls (shrimp, basil, bean sprouts, and romaine wrapped in rice paper); steamed salmon with garlic, chili, and fresh lime juice.

Summary & comments: Style meets substance at these chic siblings. Prices are high and portions small by Thai-food standards, but the service, setting, and cooking all deliver. In proper L.A. fashion, the kitchen strays from the straight and narrow, adding dashes of pan-Asian flair to the collection of Thai standards—which are anything but standard.

262

TAY HO

<table>
<tr><td></td><td>Vietnamese</td></tr>
<tr><td>Zone 9   Orange County North</td><td>★★½</td></tr>
<tr><td>9242 Bolsa Avenue, Westminster</td><td>Inexpensive</td></tr>
<tr><td>(714) 895-4796</td><td>Quality 75   Value A</td></tr>
</table>

Reservations:	Not accepted
When to go:	Lunchtime
Entree range:	$4–6.50
Payment:	No credit cards
Service rating:	★★
Friendliness rating:	★★
Parking:	Self
Bar:	None
Wine selection:	None
Dress:	Casual
Disabled access:	Limited
Customers:	Vietnamese locals
Lunch / Dinner:	Every day, 11 A.M.–9 P.M.

Atmosphere / setting: A hole-in-the-wall, minimall noodle house smack in the middle of Little Saigon.

House specialties: Delicious banh cuon (rice noodle) dishes—wide, lasagne-style flat noodles that are rolled up, sliced, and topped with such things as roast pork with tree ear mushrooms, or tasty chopped shrimp, or strange Vietnamese pâté.

Other recommendations: Various noodle soups; banh xeo, a wonderful bright orange (from turmeric) rice-flour pancake with shrimp, pork, and bean sprouts; banh tom chien, a light sweet potato patty; sweet red bean in coconut milk.

Summary & comments: This fine noodle house is a perfect launch for a walking tour of Little Saigon, located right between the two huge Vietnamese malls. All the noodle dishes are worthy, but the banh cuon is extraordinary.

TERRAZZA TOSCANA

Zone 8 San Fernando Valley West	Italian
17401 Ventura Boulevard, Encino	★★½
(818) 905-1641	Moderate
	Quality 79 Value C

Reservations:	Accepted
When to go:	Any time
Entree range:	$9.50–22.50
Payment:	Major credit cards
Service rating:	★★★
Friendliness rating:	★★★★
Parking:	Valet available
Bar:	Full service
Wine selection:	Good Italians
Dress:	Casual chic to upscale
Disabled access:	Yes
Customers:	Encino upper-crust
Lunch:	Monday–Friday, 11:30 A.M.–3 P.M.;
	Saturday, 11:30 A.M.–2:30 P.M.
Dinner:	Monday–Friday, 5:30–10 P.M.;
	Saturday, 5:30–10:30 P.M.;
	Sunday, 5–9:30 P.M.

Atmosphere / setting: A long, cool, noisy Italian on the second floor of an upscale mall, with washed terra cotta walls, tiled counters, open kitchen, wood-burning oven, Italian staff, and large terrace overlooking Ventura Boulevard.

House specialties: An appealing fixed-price family-style menu (Sunday through Thursday), including such dishes as bruschetta, artichokes cooked in garlic and risotto with rosemary and veal sauce; an excellent antipasto buffet at lunch.

Other recommendations: Any of the carpaccios; spaghetti with seafood; grilled lamb chops with radicchio; sausage and red bean stew; pear tart.

Summary & comments: You'd never confuse the Courtyard Shops of Encino mall for a Tuscan villa, but once you're inside this high-style ristorante, the Italian accents and the aromas of rosemary and wood-fired meats make even Ventura Boulevard look attractive. The food is more uneven than at the parent restaurant in Brentwood, but the space and service are more welcoming.

Teru Sushi

	Japanese
	★★★
	Moderate
	Quality 80 Value D

Zone 7   San Fernando Valley East
11940 Ventura Boulevard, Studio City
(818) 763-6201

Reservations:	Advised
When to go:	Any time
Entree range:	$15–23 for complete dinner; sushi $4–6
Payment:	Major credit cards
Service rating:	★★
Friendliness rating:	★★★★
Parking:	Valet available
Bar:	Beer and wine
Wine selection:	Decent
Dress:	Casual
Disabled access:	Yes
Customers:	Date-night Valleyites
Lunch:	Monday–Friday, noon–2:30 P.M.
Dinner:	Monday–Thursday, 5:30–11 P.M.;
	Friday and Saturday, 5:30–11:30 P.M.;
	Sunday, 5–10 P.M.

Atmosphere / setting: A large, frenzied sushi bar manned by a team of costumed chefs who greet each new diner with whoops and hollers. A back enclosed patio offers a pond and some relative peace and quiet.

House specialties: All the California-sushi standards: spicy tuna roll, California roll, tiger's eye, and such; sashimi combinations; some very good non-sushi dishes, like beef sashimi with garlic-soy-ginger sauce and chicken in crushed sesame sauce.

Other recommendations: The cooked dishes—tempura, noodles, teriyakis—are as well prepared as the sushi.

Summary & comments: Sure, Teru Sushi is hokey and theatrical, with all those grandstanding sushi chefs being egged on by saké-fueled partiers. The surprise is that after all these years, after sushi mania peaked and ebbed, Teru Sushi has maintained its standards. Some of the rolls and combinations may be silly, but the fish sparkles with freshness and the flavors are good.

Thai Ranch

Zone 8   San Fernando Valley West
1145 Lindero Canyon Road, Westlake
(818) 991-4499

Thai	
★★½	
Inexpensive	
Quality 77	Value B

Reservations:	Accepted
When to go:	Any time
Entree range:	$6.95–14.95
Payment:	VISA, MC
Service rating:	★★
Friendliness rating:	★★
Parking:	Self
Bar:	Beer and wine
Wine selection:	Limited
Dress:	Casual
Disabled access:	Yes
Customers:	Solid West Valley suburbanites
Open:	Every day, 11:30 A.M.–10 P.M.

Atmosphere / setting: A pleasant pod-mall room enlivened with turquoise linens, Thai wall hangings, and hip flatware.

House specialties: Tom yum koong, a soup of shrimp and lemongrass; beef panang, a curry dish with peas and coconut milk; deep-fried whole catfish with spicy sauce.

Other recommendations: Yum yai salad, a toss of romaine, shrimp, chicken, cabbage, egg, and peanut dressing; most of the curry dishes.

Summary & comments: Despite a tendency to make dishes too sweet, the cooking is better than one might expect out here in nonethnic suburbia. Thai Ranch isn't worth a long drive, but it's a great West Valley alternative to the chain restaurants.

Tommy Tang's

	Thai
	★★★
	Moderate
	Quality 82 Value C

Zone 6   San Gabriel Valley
24 West Colorado Boulevard, Pasadena
(818) 792-9700

Reservations:	Accepted
When to go:	Any time
Entree range:	$7.50–13.95
Payment:	Major credit cards
Service rating:	★★★
Friendliness rating:	★★★
Parking:	Valet available
Bar:	Beer and wine on Melrose, full bar in Pasadena
Wine selection:	Pretty good
Dress:	Casual chic
Disabled access:	Yes
Customers:	All sorts
Lunch/Dinner:	Tuesday–Thursday, 11:30 A.M.–10 P.M.;
	Friday and Saturday, 11:30 A.M.–midnight;
	Sunday, 1–10 P.M.

Atmosphere / setting: Brick walls contrast with stark, unadorned plaster walls, bare hardwood floors, and white-clothed tables. A quiet, almost secret spot in the middle of crowded Old Town.

House specialties: Spicy, savory Thai beef salad with lemongrass vinaigrette; tom kha kai, delicious chicken-coconut soup with galanga and lemongrass; the exceptional Tommy duck with honey-ginger sauce.

Other recommendations: Chicken satay with an extraordinary peanut sauce; crispy oysters with kaffir lime sauce; rice noodles sautéed with a lively blend of shrimp, garlic, and fresh mint.

Summary & comments: Back when Thai food was still news, Tommy Tang acheived national acclaim for his bright, fresh Thai cooking influenced by California-style innovation. The faddish crowds have moved on and the original Melrose restaurant has closed, but Tang's cooking remains skilled and appealing.

TOSCANA

Zone 1 Westside	Italian
11663 San Vicente Boulevard,	★★★
Brentwood	Moderate
(310) 820-2448	Quality 83 Value C

Reservations:	Advised
When to go:	Any time
Entree range:	$9–22.50
Payment:	Major credit cards
Service rating:	★★★
Friendliness rating:	★★
Parking:	Valet available
Bar:	Beer and wine
Wine selection:	Not cheap, but interesting
Dress:	Casual chic
Disabled access:	Yes
Customers:	Entertainment attorneys, investment bankers, celebs
Lunch:	Monday–Saturday, 11:30 A.M.–3 P.M.
Dinner:	Every night, 5:30–11 P.M.

Atmosphere / setting: A simple, crowded trattoria (with requisite open kitchen) that's humbler than its high-powered clientele.

House specialties: Good Tuscan bruschetta; risotto with white truffles in season, or with rosemary and veal sauce, or with shrimp and saffron; a superb rib-eye steak cooked in the wood-burning oven; any of the special game dishes.

Other recommendations: Trenette al pesto; tagliolini with crab and tomato sauce; memorable veal chop sautéed with butter and sage; ricotta cheesecake.

Summary & comments: Progenitor of a budding restaurant empire (including Rosti and Terrazza Toscana), this no-frills, high-energy trattoria serves some mighty fine risotti, pastas, and grilled meats and game. The experience isn't relaxed, but the food usually delivers.

Toto Caffe Spaghetteria

Zone 1 Westside	Italian
11047 Santa Monica Boulevard,	★★½
West L.A.	Inexpensive
(310) 312-6664	Quality 78 Value A
Zone 7 San Fernando Valley East	
5658 Sepulveda Boulevard, Van Nuys	
(818) 781-0144	

Reservations:	Not accepted
When to go:	Any time
Entree range:	$6.50–12.95
Payment:	VISA, MC, AMEX
Service rating:	★★
Friendliness rating:	★★
Parking:	Self
Bar:	Beer and wine
Wine selection:	Limited
Dress:	Casual
Disabled access:	Yes
Customers:	Regular folks of all types
Lunch:	Monday–Friday, 11:30 A.M.–3 P.M.
Dinner:	Monday–Friday, 5:30–10 P.M.;
	Saturday, 5–10 P.M.; Sunday, 5–9:30 P.M.

Atmosphere / setting: A no-frills Italian diner with black-and-white tile floors, an open kitchen, and an acoustical tile ceiling.

House specialties: Spaghetti in every imaginable form: vecchio style, with a ragu sauce and small meatballs; alla checca, with a chop of fresh tomatoes, basil, garlic, and olive oil; alla puttanesca, with tomatoes, garlic, black olives, capers, and chilis.

Other recommendations: Simple salads; tasty, homey pizzas topped with classic combinations, from mushrooms and prosciutto to smoked mozzarella and sun-dried tomatoes.

Summary & comments: Spaghetti 15 ways is the specialty of this humble neighborhood cafe, and every variety is tasty, generously served, and inexpensive. Ditto for the pizzas. A satisfying, homey choice when you don't feel like cooking your own pasta.

Trattoria Farfalla

Zone 5   Central City
1978 Hillhurst Avenue, Los Feliz
(213) 661-7365

Italian
★★★
Inexp/Mod
Quality 83   Value B

Reservations:	Not accepted
When to go:	Early or late to avoid crowds
Entree range:	$8–15
Payment:	Major credit cards
Service rating:	★★
Friendliness rating:	★★
Parking:	Self
Bar:	Beer and wine
Wine selection:	Decent
Dress:	Casual
Disabled access:	Yes, but it's crowded
Customers:	Los Feliz/Silverlake intelligensia
Lunch:	Monday–Friday, 11:30 A.M.–2 P.M.
Dinner:	Monday–Thursday, 6–10 P.M.;
	Friday and Saturday, 6–11 P.M.;
	Sunday, 5:30–10 P.M.

Atmosphere/setting: A simple, noisy, always-crowded storefront with brick walls, plain tables, and Italian waiters.

House specialties: Insalata Farfalla, a romaine-radicchio mix served atop crisp pizza bread; the simple, perfect tagliolini with shrimp, garlic, and olive oil; roasted free-range chicken with garlic, herbs, and wild mushrooms.

Other recommendations: Pasta alla Norma, with eggplant; rich gnocchi with chicken, sun-dried tomatoes, and a bit of cream sauce; thin-crusted pizzas.

Summary & comments: The terrific, homey, inexpensive Italian cooking has brought Farfalla several years of constant crowds and a larger, fancier spin-off restaurant over on La Brea. But this little storefront remains the friendlier and more consistent of the two.

Tung Lai Shun

Zone 6 San Gabriel Valley	Chinese
140 West Valley Boulevard,	★★★
No. 118C, San Gabriel	Inexp/Mod
(818) 288-6588	Quality 82 Value B

Reservations:	Accepted for large parties
When to go:	Any time
Entree range:	$5.95–16.95
Payment:	VISA, MC
Service rating:	★★
Friendliness rating:	★★
Parking:	Self
Bar:	None
Wine selection:	None
Dress:	Casual
Disabled access:	Yes
Customers:	Chinese, Muslims
Lunch/Dinner:	Every day, 11 A.M.–10:30 P.M.

Atmosphere/setting: A large, pleasant, but not luxurious Chinese setting with a constant crush of humanity.

House specialties: Lamb with China cabbage soup; sesame bread with green onion; succulent lamb with green onion or pickled cabbage; steamed dumplings and buns.

Other recommendations: Cold lamb with garlic sauce; house special chicken; beef with scallion in Beijing sauce; robust Hunan bean curd.

Summary & comments: Bereft of both pork and alcohol, this northern-style Chinese Islamic restaurant serves a robust cuisine that's big on lamb, brown sauces, and spices. The dense sesame bread is famous, and most everything is delicious.

Tutto Mare

	Italian
Zone 9 Orange County North	★★★
Fashion Island,	Moderate
545 Newport Center Drive, Newport	
(714) 640-6333	Quality 80 Value C

Reservations:	Advised
When to go:	Any time
Entree range:	$8.95–23.95
Payment:	Major credit cards
Service rating:	★★★
Friendliness rating:	★★★★
Parking:	Self
Bar:	Full service
Wine selection:	Good
Dress:	Stylish
Disabled access:	Yes
Customers:	Shoppers, businesspeople, chic tourists
Lunch/Dinner:	Monday–Thursday, 11:30 A.M.–11 P.M.;
	Friday and Saturday, 11:30 A.M.–midnight;
	Sunday, 11 A.M.–10 P.M.

Atmosphere / setting: Dark wood columns, a long bar, French windows overlooking Fashion Island, open kitchen, and art deco posters—all in all, a glowing, handsome trattoria.

House specialties: Exceptional antipasto misto, with such luxurious additions as poached scampi and poached endive; green raviolini with spinach and ricotta in brown butter, sage, and Parmesan; whole baked branzino, boned tableside; daily fresh-fish specials, such as grilled ono or swordfish.

Other recommendations: Heady clams with white wine and garlic-clam broth; special risotto of the day, particularly the simple ones; ricotta tart.

Summary & comments: It may lack mama-and-papa soul, since it's part of the great Prego-Il Fornaio Spectrum chain, but Tutto Mare doesn't lack much else. The great Italian seafood, rewarding pastas, feel-good interior decor, and amusing people-watching all add up to big fun.

TwiN PaLMs

	French/American
Zone 6 San Gabriel Valley	★★★½
101 West Green Street, Pasadena	Moderate
(818) 577-2567	Quality 86 Value B

Reservations:	Advised
When to go:	Warm evenings, Sunday brunch
Entree range:	$8–17
Payment:	Major credit cards
Service rating:	★★★
Friendliness rating:	★★★★
Parking:	Valet available
Bar:	Full service
Wine selection:	Good
Dress:	Casual chic
Disabled access:	Yes
Customers:	A wonderful mix
Brunch:	Sunday, 10:30 A.M.–3 P.M.
Lunch:	Monday–Saturday, 11:30 A.M.–2:30 P.M.
Dinner:	Every night, 5–10:30 P.M.

Atmosphere / setting: One of the largest restaurants in Southern California, seating some 400. Built around two palm trees, the huge central patio is surrounded by two bars, a bandshell, a huge rack of rotisserie spits, and a long, front porch–style covered terrace. Retractable canvas tenting protects diners from the elements. There's also a more formal indoor dining room.

House specialties: Brandade (mashed potato with salt cod); "grand" vegetable platter, a fine grilled vegetable mix with aioli and, if desired, smoky grilled shrimp; garlicky rotisserie chicken with great, crisp shoestring fries; French toast brûlée, a dreamy melange of French toast, fresh fruit, and crème brûlée.

Other recommendations: Tasty baguette sandwiches; a fine bouillabaisse; rotisserie loin of pork with mustard and sage; cassoulet.

Entertainment & amenities: Superb gospel groups at the joyous Sunday brunch; live music Tuesday–Sunday, with more upbeat music on weekends.

Summary & comments: It took a good six months or so for the cooking to shape up at this high-profile, mostly open-air new restaurant owned by acclaimed chef Michael Roberts and Cindy Costner (Kevin's ex). But now the rustic southern French food is consistently good, and the experience couldn't be more fun, particularly when the weather's fine. Great people-watching, great live music, and great French-Mediterranean comfort food, at very fair prices. Just opened at press time was an even larger Twin Palms in Newport Beach.

273

Typhoon

Zone 1   Westside
3221 Donald Douglas Loop South,
   Santa Monica
(310) 390-6565

Pacific Rim
★★½
Inexp / Mod

Quality 79   Value B

Reservations:	Advised
When to go:	Before sunset if skies are fair
Entree range:	$11.75–17.50
Payment:	VISA, MC, AMEX
Service rating:	★★
Friendliness rating:	★★
Parking:	Self
Bar:	Full service
Wine selection:	Decent
Dress:	Casual chic, young
Disabled access:	Yes
Customers:	All sorts, with a fair number of the young and ebullient
Lunch:	Monday–Friday, noon–3 P.M.
Dinner:	Every night, 5:30–10:30 P.M.

Atmosphere / setting: Hidden on the south side of the Santa Monica Airport, this second-floor restaurant has a swell view of the old prop planes and the Santa Monica Mountains. The modern look—concrete floors, slick cherry paneling—is warmed by some old aeronautical touches, like flight mechanics' jumpers hanging on coathooks.

House specialties: Shu mai dumplings; Philippine wonton soup with shredded chicken and shrimp; fiery Burmese fish with curry sauce; rich, spicy Szechwan eggplant with ground pork and basil; garlic rice.

Other recommendations: Lemongrass chicken tender with Vietnamese salad tray and rice paper; beef rib eye topped with Thai salad; Taiwanese oysters with chili.

Summary & comments: A food-lover's tour of Southeast Asia and China is held daily in this fun, atmospheric spot overlooking Santa Monica Airport. Seductive party drinks are part of the draw, but even the stone-cold sober have lots of fun sampling these good tastes from Thailand, Korea, the Philippines, Hong Kong, and beyond.

Uzbekistan

Zone 5   Central City
7077 Sunset Boulevard
(213) 464-3663

Russian
★★
Inexpensive

Quality 75   Value B

Reservations:	Accepted
When to go:	Any time
Entree range:	$7–11
Payment:	Major credit cards
Service rating:	★
Friendliness rating:	★★
Parking:	Self
Bar:	Full service
Wine selection:	Limited
Dress:	Casual
Disabled access:	Yes
Customers:	Homesick Russians
Lunch/Dinner:	Every day, 11:30 A.M.–1 A.M.

Atmosphere / setting: Yet another modest, minimall ethnic restaurant, no different from many others.

House specialties: All sorts of dumplings, like samsa and pelemeni; hunum, a hearty potato dumpling; eggplant in several tasty guises; kaurmalagman, thick hand-cut noodles fried with various meats and vegetables; stews of many kinds, from oxtail to plaov (a rice-based stew).

Other recommendations: Pickled vegetable plate; thinly sliced salad of tomato and onion; such Russian standards as chicken Kiev and shashlik.

Entertainment & amenities: Live Russian music Friday–Sunday evenings.

Summary & comments: The hearty, stewy, little-known food of Uzbek, a former Soviet Republic just north of Afghanistan and Iran, is reason enough to visit this authentic Russian restaurant—the vodka, heavily accented diners, authentically oblivious service, and live Russian music only add to the experience.

U-Zen

Zone 1 Westside	Japanese
11951 Santa Monica Boulevard,	★★★
West L.A.	Moderate
(310) 477-1390	Quality 84 Value C

Reservations: Not accepted
When to go: Any time
Entree range: $3–8 for small dishes and sushi, $11.80–13.50
                       for set dinners
Payment: VISA, MC
Service rating: ★★★
Friendliness rating: ★★★
Parking: Self
Bar: Beer and saké
Wine selection: Good sakés
Dress: Casual
Disabled access: Yes
Customers: Japanese businesspeople, assorted sushi lovers
Lunch: Monday–Friday, 11:30 A.M.–2 P.M.
Dinner: Monday–Thursday, 5:30–10 P.M.;
                       Friday and Saturday, 5:30–10:45 P.M.;
                       Sunday, 5:30–9:30 P.M.

Atmosphere / setting: A 20-seat sushi bar, several booths, and a large family-style table in the middle of the room accommodate all sorts of groups. An attractive, comfortable, and informal spot.

House specialties: Very good sushi and sashimi, including yellowtail flown in from Japan, jack knife clam, Spanish mackerel and such complex creations as the U-Zen roll and the soft-shell crab roll, with carrot and asparagus.

Other recommendations: An appealing collection of small, high-quality pub-food dishes: fried spicy tofu; baked green mussels; salmon skin salad; tempura.

Summary & comments: A little more upmarket than the typical pod-mall sushi joint, but not pretentious or overpriced, U-Zen has something for everyone: excellent sushi, including some hard-to-find fish; lots of tasty ippin-ryori dishes, designed to snack on with a beer or shot of saké; and traditional tempura-teriyaki combo dinners.

VALENTINO

Zone 1   Westside
3115 Pico Boulevard, Santa Monica
(310) 829-4313

Italian
★★★★★
Exp/Very Exp

Quality 96   Value C

Reservations:	Advised
When to go:	Any time
Entree range:	$17.50–25, less for pasta
Payment:	Major credit cards
Service rating:	★★★★★
Friendliness rating:	★★★★★
Parking:	Valet available
Bar:	Full service
Wine selection:	One of the best wine lists in the country
Dress:	Upscale
Disabled access:	Yes
Customers:	Well-heeled regulars, special-occasion celebrants
Lunch:	Friday, noon–2:30 P.M.
Dinner:	Monday–Saturday, 5:30–11 P.M.

Atmosphere / setting: Three quiet rooms that skillfully combine a modern aesthetic with old-fashioned comfort. Colors are muted, banquettes are roomy, tables are well set, and lighting is flattering.

House specialties: The best dishes are culled from the long list of nightly specials—such things as risotto with white truffles, grilled quail wrapped in pancetta, fettuccine with rabbit, or orange créme caramel. Regulars either order strictly from the specials list or ask for the chef to design a meal around small tastes.

Other recommendations: Porcini tortino, a little mushroom tart topped with cheese; risotto with seafood (or any of the risotti); and calves' liver alla veneziana.

Summary & comments: The uninitiated settle into luxurious seats at one of the country's most acclaimed Italian restaurants, open the menu, and look confused. All this fuss over a place serving Caesar salad, rotelli with sausage, and eggplant parmigiana? Granted, all those shopworn standards are prepared better here than most anywhere else, but that's not why you go to Valentino. You go for the specials menu, a nightly roster of dishes that reflect the creativity and passion for world-class ingredients that drive owner Piero Selvaggio and chef Angelo Auriana. With the help of your waiter or, preferably, the handsome and effusive Selvaggio, craft a meal out of the specials, or ask that chef Auriana surprise you. After a meal at Valentino, your wallet will be poorer for the experience, but your soul will be richer.

Honors / awards: Rated as one of "America's Best Restaurants" by *Condé Nast Traveler.*

Versailles

Cuban	
★★	
Inexpensive	
Quality 75	Value A

Zone 4   City South
10319 Venice Boulevard, Culver City
(310) 558-3168

Zone 5   Central City
1415 South La Cienega Boulevard
(310) 289-0392

Zone 8   San Fernando Valley West
17410 Ventura Boulevard, Encino
(818) 906-0756

Reservations:	Not accepted
When to go:	Any time
Entree range:	$6.50–9
Payment:	VISA, MC, AMEX
Service rating:	★
Friendliness rating:	★★
Parking:	Self
Bar:	Beer and wine
Wine selection:	Limited
Dress:	Casual
Disabled access:	Limited
Customers:	Some Cubans, lots of the young and hungry
Lunch/Dinner:	Every day, 11 A.M.–10 P.M.

Atmosphere / setting: Raucous, bare-bones roadhouses with Cuban music on the stereos and a constant crowd.

House specialties: Perhaps the best roast chicken in town: a huge, juicy and crisp-skinned half bird, steeped in a citrus-garlic marinade and served with black beans and rice, fried plantains, and raw onion.

Other recommendations: Mango shakes; marinated roast pork, sometimes greasy but always tasty.

Summary & comments: Versailles is always a revelation to young Angelenos who discover it for the first time. What incredible chicken! What a bargain! What a great people-watching scene! Originally a simple neighborhood Cuban joint in Culver City, Versailles has grown into a mini-empire, thanks to its irresistible roast chicken and dirt-cheap prices.

Vid**A**

Zone 5   Central City
1930 North Hillhurst Avenue, Los Feliz
(213) 660-4446

International
★★★½
Moderate

Quality 86   Value C

Reservations:	Accepted
When to go:	Dinner
Entree range:	$9–19
Payment:	Major credit cards
Service rating:	★★★
Friendliness rating:	★★★
Parking:	Valet available
Bar:	Full service
Wine selection:	Pretty good
Dress:	Inventive
Disabled access:	Yes
Customers:	Eclectic, artistic, intellectual
Dinner:	Every day, 6–11:30 P.M.

Atmosphere / setting: Strange and a bit cramped, but pleasantly hip, with bamboo tatami walls and an Asian minimalism.

House specialties: The New Yorkshire, a huge New York steak with Yorkshire pudding; Jiffy Pop clams, Manila clams baked with varying herbs and sauces; Ty Cobb, a Thai-style Cobb salad made with crispy duck; shrimp done three ways; banana–chocolate crêpe sundae.

Other recommendations: Three oysters, one each with wasabe, curry, and ponzu; vegetarian spring roll with fresh plum sauce; roasted smoked salmon with a barley-mushroom risotto and cream of spinach; cookies and milk.

Summary & comments: Fred Eric's food is whimsical and fun, but it's not silly—this guy really knows how to cook. From the hominess of his macaroni and cheese update to the inventiveness of his Asian noodle dishes, Eric's taste is impeccable. Quirky people, quirky food, and a great L.A. experience. The bar is cool, too.

VIM

Zone 5   Central City
831 South Vermont Avenue
(213) 480-8159

	Thai-Chinese
	★★½
	Inexpensive
	Quality 80 Value A

Reservations: Not accepted
When to go: Any time
Entree range: $6–7.50
Payment: No credit cards
Service rating: ★
Friendliness rating: ★
Parking: Self
Bar: Beer and wine
Wine selection: Stick with beer
Dress: Casual
Disabled access: Limited
Customers: Thais and a multicultural mix
Lunch/Dinner: Every day, 11 A.M.–10 P.M.

Atmosphere / setting: A stark room with Formica tables, located in a rather grubby (but interesting) midcity neighborhood.

House specialties: Oysters with ginger and oyster sauce; many wonderful soups, like the seafood soup thick with crab, shrimp, snapper, and more; catfish with spicy hot sauce; pineapple rice (by special request).

Other recommendations: Hot and sour shrimp salad; chicken with green chili, garlic, and mint; excellent pad thai noodles.

Summary & comments: Some of the best soups in town are found at this midcity dive serving the Chinese-influenced Thai street food that's so plentiful in Bangkok. And there's more than soup—from the noodle and rice dishes to the salads and stir-frys, Vim's food is uniformly good and amazingly cheap.

WARSZAWA

	Polish
	★★½
Zone 1 Westside	Inexp/Mod
1414 Lincoln Boulevard, Santa Monica	
(310) 393-8831	Quality 78 Value B

Reservations:	Accepted
When to go:	When you're really hungry
Entree range:	$8.95–17.50
Payment:	Major credit cards
Service rating:	★★★
Friendliness rating:	★★★
Parking:	Self
Bar:	Full service
Wine selection:	Pretty good, but vodka's the drink here
Dress:	Casual
Disabled access:	Yes
Customers:	All sorts
Dinner:	Every night, 5:30–10:30 P.M.

Atmosphere / setting: Several homey, warm dining rooms in a converted old bungalow, with lace curtains, candlelight, and Polish posters.

House specialties: Zczerwonej kapusty, a salad of red cabbage, bell peppers, leeks and walnuts; fabulous roast duck stuffed with apples and served with dumplings; bigos, the traditional hunter's stew with sauerkraut, various meats, and potatoes.

Other recommendations: Pierogi (Polish ravioli) of all sorts; fresh rainbow trout simmered with leeks, tomatoes, lemon, and dill; roasted game hen polonaise with herb stuffing; chocolate cream walnut cake.

Summary & comments: L.A.'s best Polish restaurant is also L.A.'s *only* Polish restaurant—but Warszawa would stand out in a crowd anyway. It fairly reeks of old-world hospitality and comfort, and the rich, deeply satisfying food will take the chill off any cold night.

Water Grill

<table>
<tr><td></td><td>Seafood/American</td></tr>
<tr><td>Zone 5   Central City</td><td>★★★½</td></tr>
<tr><td>544 South Grand Avenue, Downtown</td><td>Mod/Exp</td></tr>
<tr><td>(213) 891-0900</td><td>Quality 85   Value C</td></tr>
</table>

Reservations:	Advised
When to go:	For a chic business lunch or pre-theater dinner
Entree range:	$14–24
Payment:	Major credit cards
Service rating:	★★★★
Friendliness rating:	★★★★
Parking:	Valet available next door
Bar:	Full service
Wine selection:	Memorable
Dress:	Business at lunch, casual-chic to upscale at dinner
Disabled access:	Yes
Customers:	Attorneys, bankers, the downtown elite
Lunch/Dinner:	Monday and Tuesday, 11:30 A.M.–9 P.M.; Wednesday–Friday, 11:30 A.M.–10 P.M.
Dinner:	Saturday, 5–10 P.M.; Sunday, 4:30–9 P.M.

Atmosphere/setting: One of L.A.'s best-looking restaurants, marred only by a daunting noise level. Burnished dark woodwork, modern lighting, white linens, and a sleek, rounded bar and oyster bar all add to the modern brasserie feel.

House specialties: One of the best oyster bars anywhere, stocked with the finest Fanny Bays, Chiloes, and Malpeques, along with a dazzling array of other shellfish, from Santa Barbara spot prawns to exotic scallops.

Other recommendations: Menu changes weekly. Good possibilities include excellent clam chowder; planked wild sockeye salmon with tomato-basil salsa; trout fillets with applewood-smoked bacon; roasted tilefish with asparagus.

Summary & comments: The Water Grill has become the leading light in a restaurant group that includes Ocean Avenue Seafood, I Cugini, and Pine Avenue Fish House, thanks to its knockout decor, big-city buzz, exceptional oyster bar, and generally very good preparations of fish from around the country. Sometimes dishes get too fussy, and the pastas can disappoint, but for the most part the Water Grill does seafood very proud indeed.

Wei Fun

Zone 6   San Gabriel Valley
708 East Las Tunas Drive, San Gabriel
(818) 286-6152

Reservations:	Accepted
When to go:	Any time
Entree range:	$6.50–10.50
Payment:	VISA, MC
Service rating:	★★★
Friendliness rating:	★★★
Parking:	Self
Bar:	Beer and wine
Wine selection:	Limited
Dress:	Casual
Disabled access:	Yes
Customers:	Chinese, Chinese-Americans
Lunch:	Monday–Friday, 11:30 A.M.–3 P.M.
Lunch/Dinner:	Saturday, 11:30 A.M.–10 P.M.;
	Sunday, 11:30 A.M.–9:30 P.M.
Dinner:	Monday–Thursday, 4:30–9:30 P.M.;
	Friday, 4:30–10 P.M.

Atmosphere / setting: A large, plain, square room devoted to eating.

House specialties: Hundred-layer pancake—a steaming, layered bread that replaces rice as the meal's accompaniment; cold jellyfish with turnip; house special chicken, fried and bathed in a tangy-sweet-spicy sauce; sea bass with hot bean sauce; house special bean curd, in a robust sauce.

Other recommendations: Smoked fish; sliced lamb with hot sauce, a wonderful Hunanese dish; string beans with ground pork.

Summary & comments: It doesn't look like much, but this busy restaurant serves some of the finest northern Chinese food around, full of potent (but not overused) chilis and complex sauces. The hundred-layer bread alone is worth the trip.

Woodside

<table>
<tr><td></td><td>New American</td></tr>
<tr><td>Zone 1   Westside</td><td>★★★½</td></tr>
<tr><td>11604 San Vicente Boulevard,
    Brentwood</td><td>Moderate</td></tr>
<tr><td>(310) 571-3800</td><td>Quality 85   Value B</td></tr>
</table>

Reservations:	Advised
When to go:	Any time
Entree range:	$11–19
Payment:	Major credit cards
Service rating:	★★★
Friendliness rating:	★★★★
Parking:	Valet available
Bar:	Beer and wine
Wine selection:	Good by-the-glass selection
Dress:	Casual chic
Disabled access:	Yes, but space is tight
Customers:	Glowing Westsiders of all ages
Dinner:	Monday–Thursday, 5:30–10 P.M.; Friday and Saturday, 5:30–11 P.M.; Sunday, 5–10 P.M.

Atmosphere / setting: With its exposed brick walls, wooden library chairs, wood floors, and open kitchen, Woodside looks like it should be in Soho. At peak hours, the hard surfaces and crowd make for an ear-ringing roar.

House specialties: Menu changes seasonally. The fall menu, for example, might include French butter pear salad with gorgonzola, balsamic, endive, rocket, and spiced pecans; wild mushroom risotto, a knockout of mushroom flavor; roast rack of lamb with pumpkin raviolis and autumn vegetables; a huge grilled portobello mushroom with an assortment of roasted and grilled vegetables.

Other recommendations: Bouillabaisse with shellfish, rock shrimp, and fresh fish; grilled chili-rubbed gulf shrimp with a bright green mash of potatoes and poblano chilis; a side dish of spicy sautéed spinach; apple crumble pie with vanilla ice cream.

Summary & comments: One of L.A.'s most notable young chefs has created one of the best new restaurants L.A. has seen in a long time. Woodside bursts with American warmth and enthusiasm, and chef Louise Branch displays considerable respect for good seasonal ingredients. Contemporary her cooking may be, but it's also the best sort of American comfort food.

Xiomara

Zone 6   San Gabriel Valley
69 North Raymond Avenue, Pasadena
(818) 796-2520

French
★★★½
Moderate

Quality 88   Value D

Reservations:	Accepted
When to go:	Any time
Entree range:	$15–23
Payment:	Major credit cards
Service rating:	★★★★
Friendliness rating:	★★★★
Parking:	Valet available
Bar:	Full service
Wine selection:	Good
Dress:	Stylish to upscale
Disabled access:	Yes
Customers:	An older, better-dressed crowd than the typical Old Town crew
Lunch:	Monday–Friday, 11:30 A.M.–2:30 P.M.
Dinner:	Every night, 5:30–10:30 P.M.

Atmosphere / setting: A small, stylish storefront that's more contemporary than the cooking, with a sleek bar counter, smooth, rich woods, and roomy chairs.

House specialties: Menu changes seasonally, but many dishes are constant. Winners have included crispy duck confit salad with frisse and green beans; an excellent cassoulet with lamb shoulder, duck confit, slab bacon, pork ribs, sausage, and white beans; an unbelievably tender and buttery Provençal lamb daube, marinated for days and cooked with vegetables and noodles in a cast-iron casserole sealed with bread dough.

Other recommendations: Country terrine of duck and foie gras; simple green salad with watercress; dreamy poule au pot (chicken) with five vegetables cooked in clay.

Summary & comments: After a rocky start with two other chefs, dedicated restaurateur Ardolina Xiomara (pronounced "cee-o-mara") snagged Patrick Healy, ex of Champagne, and the two are a match made in heaven—or were, until he started dividing his time recently between this and his groovy new Buffalo Club. He produces a meaty, labor-intensive, old-fashioned French cuisine of the homiest, most soul-satisfying kind, while she keeps the place inviting and well run. Time will tell if the culinary standards stay as high as they've been.

Yang Chow

Zone 5   Central City
379 North Broadway, Chinatown
(213) 625-0811

Chinese
★★★
Inexpensive

Quality 83   Value B

Reservations:	Advised
When to go:	Any time; peak lunch is mobbed
Entree range:	$7.95–11.95
Payment:	VISA, MC, AMEX
Service rating:	★★★
Friendliness rating:	★★★
Parking:	Valet available
Bar:	Beer and wine
Wine selection:	Limited
Dress:	Casual
Disabled access:	Yes; it's a bit tight
Customers:	Mostly non-Chinese—downtown businesspeople, loyal fans from all over
Lunch / Dinner:	Sunday–Thursday, 11:30 A.M.–9:45 P.M.; Friday and Saturday, 11:30 A.M.–10:45 P.M.

Atmosphere / setting: Two pinkish, comfortable but plain rooms, with booths and some round tables for large groups.

House specialties: Szechwan dumplings in a potent red-chili broth; juicy pan-fried dumplings; lamb and broccoli in a brown sauce; nearly every table gets fried "slippery" shrimp bathed in a tangy-sweet-hot sauce, and for good reason.

Other recommendations: Memorable cashew chicken; dried-fried string beans; crunchy-soft pan-fried noodles, with vegetables or with assorted meats.

Summary & comments: People have been known to drive 20 miles just for a taste of Yang Chow's slippery shrimp, one of the most addictive dishes in town. The rest of the food is damn good, too, but no meal is complete without that shrimp.

Ye Olde King's Head

Zone 1 Westside	English
116 Santa Monica Boulevard,	★★
Santa Monica	Inexpensive
(310) 451-1402	Quality 76 Value

Reservations:	Not accepted
When to go:	When you are dreaming of the Queen Mum
Entree range:	$7.65–15
Payment:	Major credit cards
Service rating:	★★
Friendliness rating:	★★
Parking:	Self
Bar:	Full service
Wine selection:	Beer's the drink here
Dress:	Casual
Disabled access:	Yes
Customers:	Expatriate Brits, lively groups
Open:	Monday–Friday, 10:30 A.M.–10:30 P.M.;
	Saturday and Sunday, 9:30 A.M.–10:30 P.M.

Atmosphere / setting: A well-worn, working-class pub with lots of nooks and crannies, assorted English knickknacks, and photos of local soccer teams. The adjacent bar is loud, smoky, and convivial, packed with darts players, beer drinkers, and pub fans.

House specialties: First-rate fish and chips, as good as you'll find on the Pacific; shepherd's pie, topped with creamy mashed potatoes; Scotch eggs; Midland English trifle.

Other recommendations: Great beers on tap: Watney's, Bass, Harp, Guinness, and more.

Summary & comments: English and Irish pubs have proliferated on the Westside—Santa Monica is home to many émigrés from the British Isles—but the King's Head remains the favorite for fish and chips. Solid food, excellent fish and chips, great beer on tap, and a warm pubby atmosphere.

Yujean Kang's

San Gabriel Valley
67 N. Raymond Avenue, Pasadena
626-585-0855

		Chinese
		★★★★
		Moderate
		Quality 92 Value B

Reservations:	Advised
When to go:	When you're sick of kung pao
Price range:	$11–17
Payment:	Major credit cards
Service rating:	★★★★
Friendliness rating:	★★★★
Parking:	Valet available
Bar:	Beer and wine
Wine selection:	Outstanding
Dress:	Casual chic to upscale
Disabled access:	Yes
Customers:	Kang fans from all over L.A.
Lunch:	Every day, 11:30 A.M.–2:30 P.M.

Atmosphere / setting: Another old storefront space next door to Xiomara, warmed with a few antiques, splashes of red, formal service, and rosewood chopsticks.

House specialties: Chinese eggplant with garlic and cilantro; an appetizer of Pacific snapper with kumquat and passion fruit sauce, a twist on the old sweet 'n' sour; lobster with fava beans, mushrooms, and caviar, sautéed with garlic, ginger, fresh tomato juice, and chili sauce.

Other recommendations: Picture in the Snow, a rich soup with chicken, ham, and enoki topped with a meringue-vegetable village scene; Hunan-style lamb with garlic, ginger, soy, and red date sauce, topped with crisped prosciutto and accompanied with baby bok choy and bean curd rolls.

Summary & comments: If anyone doubts that Chinese food deserves as much respect as the finest French and Italian, send them to Yujean Kang, where they'll be dazzled with a meal that defies all Chinese clichés. Owner / chef Kang stays true to the dictums of Chinese cooking but takes license with some of the ingredients and combinations. His is a cuisine that somehow combines startling innovation and rigorous tradition, with results that are always nothing short of delicious. Kang is an oenophile as well as a chef, and his wine list attracts almost as many customers as his cooking. Worth a trip, well worth the money.

288

YUU

Japanese
★★★
Inexp / Mod

Zone 1   Westside
11043 Santa Monica Boulevard,
    West L.A.
(310) 478-7931

Quality 83   Value

Reservations:	Not accepted
When to go:	Any time
Entree range:	$5.50–9.50 for smallish dishes
Payment:	VISA, MC, AMEX
Service rating:	★★★
Friendliness rating:	★★★
Parking:	Valet available
Bar:	Beer and saké
Wine selection:	Very good sakés
Dress:	Casual
Disabled access:	Yes
Customers:	Asian and multiethnic Westsiders
Dinner:	Sunday–Thursday, 6–10 P.M.; Friday and Saturday, 6–10:30 P.M.

Atmosphere / setting: Hidden in a Westside strip mall, Yuu is a good-looking spot, with a sushi bar, blonde wood, and exposed beams.

House specialties: Consommé of clam and shiitakes; excellent grilled Japanese eggplant with soybean paste; tofu cakes with chili slivers; shirome isobe, deep-fried whitefish wrapped in nori; delectable grilled cod marinated in saké lees.

Other recommendations: Very good sushi and sashimi; fried soft-shell crabs; ebi shinzo, fried balls of shrimp and vegetables; steamed pork with sweet sauce.

Summary & comments: Yuu is an izaka-ya, specializing in the small pub-food dishes that are so common in Japan but little known in the United States. Seafood, vegetables, and saké are particular specialties, and the sushi is admirable.

Z̲itside

‾venue, Santa Monica

‾‾5

	Pacific Rim
	★★★
	Mod/Exp
	Quality 84 Value D

̲ns:	Accepted
̲go:	Any time
̲nge:	$18–26
̲t:	Major credit cards
̲ rating:	★★★★
̲dliness rating:	★★★★
̲ing:	Valet available
̲ar:	Full service
Wine selection:	Good
Dress:	Stylish
Disabled access:	Yes
Customers:	Westside hipsters, showbiz
Lunch:	Monday–Friday, 11:30 A.M.–2 P.M.
Dinner:	Monday–Friday, 6–10 P.M.;
	Saturday, 6–10:30 P.M.; Sunday, 5:30–9 P.M.

Atmosphere / setting: Zenzero occupies the prime Ocean Avenue spot once filled by Fennel. It's a great-looking space, minimalist but not cold, with curving blonde wood, white linens, an open kitchen, glassed-in patio lined with greenery, and a sleek bar.

House specialties: Excellent cilantro-cured salmon with a delicate potato salad and a salmon-roe vinaigrette; fried whole fish with ponzu dipping sauce; wok-seared mahi mahi with wasabe crust; stir-fried eggplant in a rich brown sauce.

Other recommendations: Smoky grilled shrimp salad with a cucumber-frisse salad; salty but otherwise terrific sautéed Chilean sea bass dusted with Chinese black beans and served with a red and yellow tomato salsa; dramatic almond tuile filled with sautéed bananas and ice cream.

Summary & comments: After years of brilliantly manning the kitchen at Puck's Chinois on Main, Kazuto Matsusaka is on his own, thus far with respectable success. His Asian-blend cuisine is served family style, with larger-than-usual portions on platters, though not too many families can pay his prices. Exciting Pacific Rim tastes, served in an austere space perched on the rim of the Pacific.

Eclectic Gourmet Guide to Los Angeles
Reader Survey

If you would like to express your opinion about your Los Angeles dining
experiences or this guidebook, complete the following survey and mail it

> Eclectic Gourmet Guide Reader Survey
> P.O. Box 43059
> Birmingham, AL 35243

	Diner 1	Diner 2	Diner 3	Diner 4	Diner 5
Gender (M or F)	_____	_____	_____	_____	_____
Age	_____	_____	_____	_____	_____
Hometown	_____	_____	_____	_____	_____

Tell us about the restaurants you've visited . . . .

You're overall experience:

Restaurant

Comments you'd like to share with other diners: